INVESTING

―― AT ――

LEVEL3

INVESTING
— AT —
LEVEL3

Higher Returns With Minimal Risk
for the Long-Term Individual Investor

James B. Cloonan

The content of this book is solely the opinion of author, who is not a registered investment adviser or a broker/dealer. This book is solely for informational purposes and should not be construed as an offer to sell or the solicitation of an offer to buy securities. No one area of investment is suitable for all investors and no single method of evaluating investment opportunities has proven to be successful all of the time.

The opinions and analyses included herein are based on sources believed to be reliable and written in good faith, but no representation or warranty, expressed or implied, is made as to their accuracy, completeness, timeliness, or correctness. The author shall not be liable for any errors or inaccuracies, regardless of cause. All information contained in this book should be independently verified.

Printed in the U.S.A.

10 9 8 7 6 5 4 3 2

Book code: 35171

American Association of Individual Investors

625 North Michigan Avenue
Chicago, Illinois 60611
(312) 280-0170; (800) 428-2244
www.aaii.com

ISBN: 978-1-883328-29-0

To Edie, and to the two million current and former members of AAII.

CONTENTS

Preface	1
Introduction	7
Levels of Investing	8
The Individual Investor	9
Outline of the Book	10

PART I

Where We Are: The Current State of Investment Theory and Practice ... **33**

CHAPTER 1
Problems With Modern Portfolio Theory ... **35**

Underlying Concepts of MPT	36
The Bad News/Good News	48
A Real-World View	57
Questions About Random Walk Theory	60
Consider Other Opinions	70

CHAPTER 2
The Limits of Fundamental and Technical Analysis ... **73**

Technical Analysis	73
Fundamental Analysis	81
Summary	87

CHAPTER 3
The Financial Services Industry: Friend or Foe? ... **89**

Asset Managers and Their Obligation	89
Categories of Advisers	91
Products and Their Problems	99
Summary	115

PART II
Where We Should Be: Investing at Level3   *117*

CHAPTER 4
The Nature of Real Investment Risk   **119**

Level 2 Risk Concepts   120
Risk Concerns for the Long-Term Investor   121
Real-World Examples   139
A Look at Past Crashes   143
Accounting for Unknown Risks   147
Other Views   148
Summary   148

CHAPTER 5
Real Risk in the Withdrawal Stage   **151**

The Level3 Approach to Short-Term Asset Allocation   152
The Cost of Risk Reduction   159
Level3 Rules for Withdrawal Stage   161
The Strategy in Down Markets   166
A More Generalized Defensive Approach   169
Do You Need a Defensive Strategy?   169
What Should Be in the Defensive Portfolio?   173
Withdrawals for Other Objectives   174
Summary   175

CHAPTER 6
Obtaining Higher-Than-Market Returns   **179**

Setting the Stage   180
Passive Approaches   188
Active Approaches   194
Intermediate Approaches   206
The Use of Leverage   207
Market Timing   211
Possible Scenarios   212
Addressing the Rare Risks   218
A Summary of the Approaches   220

CHAPTER 7
Implementing and Controlling Long-Term Investment Strategies   **225**

    Rule 1: Choose a Well-Defined Strategy   225
    Rule 2: Stick to the Strategy   227
    Behavioral Challenges to Level3 Investing   229
    Overcoming Psychological Pressures   239
    Summary   249

Postscript   **251**

Appendix: AAII Resources   **253**

    AAII Model Shadow Stock Portfolio   253
    AAII Stock Screens   261
    Stock Investor Pro   263
    AAII Local Chapters   265
    Related Articles   267

Level3 Investing Website   **269**

Glossary   **271**

Bibliography   **301**

List of Exhibits   **307**

Index   **311**

About the Author   **321**

About AAII   **323**

PREFACE

*It seems to me more important to read stuff you
disagree with than to read stuff you agree with."*

-Milton Friedman

Eight years ago, I decided that I should write a book prior to
my retirement summarizing what I felt were the key concepts
of investing as observed over the past 36 years. These would
be the concepts that I believed could help individual investors
successfully manage their own investment portfolios. And by
successfully, I mean achieving "abnormal" returns—returns in
excess of what can be achieved by chance alone or by buying
the market portfolio.

We cover those concepts on a daily basis at the American
Association of Individual Investors (AAII) in our publications
and on our website (www.aaii.com), and they evolve from *AAII
Journal* articles by academics and investment professionals,
from insights and experiences of our members, and from our
internal research. I intended to integrate the most important of
them into a book.

Just when I thought I had the content settled, along came the
Great Recession of 2007–2009. As I watched the worst stock
market since the 1930s unfold, I realized that the focus of my
book must change.

I came to believe that a bit-by-bit shoring up of our approaches
to investing was no longer sufficient; individual investors needed a major strategy revision. There has been enough investment
history and research that a major step forward in thinking was

necessary and possible.

At AAII, we make an effort to point out the weaknesses of contemporary approaches to investing, but we had not looked at them in totality. Truly bad times should provide a new blueprint for effective strategy, not an experience to be forgotten with the next up market.

Truly bad times should provide a new blueprint for effective strategy, not an experience to be forgotten with the next up market.

When I began to review the weaknesses of current approaches to portfolio management, it became evident that their deficiencies had grown to the point that bandages were not enough. We needed major surgery on current investment practice—particularly for the individual investor.

I re-examined every aspect of investing to see if current approaches really are relevant to the success of the individual long-term investor. In my opinion, the three primary approaches commonly used for asset selection and portfolio management have largely become ineffective in helping individual investors achieve superior results: modern portfolio theory (MPT), technical analysis and fundamental analysis.

Modern portfolio theory (MPT) is the systematic scientific approach begun by Harry Markowitz between 1952 and 1959 and continued primarily in the finance and economics departments of academia. The objective of MPT is to discover approaches to investing that will maximize returns at a given level of risk or minimize risk at a given level of return. It also presents measures of portfolio performance that combine risk and return. However, it provides only incidental assistance to the individual investor since it relies on measurements of risk that are appropriate for institutions and short-term traders but largely meaningless for the individual.

Technical analysis is based on the belief that the most significant information necessary for determining what assets to buy and sell and when to buy and sell them is in the historical price and trading volume data of the market itself. The approach continues to draw the attention of investors. You can't read or listen to a discussion of the future direction of some stock or the entire market without coming across a comment about a technical indicator—resistance, support, triple bottom, head and shoulders, etc. This knee-jerk use of technical analysis is almost all nonsense, and yet mature experts tout it as being effective. However, there is evidence that past price and volume history, properly analyzed, can be useful in increasing returns.

Fundamental analysis asks us to look at all the characteristics of a company and use them to predict the future earnings and stock price, or at the very least help us avoid bad investments. It has a sensible foundation, but in practice very few investors or mutual funds have been able to turn these sensible measures into portfolios that can beat throwing darts at a list of stocks.

I examine these three approaches and their limitations in more detail in Chapters 1 and 2 of this book. In Chapter 3, I also look at the financial services industry and the role it plays in your investment success, or rather the lack thereof.

The picture that emerges is not pretty. The guidance we are receiving is mostly wrong or inappropriate for the individual investor. We are paying ridiculous sums of money to be misguided.

But getting rid of poor strategy is not a solution to the challenges of effective portfolio management. In Chapters 4 through 7, I pull together the theories and strategies that I feel can help investors obtain the highest level of return consistent with an appropriate level of real risk. These strategies make up the "Investing at Level3" approach.

I pull together the theories and strategies that I feel can help investors obtain the highest level of return consistent with an appropriate level of real risk.

The risk and return concept that I lay out

in these pages is quite different from the strategies of modern portfolio theory or fundamental analysis. Also, the focus here is on the individual rather than the institutional investor, and there is a significant difference between strategies that are appropriate for the individual and those that are necessary for institutions and the investment services industry.

My orientation toward the individual investor, of course, stems from the purpose and activities of AAII. In the 38 years since I founded AAII, it has provided extensive educational materials to investors, always in the belief that the motivated and disciplined individual can obtain far better investment results than most institutions.

This book is a continuation of that effort to support the individual investor. My focus is on the best ways to communicate the concepts that I think are vital. I have tried to make the book readable by minimizing mathematical nomenclature and formulas. (As I show, mathematical modeling is rather useless anyway.)

Throughout the book, I refer to professional books or academic research. In many cases, the original work I refer to is in scholarly journals that are not easily be available to most investors. Full titles and authors are provided in the bibliography. Links to works that are available online are provided at the website Level3investing.com. Alternatively, an internet search of a citation should provide a basic description plus commentary.

One of the most difficult parts of writing this book was the necessity of abandoning many previously held beliefs. I have advocated many of the approaches that I now find insufficient at best and often harmful. Traditional investment approaches are so ingrained that, even if I could prove them useless beyond any doubt, most investors would still cling to them out of habit.

Many of the weaknesses with current approaches that I discuss have been covered by other writers one or two at a time but, to my knowledge, have not been combined in a complete dismissal of current investment theory and practice. Some of the alternative approaches I suggest have likewise been previously discussed but never, I believe, integrated into an overall strategy or strategies.

Many will disagree with various aspects of my approach. Some will disagree because I am 'goring their ox'; others will have a genuine conceptual disagreement. Ultimately, investment theories cannot be proved absolutely because chance can affect results into eternity. What is true now may not be true in a changing future, so there can never be complete certainty about the effectiveness of an investment approach. We must always be willing to accept reasonable evidence if we are to make any decisions.

Even if the content of this book goes against your current beliefs and approaches, I ask that you give the ideas some thought. I don't expect that everyone will rush to adopt my approaches. In fact, they would not work if everyone did. But perhaps you will find a few ideas here that are helpful. I truly believe that the strategies of Level3 Investing have the potential to add significantly to your wealth and the quality of your life in retirement.

> *Even if the content of this book goes against your current beliefs and approaches, I ask that you give the ideas some thought.*

Ultimately, I am responsible for the opinions and strategies in this book. My opinions are not the opinions of AAII, which focuses on exploring all relevant approaches to investing. Much of the content flies in the face of conventional beliefs. My neck is out there, so feel free to chop at jbc.level3@aaii.com. However, it is my firm belief that the approaches covered in this book can result in a young person's ultimate retirement wealth being at least twice what it would be following the current "best practices" of investing and can add significantly to the assets of those closer to or in retirement.

I want to thank the staff of AAII and the two million individual investors who have been members of AAII over the years and have helped expose me to so many challenging ideas. Particular thanks go to those who have helped me with the ideas in this book and have provided editorial support: Arthur Susman, John Markese, Charles Rotblut and John Bajkowski provided guidance on content throughout the writing of the book.

For the copy editing, layout and design and extensive checking of calculations, thanks go to Wayne Thorp, Jaclyn McClellan, Kate Peltz and Annie Prada. The website Level3investing.com is an integral part of the book and thanks go to Peter Nguyen for putting it together. Finally, special thanks to Jean Henrich who has edited, overseen and integrated it all.

James B. Cloonan
Chicago
May 2016

INTRODUCTION

*"If you stay rational yourself, the
stupidity of the world helps you."*

—Charles Munger

This book has four objectives:

1. To show that the vast majority of what we have been
   taught about investing is not effective for the long-term
   individual investor. While the combination of modern
   portfolio theory and fundamental analysis (which I call
   "Level 2 investing") is a vast improvement over the unorganized, always changing, emotion-driven practices
   (which I call "Level 1 investing"), it falls far short of
   achievable levels of return.

2. To offer alternative approaches that can, I believe, significantly increase the ultimate wealth and retirement income
   of investors using reality-based rather than theoretical
   models.

3. To show how this can be done while effectively controlling real risk as opposed to the "ghost" risk of short-term
   volatility. The combination of these last two points is what
   I define as "Level3 Investing."

4. To provide a framework for accomplishing the above
   objectives while overcoming significant psychological barriers and ignoring the continuous excess costs, harmful
   noise and misdirection coming from the investment services industry.

To do this, a series of beliefs that have become accepted over the years as appropriate must first be torn down. The approaches to investing that we are exposed to on a daily basis have major flaws. These flaws significantly reduce the effectiveness of individual investors in their effort to increase their standard of living through their working years and in their retirement. While Level 2 investing may be suitable for institutional and short-term investors, it severely handicaps the long-term individual investor.

LEVELS OF INVESTING

Level 1 is unorganized investing driven by impulse and emotion. It is influenced by random observations and advice and is in a constant state of flux. Unfortunately, this is still the level of investing of too many individual investors.

Level 2 represents the investing strategy that has evolved from modern portfolio theory and is academic in origin. It is based on measures of return and risk and seeks optimal outcomes from models assuming an efficient market, rational actions and the effects of random chance. It has also been formulated without these models but maintaining academic measures of risk. Variations of this model are considered best practices by most investment advisers.

Level3 Investing is a new strategy that I offer as a substitute for current practice. It is reality-based rather than mathematically based in that return and risk are derived directly from actual historical data and common sense without attempting to force them into a mathematical distribution or model first.

Each of the three investing levels is actually a continuum, as there is a range of approaches and theory within each level. A significant portion of academia has abandoned the efficient market hypothesis and has accepted adjustments to the traditional measures of risk. I expand on each approach throughout the book.

THE INDIVIDUAL INVESTOR

In 1978, I founded AAII because I believed that the individual investor had significant advantages over institutions and could use those advantages to realize higher returns. This has become truer over the years as online commissions have been reduced to insignificance for the long-term investor, bid-ask spreads have narrowed, no-load mutual funds have proliferated, and exchange-traded funds (ETFs) have come into existence.

However, the increased flow of information has not helped individual investors realize higher rates of return. It has just reinforced short-term, emotional actions that hurt long-term performance.

Today, I think individual investors not only have significant advantages over institutional investors, but they can capitalize on the limitations of institutions to increase their individual returns. Following the strategies outlined in this book, I believe it is not unreasonable to think that typical individual investors can arrive at retirement with more than twice the assets they would have under today's suggested best practice approaches.

Following the strategies outlined in this book, I believe it is not unreasonable to think that typical individual investors can arrive at retirement with more than twice the assets they would have under today's suggested best practice approaches.

The problem is that while individuals have the ability to get out from under the burdens institutions must bear, the investment services industry (with frequent support from the investment press) has been able to convince individual investors to voluntarily accept and bear the same burdens as the institutions. These burdens include:

- short- to intermediate-term investment horizons,

- the need to perform relative to competition,

- the need to take very large positions,

- the need to appear competent by complying with current academic theory and, most importantly,

- the acceptance of meaningless measures of risk.

All of these are burdens the individual can unload in order to excel.

OUTLINE OF THE BOOK

When attempting to organize this book to make it as understandable as possible, I was faced with the problem that trying to explain any part seemed to require having already explained another part. The approach I have taken to overcome this conundrum is to cover almost all the content of the book in overview form at the beginning. So this chapter is not only an introduction but also a summary of the entire book.

In the chapters to follow, I discuss in detail the problems contributing to the less-than-optimal performance of most individual investors, followed by the strategies for overcoming these problems.

Major Obstacles to Optimal Performance

I feel there are four major obstacles blocking optimal performance by the individual investor:

Major Obstacle One: Current academic research and modeling is largely inappropriate or misapplied.

Modern portfolio theory (MPT) is the effort over the last 60 years to provide a mathematical model of security market behavior in order to determine the highest return for a given level of risk or the least risk for a given level of return. In some cases the impact of risk and reward are combined in a single score—for example, the Sharpe ratio. From the viewpoint of the individual investor, the problems are extensive.

- The various MPT models are inadequate to explain real-world phenomenon.

- The research that might be of value to individuals is not translated into useful formats. While it is likely not the responsibility of academia to do this, those who have attempted to translate research into actionable form have done an inadequate job (whether accidentally or on purpose).

- The assumptions underlying almost all of the MPT models have significant weaknesses in the real world in which individuals operate. While academic researchers understand and footnote this, the models are put to use by analysts and advisers who don't understand the limitations or choose to ignore them.

- Probably most important, modern portfolio theory, in almost all of its models, has misconstrued or run away from the real nature of investment risk. There are many types of risk in the financial world. Throughout this book, I use the word risk to describe the variations in stock prices and how that impacts the availability of assets.

The use of volatility as a suitable measure of risk in virtually all models of asset behavior is a critical failing of modern portfolio theory. I examine all the ramifications of this flaw in Chapter 1, including how it leads to too much diversification and needless asset allocation and thereby reduces portfolio returns.

My view of real risk is not short-term volatility but rather the possibility that the assets we expected to have for consumption will not be there when we need them.

In Chapter 1, I also discuss how real-world market behavior has called into question the major underpinnings of MPT—the efficient market hypothesis (the belief that asset prices reflect all information about the asset) and the normal (or even near normal) distribution of returns.

Major Obstacle Two: Fundamental analysis and technical analysis—the conventional and popular approaches to stock selection and portfolio management—are largely ineffective as practiced.

While the underlying concepts of fundamental analysis (the analysis of all hard data known about a company) make sense, and its "father" Benjamin Graham is held in high regard by many famous investors, fundamental analysis has been largely ineffective in obtaining above-average portfolio returns in real-world applications. This is true even of many of Graham's own strategies. Virtually all stock mutual funds are managed using models that apply different fundamental factors, but they rarely perform better than an index fund over the long run, especially net of fees.

Virtually all stock mutual funds are managed using models that apply different fundamental factors, but they rarely perform better than an index fund over the long run.

This is a strange phenomenon. The best investors of our time all talk about the importance of fundamentals in picking stocks destined to provide higher returns. Yet using fundamental data doesn't seem to work for most individual investors or institutions. I feel that the way fundamentals are applied in decision-making may be creating the problem.

One example is the use of too many fundamental criteria to select stocks without regard for their varying levels of importance. This can result in eliminating a stock that is exemplary on the most important criterion because it fails on some criterion that is only marginally important. Other problems with using fundamental analysis are explored more fully in Chapter 2. However, all is not lost. I show individual investors which active approaches have been successful in outperforming passive approaches in Chapter 6.

It is one of the great mysteries of contemporary investment practice that there is very strong evidence of superior returns from a variety of fundamental approaches, but mutual funds and other institutions misinterpret them, choose not to use them or are limited by their own business model from properly implementing them.

Technical analysis is broadly defined as the attempt to find stocks that will provide above-average returns based on their historical price movement and trading volume. There is significant evidence that momentum analysis can be used to obtain returns above those possible in an efficient market. Momentum analysis rates stocks based on how much their price has gone up over recent periods of time compared to the market as a whole or compared to other stocks.

It is possible that advanced analytic approaches using historical price and volume statistics may lead to strategies that provide above-market returns. I examine such approaches in detail in Chapter 2 and explore why research in this area is migrating out of finance and economics departments and into the hard sciences.

However, the major tools of the popular technical analysis forms—such as point & figure charting or Japanese candlesticks—are mostly myth and have no provable value. I have never seen a fund, or even a portfolio, that is governed primarily by charting produce long-term results even equal to market averages. There is some evidence that charting might work for some commodities, but not for stocks.

The major tools of the popular technical analysis forms are mostly myth and have no provable value.

I have a hard time containing myself when I see gurus on CNBC drawing strange pictures on price charts with funny names like "dark cloud," "head and shoulders" or "triple bottoms" and then predicting future market moves. All of these formations will appear in the generation of random numbers.

Even if charting had some underlying validity, it would be difficult to justify crude charts in the era of high-speed computers.

Major Obstacle Three: The investment services industry and its employees follow their own profit models; for the individual investor, they are often more of a competitor than a teammate.

While those who comprise the investment services industry may not deliberately try to harm the individual (except in extreme cases like Bernard Madoff, or as in the movie "The Wolf of Wall Street"), the actions that help advisers maximize their profits frequently diminish the returns of the individual investor. For example, investment advisory firms will try to charge fees that maximize their profit, as any company tries to do. We, the customers, can control the demand curve (which determines price) if we act rationally. However, as discussed in Chapter 3, we often don't act rationally or are too timid to negotiate.

Mutual funds charge an average of about 1% for managing what is only a portion of an investor's portfolio, and they do not deal with individual circumstances or asset allocation. Meanwhile, individual investment advisers and financial planners typically charge 1% or less depending on portfolio size to select assets, consider individual circumstances, establish proper asset allocation and deal with the tax ramifications of decisions. In most cases, these charges are also too high for reasons shown below, but they are significantly lower than the average mutual fund. (To put this in context, $100,000 invested at just 1% over 20 years would generate over $22,000 in gains.)

Commission-reimbursed advisers simply do not advocate "buy and hold" even for the intermediate term. Advisers whose pay is not tied to turnover (commissions and fees from buying and selling) will trade less but enough to make it look like they are earning their keep. It is human nature to rationalize behavior that helps us achieve our own goals, and the cohorts of the investment services business are very human that way.

Understand that I don't object to companies trying to maximize profits. They have an obligation to their stockholders to do so as long as they are within the law and the ethical guidelines that govern their relationship with their clients. The problem lies with the need for clients to drive their own costs down by being discriminating consumers of investment services.

Institutional advisers try to persuade companies with 401(k) retirement plans and state lawmakers designing 529 educational savings plans to permit unnecessary fees and restrict the choices to those that are more favorable to the adviser and less favorable to the investor. In many cases, the ineffectiveness of the plans more than offsets the tax advantage.

As I examine in Chapter 3, even advisers who want to be on your side with no ax to grind can wind up reducing your investment success because they have been sold on approaches that don't make sense for the individual investor with a long-term planning horizon.

Advisers can wind up reducing your investment success because they have been sold on approaches that don't make sense for the individual investor with a long-term planning horizon.

Major Obstacle Four: Our own psychological processes work against us, which may be the biggest hindrance to successful long-term investing for the individual.

While it is difficult to pinpoint exactly, it is likely that the typical individual investor makes trading decisions that reduce annual return by 2% to 3% a year. Many researchers would say it is even more. I am not talking about the extreme cases of "nutty" trading, but the everyday behavior of investors who are driven to panic on downside market moves and become too ecstatic during upward moves.

There are well-established behavioral tendencies that are self-defeating. In Chapter 7, I examine these phenomena of behavioral finance along with possible ways to neutralize their return-reducing impact.

The State of Contemporary Portfolio Management

Even the best money managers are victims of the weaknesses

discussed above. It is hard to blame them, because they have been continuously taught approaches that might be proper for institutions but are grossly inadequate for the long-term individual investor. In addition, the fees—both hidden and admitted—are unreasonably high.

> *Money managers have been continuously taught approaches that might be proper for institutions but are grossly inadequate for the long-term individual investor.*

This is particularly true of mutual funds, where average annual expense fees run 1% a year and transaction and other costs further reduce final performance. It is even truer of hedge funds, where the current fees typically are 2% of assets plus 20% of the profit (they do not give back 20% of any losses). Both hedge funds and regular mutual funds on average perform about equal to each other and slightly underperform the market after fees.

I want to clarify who I am talking about when I use term "money managers." By that term, I mean mutual funds, hedge funds, investment advisers, and financial planners—but only the part of their activities that involves the selection of publicly traded investment assets and the allocation of wealth among those assets.

I do not include professional help that is fee-based and provides advice in areas such as wills, trusts, transfer of assets, and matters related to the proper format of retirement plans. These latter issues require specific professional knowledge that individual investors probably don't have and must depend on others for.

That is not the case with money managers. They may be professional in the sense that they get paid for their advice, but their advice is essentially worthless, and in most cases worse than worthless, because it underperforms random chance and adheres to concepts that are flawed.

There is a story about a group of men trying to escape the

Spanish Inquisition. Their efforts to secure passage on any ship are not meeting with success because of the multitudes attempting to flee. Finally, they come across a ship's captain who tells them that because of sickness he is short a number of prisoner rowers and since he is often sailing against the wind this is a problem.

He tells the group that he will transport them free to the next port that will be safer for them if they will take over the rower vacancies. He emphasizes that while passage is free they will be treated the same as the regular convict rowers.

After a brief consultation, the group in desperation agrees to the terms and are escorted to the ship's hold and chained to the rowing seats. A few hours later the ship pushes off and they are told to begin rowing. A giant of a man stands behind them and cracks a whip across the back of anyone slacking in their effort.

This goes on for 10 to 15 hours a day, whenever the wind is not right. Day after day they row and the giant continuously lashes them to pull harder. Finally, they hear sounds and voices indicating they are coming to port, and they are told to stop rowing.

Shortly later the captain comes down into the hold, unlocks their chains and tells them they have arrived at port and are free to go. As they slip their chains and head toward the hatch, the leader of the group approaches the captain and asks, "Pardon me, captain, but how much do we *tip the whipper?*"

As individual investors, we are continually paying for advice that provides returns worse than average market returns and much worse than the returns we would get on average from throwing darts. We are "tipping the whipper" to do worse.

The Impact of Various Approaches

Let's look at an estimate of what different investment inefficiencies cost us.

I use the hypothetical life conditions of John and Mary Smith to calculate the rates of return under various approaches over their lifetime. Readers can make adjustments for their own situations as a percentage of the Smiths'. The assumptions about the Smiths are detailed in the box below.

HYPOTHETICAL SMITH FAMILY ASSUMPTIONS

Investor John Smith is the oldest of the Smith couple and is approaching 70 when he plans to retire. Mary Smith is 67 and is no longer working. They have managed to put away $250,000 (initial saved dollars) over the years and have their Social Security, which they both will start receiving when he retires. Their retirement fund is the $250,000 plus the investment returns on those savings over the years that John Smith has been working.

While there is a nearly 50-year span during which the Smiths tried to put aside money for their retirement, not much was saved in the early years beyond what went into the down payment on a house; the children's education took money out of possible savings in the middle years. More was put away as their income increased, so the average dollar has only been invested for 18 years. To make the example simple, the assumption is that $250,000 was invested and allowed to earn an investment return that was reinvested at the compound annual growth rate over an 18-year time period.

The amount in the retirement fund depends on how they invested their savings over the years (Table I.1).

In Chapter 5, I look at the Smiths' future needs and plans as well as the change in approach required as they near retirement, but for now I simply want to show in Table I.1 the impact of their past investing on the size of their retirement fund.

TABLE I.1

Potential Investment Returns for the Smiths Over the Very Long Term

Assumptions: $250,000 portfolio invested for 18 years

Strategy	Estimated Long-Term Annual Return	Portfolio Value at Retirement
Level 1 investing	4%	$506,000
Level 2 investing	8%	$999,000
Passive Level3 Investing	12%	$1,922,000
Active Level3 Investing	16%	$3,616,000

Returns are based on stock selection only, without leverage. The examples are presented on a pretax basis. See the box on page 20 for portfolio value (future value) formula.

Level 1 investing: Individual investor playing the market, getting in and out, acting on emotions, and following different advice at different times.

Level 2 investing: Portfolio invested 60% in large-cap stocks (primarily S&P 500 index) and 40% in bonds. Assumes stock-picking ability is above average enough to offset the fees. Typical outcome for investors using a good money manager or following generally accepted investment practice on their own.

Passive Level3 Investing: Reasonable possibility for Level3 Investing approach when investor prefers a more passive stance or doesn't feel able to maintain the necessary discipline. As an example, see the Plan Z approach described in Chapter 6.

Active Level3 Investing: Maximum achievable expectation for investor following the guidance in this book. Requires active participation, absolute adherence to strategies and control of emotions. This approach is described in Chapter 6.

Table I.1 shows estimates of possible rates of return for the Smiths under different approaches. I discuss the basis for these estimates throughout the book.

The figures in Table I.1 will vary with the amount spent on advice and transaction costs. This can vary from a few hundred dollars for data and information to upward of 3% a year with a full-service broker. *The estimated long-term returns create quite a range between portfolio values of $500,000 and $3 million and quite a difference in potential retirement lifestyle.*

The scenarios in the table are four points on what is really a continuum, and mixed strategies will show results between the sample points. For example, many researchers in academia have abandoned the efficient market hypothesis (EMH) but still adhere to other concepts of modern portfolio theory. They support anomalies (such as the small-cap effect) and believe that

---

FUTURE VALUE FORMULA TO CALCULATE PORTFOLIO VALUE AT RETIREMENT

Future value   =   Present value $\times (1 + r)^n$

Where:

Present value   =   initial investment amount
r   =   assumed rate of return
n   =   compounding periods

Example Using Active Level3 Investing Scenario in Table I.1:

(See Smith family assumptions on page 18.)

Present value   = $250,000
r   =   16%
n   =   18 years

Future value   = $250,000 $\times 1.16^{18}$
= $3,616,000

returns above those of the S&P 500 index can be achieved. This might be called Level 2.5 investing and could generate returns above the 8% level estimated for the pure Level 2 approach.

I want to emphasize that these are long-term total returns from the selection of publicly available assets without leverage. Many hedge funds, private equity funds, and other investing processes add to returns by adding value in other ways. High-speed trading, arbitrage, conversion activity and buying, reorganizing and selling companies can all add to an investment firm's returns. Some investors impact the market by their very presence.

When Warren Buffett takes a position in a company, the volatility in that company's stock goes down because he is a long-term investor and, in addition, performance may well go up based on his managerial advice and oversight (or simply the belief in it). The additional returns he achieves are not just from stock selection but from expertise and effort. He also leverages significantly. The estimates in Table I.1 are based only on the returns from decisions as to what is in the investment portfolio.

A Simple Alternative

If you don't want to be or don't have the time to be involved in the analysis and discipline necessary to attain the maximum return for your portfolio, I offer you the opportunity to go no further in this book and adopt a simple plan that will outperform most mutual funds, hedge funds and money managers. It is a variation of Level3 investing I call Plan Z and it will provide a long-term annualized return, in my estimation, of approximately 12% per year with little effort. Here are the rules:

1. You may stop reading this book until you are five years from retirement, and then read Chapter 5.

2. Tomorrow, open an online discount brokerage account with one of the well-known and financially strong online brokers (Schwab, E*Trade, TD Ameritrade, Scottrade, etc.)

3.   Invest all your funds in the Guggenheim S&P 500 Equal Weight (RSP) exchange-traded fund and arrange to have future savings sent and invested in the fund. This ETF seeks to replicate as closely as possible the performance of the S&P 500 Equal Weight Index.

4.   Arrange for reinvestment of distributions.

5.   If you will need withdrawals for reasons other than retirement (college tuition, for example), read Chapter 5 five years before such withdrawals. Exceptions: If funds are in a taxable account, you will have to pay taxes each year and make estimated payments. If you are over 70, you will have to make required minimum withdrawals (RMDs) from any tax-deferred accounts, pay tax on the withdrawal, and reinvest the balance in a taxable account.

6.   Try to avoid following the stock market on a frequent basis; if you must watch financial television, turn off the sound and just pay attention to the data.

7.   Check for revisions to this book. If new ETFs appear exploiting value or cap-size effects, they will be included in future editions of this book and posted at Level3investing.com.

Once again, all of the above refers to investments held for the long term (five years or longer). When money is needed from investments in the short term, the short-term funds must be treated differently. This is described in Chapter 5.

Evidence That a Higher Return Is Achievable

Is it possible to achieve a 12% return with virtually no effort? And is it possible to do even better with effort and discipline?

Achieving a 12% return over the long run would pretty much put an investor ahead of the vast majority of mutual funds and hedge funds. (Since the typical hedge fund or stock mutual fund investor also has investments in bonds and cash, their overall return is likely lower than that of their funds.)

It will also put the investor ahead of the average stock investor's return of 10% based on long-term performance of the market-cap-weighted S&P 500 (less fees for advice and transactions).

I believe a 12% return is possible because the average stock in the broad-based Wilshire 5000 index was up an annualized 17.1% over the past 45 years (the longest the data is available). So on average over the years dart throwers would have received a 17.1% return (less a significant transaction cost) if they invested an equal amount in each stock.

Real Portfolios

Can the active disciplined investor obtain an annualized 16% a year? I believe so. Here are two examples in the area of small-cap value stocks.

- The Model Shadow Stock Portfolio, which is maintained at AAII, has returned an annualized 15.4% over the past 23 years, and this has been a below-average period for the stock market as a whole (through year-end 2015). This real portfolio (not a simulation) invests in attractively priced small-company (micro-cap value) stocks with specific rules. I discuss this approach in later chapters and describe it completely in the Appendix.

- A small-cap value portfolio following the recommendations of The Prudent Speculator advisory newsletter has had an annual return of 16.3% over the past 20 years net of transaction costs, as tracked by the Hulbert Financial Digest.

Model Shadow Stock Portfolio has returned an annualized 15.4% over the past 23 years.

There are other real-time examples providing returns at or above the 16% level that I discuss in Chapter 6. I certainly believe that if you follow the strategies of Level3 Investing you can approach the 16% return indicated, but this is the upper end of reasonable expectations and it demands effort and discipline.

Research Studies

In addition to the above examples of real portfolios, there is also extensive research performed on historical data that provides indications of above-average returns. The 1992 Fama/French study examined returns for small-cap and high-value stocks for 27 years, during which time the combination of the smallest 10% in capitalization size and the best 10% in value returned 23.0% per year (less transaction costs).

The study period was a strong period for stocks, but the small-value group outperformed the overall market by over 10% a year. Even using a combination of the best 20% for each category provided a return of 20.9% a year.

> *Extensive research performed on historical data provides indications of above-average returns.*

James P. O'Shaughnessy, in his book "What Works on Wall Street" (2012), examined a multitude of strategies over a 44-year period, and there are an extensive number that exceed the S&P 500 by over 4% a year. O'Shaughnessy's work provides a great starting point for experimentation. While it is more oriented toward institutional investors, as I examine in Chapter 6 it provides additional proof that higher stock returns are very possible.

In the book "Excess Returns" (2014), Frederik Vanhaverbeke examines the results of the world's greatest investors, showing over 50 who have significantly outperformed the market for periods in excess of 15 years.

Historical research might overstate returns because of inaccurate transaction costs, particularly for portfolios that require frequent rebalancing, and exhibit some problems in accurate pricing. Well-done research provides evidence of future results, if not the exact returns that would have been received in a real portfolio. I discuss a number of approaches that consistently provide above-average long-term returns in Chapter 6.

The Basis of Higher Returns

Part of my high (compared to current practice) estimated return of the passive Level3 Plan Z approach comes from my belief that for the long-term investor there is no reason to be investing in "safer" assets than common stock or its equivalent. Throughout this book, I emphasize that unnecessary fear of volatility results in investors throwing away returns to offset risk that doesn't really exist for the long-term investor, which I call ghost risk.

Even investment practitioners who deny much of modern portfolio theory have accepted this fear of short-term volatility and pass it on to their clients. Meaningless asset allocation and over-diversification hurt the returns of the long-term investor unnecessarily.

This ghost risk is truly an advantage for the individual long-term investor. Institutions must be concerned with short-term risk, as short-term volatility is real for them. They and individual investors who invest based on ghost risk drive prices down and returns up to the benefit of long-term investors. What is the "fear index" for institutions and other short-term thinking investors (discussed further in Chapter 4) is the "opportunity index" for those who invest at Level3.

> *Unnecessary fear of volatility results in investors throwing away returns to offset risk that doesn't really exist for the long-term investor.*

The balance of the high return comes from taking advantage of the problems faced by large institutional investors. The Guggenheim S&P 500 Equal Weight ETF (RSP), which makes up the entire portfolio of Level3 Investing's Plan Z, is an index fund that buys all the stocks in the S&P 500. But it is different in that it buys equal dollar amounts of each stock, while the vast majority of S&P 500 index funds are capitalization weighted, determining quantities based on the capitalization (stock price multiplied by number of shares outstanding). If Stock A has a capitalization of $2 billion and Stock B has a capitalization of $1 billion, market-cap-weighted index funds buy twice as much

Stock A as Stock B.

There is a very interesting characteristic of a market-cap-weighted portfolio: Its gain or loss for any period is precisely the gain or loss for the average of all investors, because it captures the dollar amount of all price changes. SDPR S&P 500 ETF (SPY), with $190 billion in assets, is the largest exchange-traded fund and is cap-weighted.

The argument for using capitalization weighting is simply that buying into such an index fund guarantees you will obtain the average return with almost no costs. Or, as proponents of capitalization weighting like to say, it guarantees you get your fair share of all gains.

John Bogle, the founder of The Vanguard Group, summarizes the arguments for indexing in an interview in the *AAII Journal* ("Achieving Greater Long-Term Wealth Through Index Funds," June 2014). He has written numerous books on the subject (see Bibliography).

If it is not possible to predict which stocks will do better, then capitalization weighting is a sensible approach. However, to a significant extent, it has been amply demonstrated that certain classes of stocks do have higher-than-average returns over the long run.

The two characteristics, as we have just seen, that have provided significant and constant higher returns over the long term are capitalization size (the smaller the better) and value, most simply calculated as the ratio of the price of a share of stock to the book value per share (the lower the better).

These two characteristics are correlated, and smaller-capitalization stocks tend to have higher value than large-cap stocks. I discuss different ways of measuring value and various approaches to small-cap value investing in Chapter 6, but in general small-cap and/or value stocks provide from 3% to 6% additional return per year.

Because of this small-cap and value phenomenon, cap-weighted indexes underweight the stocks most likely to provide the higher returns. As a result, they significantly underperform equal-weighted indexes.

Cap-weighted indexes underweight the stocks most likely to provide the higher returns.

While there is no equal-weighted index fund that has been in existence for 20 years or more, Wilshire maintains its 5000 index in both cap-weighted and equal-weighted format. Over the last 45 years (to year-end 2015), the equal-weighted index has outperformed the cap-weighted index 17.1% to 10.5%, for an annualized difference of 6.6%. An investor in the equal-weighted index would now have almost 14 times the assets of the cap-weighted investor if they invested equal amounts at the beginning of 1971. On $10,000 invested, that's $12.2 million versus $894,000.

Equal weighting requires constant rebalancing, which will reduce the advantage somewhat because of transaction costs. In addition, there will be difficulty investing in some of the smaller stocks. This is particularly true for a large portfolio.

The Guggenheim S&P 500 Equal Weight ETF (RSP) has only been around since 2003, but as can be seen in Figure I.1 on the next page it significantly outperforms the cap-weighted S&P 500 index by over 3% annualized in a below-average return time period.

Equal weighting is not magical in itself. It simply gives more weight to smaller-cap stocks than capitalization weighting does. A weighting approach that gives even more weight to small caps would be even better. Advocates of cap weighting say that if you believe small-cap stocks are better, then just buy small caps. Of course the problem continues because you have to weight any small-cap index and decide on how to do it. Other problems and opportunities are discussed in more detail in later chapters.

FIGURE I.1

Equal-Weighted vs. Cap-Weighted Market ETFs

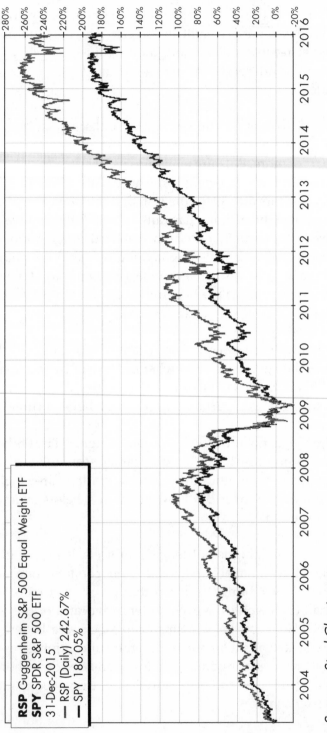

RSP Guggenheim S&P 500 Equal Weight ETF
SPY SPDR S&P 500 ETF
31-Dec-2015
— RSP (Daily) 242.67%
— SPY 186.05%

Source: StockCharts.com

To me, this is the perfect example of where the individual investor has a tremendous advantage over the institutions. Whether indexed or not, institutions cannot significantly invest in smaller-capitalization companies.

There are two different stock investment strategies. The one for institutions, Level 2 investing, has an average annual return of about 10% a year (on the equity investments) less expenses. Each institution can choose to index and accept that or try to obtain an above-average return with their own approach.

In the Level3 Investing strategy, which is limited to individual long-term investors, the average return could be up to 16% a year. With this approach, you can be passive and index to try for 12%, use your own active Level3 approach and try for 16%, or use some combination of passive and active approaches.

Institutions generally cannot invest at Level3, but individuals pay dearly to invest at Level 2. It's hard to understand why they would want to (except for their short-term funds), but unfortunately most individual investors choose to bear that handicap and pay dearly for the choice.

Institutions generally cannot invest at Level3, but individuals pay dearly to invest at Level 2.

There is another aspect of weighting indexes that largely goes unnoticed. Analysts talk about the average return on all stocks, dividing it up as if it were a pie. But the decisions to index affect the size of the pie as well as how it is divided.

To illustrate this problem and its effect on markets, imagine that at the end of this year everyone decided to index on a cap-weighted basis. From that time on, the relative prices of all stocks would stay the same. If the price of Stock A was $100 and Stock B $50, they would always stay at that 2-1 ratio. Stock A could be heading for bankruptcy and Stock B could triple its earnings and the relative prices would stay the same. Stocks would go up or down with the overall market but the ratios of all stock prices would stay the same—at least until they were delisted or went into bankruptcy.

Now, that won't happen because not everyone is going to index, but nearly $5 trillion of stock investing is indexed, most of it cap-weighted, and that must already be causing some stickiness—some tendency for prices not to respond fully to the actualities of a company's performance. With the current emphasis on indexing, I believe it may be time to start worrying about price stickiness.

Of course, equal-weighted indexing, if carried out by everyone, would also bring a ridiculous result. The equity value of every company would become the same. A small publicly held fabricator selling $1 million of goods a year would suddenly be worth the same as Apple Inc. (AAPL).

With the current emphasis on indexing, I believe it may be time to start worrying about price stickiness.

Whether they are highly successful or not, we need investors who are buying and selling stocks based on company realities, or we would not have a workable market.

There are other approaches to indexing. Fundamental indexing is basically where you vary the weights based on your favorite fundamental measures, but you buy all stocks in an index rather than only the ones with higher ratings on the factors used. Clearly, the optimal weighting would be to weight companies on the price of their stock's next period. *If we only knew.*

While my use of the term "individual investors" is generally accurate, the suitability of the approaches of Level3 is really based on portfolio size and a long-term outlook. Small institutions could use Level3 Investing and billionaires can't, but the latter have alternatives the rest of us don't.

As expanded on in Chapter 5, when you need to spend some of your money in the short term (less than five years) it is necessary for some assets to be in investments that protect against short-term risk, but even here my approach is quite different from most current wisdom.

Embracing a New Path

In this Introduction, I have stirred the pot a bit and told you what I feel is wrong with most contemporary investment practice. I have suggested that abandoning the current practices and embracing a different approach could significantly increase returns and make retirement much more comfortable. Part I expands on what is wrong with current practice (Chapters 1, 2, and 3) and Part II explores the strategies that can bring us to Level3 Investing (Chapters 4, 5, 6, and 7).

It is a strange twist for me, as I am among the many who have been trying to get individual investors away from the unorganized emotion-driven approaches (the 4% returns of Level 1 investing) and into the current organized approaches that produced the safe 8% returns of Level 2. I now that believe pushing beyond current best practice and into the reality-based long-term aggressive approaches of Level3 Investing can be just as or more important for the majority of individual investors.

I firmly believe that long-term individual investors are entitled to above-average returns because they can invest in the higher-return areas not available to large institutions and because they can ignore the short-term volatility concerns that serve to reduce the returns of institutional investors.

PART I

Where We Are: The Current State of Investment Theory and Practice

In the next three chapters, I examine the current state of investment theory and practice as well as the nature of the investment services industry in which current "best practices" operate.

As indicated in the Introduction, I believe that volatility is a poor measure of risk for the long-term investor and that real risk is the possibility of not having sufficient assets when you expected to have them for expenditure.

Out of respect for the extensive work and originality of the various models of modern portfolio theory, much of Chapter 1 is spent explaining why I disagree with the measures of volatility currently being used. I show throughout this book that volatility is only of limited interest to the long-term individual investor and that most of modern portfolio theory bears about the same relationship to real markets as chess does to actual warfare. But it is important for every investor to understand these concepts, how they are ingrained in current investment practice and their very crucial weaknesses for the long-term investor.

CHAPTER 1

PROBLEMS WITH MODERN PORTFOLIO THEORY

"Far better an approximate answer to the right question, which is often vague, than an exact answer to the wrong question, which can always be made precise."

—John W. Tukey

Modern portfolio theory (MPT) is a mathematical approach to modeling the price changes in securities over time. The MPT approach examines these changes in terms of returns (profit or loss) and risk. Return is measured as a percent change of the amount invested, and risk is measured in terms of the distribution of returns around the mean—the volatility.

The objective of MPT is to discover approaches to investing that will maximize returns at a given level of risk or minimize risk at a given level of return. It also presents measures of portfolio performance that combine risk and return.

The organized approach to accomplishing this objective is generally attributed to Harry Markowitz in an article (1952) and expanded on in his book (1959). William Sharpe (1964) formalized the approach, and the heart of the new scientific approach, the capital asset pricing model (CAPM), emerged.

It is important to note that while the organized approach may not have started until 1952 many of the insights of MPT go back much further in history. Concepts formulated by Bernoulli (1738), Bachelier (1900), Einstein (1905), and others underlie the various models.

The original capital asset pricing model is a one-factor model; that is, it determines risk and return using only a measure of volatility (market beta). It has since been supplanted by various two-, three-, and four- and (soon to be) five-factor models that use other measures in addition to volatility to measure risk. While some of these measures are important, the newer models still rely on volatility, which is poorly measured and inappropriately applied to long-term investing.

UNDERLYING CONCEPTS OF MPT

As you progress through this chapter, it will become apparent that I feel that the core of MPT is irrelevant to the success of the individual investor. The academic research that is important to us has only raised questions about MPT and its assumptions.

I feel that it is critical, however, for investors to understand the basic concepts of modern portfolio theory and why they are largely irrelevant. Every day all of us who pay attention to financial matters are exposed to concepts of investing that are meaningless and sometimes dangerous.

I feel that it is critical for investors to understand the basic concepts of modern portfolio theory and why they are largely irrelevant.

Many sources will be trying to convince us that we should follow them. As I go through these concepts, I show how they relate or don't relate to successful investing.

First, I provide a general explanation of each investing concept from an MPT point of view, and then I discuss their shortcomings and relationship to the reality-based Level3 Investing.

Efficient Market Hypothesis

The efficient market hypothesis (EMH) states that all relevant information is already in the price of the stock and therefore it is not possible to make an abnormal profit trading on information. The academic literature differentiates between three possible levels of efficiency. There are variations of these definitions, but the following generally represents the concepts.

- The *strong form* states that all information that might affect the price, including so-called insider information, is already reflected in the price of the stock, so even insiders cannot make a profit above that of a buy-and-hold strategy, at least not after transaction costs.

- The *semi-strong* version states that all public information is reflected in the price of the stock, but insiders might be able to obtain additional profits using non-public information. (This would be illegal under current law.)

- The *weak form* states that no additional profit can be derived based just on knowledge of historical stock price and volume.

The weak version of the efficient market hypothesis would eliminate the value of technical analysis, the semi-strong version would eliminate the value of fundamental analysis and the strong form would eliminate the need for laws limiting insider trading.

At the present time, academics are split over whether the efficient market hypothesis is valid as the evidence against it becomes stronger.

At the present time, academics are split over whether the efficient market hypothesis is valid as the evidence against it becomes stronger.

When I read that Eugene Fama won the 2013 Nobel Memorial Prize in Economic Sciences (along with Robert Shiller and Lars Hansen) for empirical research in asset pricing, I felt that it must be due to his extensive and valuable work on anomalies. Anomalies are patterns that point out abnormal returns not explained by the MPT model, such as the small-cap effect. When I read further that it was for empirical research in support of the efficient market hypothesis (EMH), I reacted a bit.

To me, even though Fama was an original formulator of the

efficient market hypothesis, his work has provided the strongest evidence against it, as well as against the early forms of the capital asset pricing model and other elements of modern portfolio theory.

Fama's earliest work (1965) showed that the normal distribution was not the best model of stock returns and that a stable Paretian distribution (a distribution that implies much greater volatility than the normal distribution) was better.

His research with Kenneth French (1992) showed that beta was not an efficient measure of risk and that the ratio of price to book value and capitalization size provided returns beyond what would be expected in an efficient market ("anomalies" in MPT language).

Market capitalization is the value put on a stock by multiplying its price by the number of shares outstanding. The price-to-book-value ratio is market price divided by the book value per share. It is the relationship between what the market says a stock is worth relative to what the corporate assets, if properly stated, say it is worth.

I am particularly grateful to Fama and French because I added the price-to-book ratio as a major criterion when starting the Model Shadow Stock Portfolio (a real portfolio, not a simulation) in 1993 and that has contributed greatly to its return of 15.4% annualized during the past 23 years (through 2015). With all the anomalies (returns higher than explainable by the efficient market hypothesis) researched by Fama and others, including his two co-winners of the Nobel Prize, it is hard to understand the loyalty of so many academicians to the theory.

It is almost as if the efficient market hypothesis were a religion: At some point in your education you either accept it or deny it. If accepted, it becomes a matter of faith and from then on all evidence is forced into the model.

Random Walk Theory

If all relevant information is available in an efficient market, why doesn't the price go to a specific level and stay there until there is new information instead of jumping around all of the time? There are a number of reasons. Information flows through different channels at different rates. The information affects different investors in different ways, and they react at different speeds. All sorts of events create random impacts on short-term stock prices, but in an efficient market these events are random and uncorrelated and therefore do not provide the opportunity for excess profits.

The random walk theory asserts that the past movement or trend of a stock price or market cannot be used to predict its future movements.

Think of the time it takes for you to commute to work. There is an average elapsed time but every day that time is a little (or a lot) different due to multiple random events. Since they are random, you cannot predict them. So stock prices vary randomly around what would be an equilibrium price under the efficient market hypothesis. This concept of randomness is based on the thermodynamics area of physics, where it is called Brownian movement.

Risk Aversion

The underlying assumption of modern portfolio theory in any model based on return and risk reduction is that investors want to avoid risk. While this almost has to be true under a general definition of risk as exposure to possible loss or injury, "possible" and "loss or injury" can have a variety of interpretations. In the study of investments, loss relates to financial loss; in modern portfolio theory, it is assumed that an investor wants to avoid loss and that risk avoidance should be based on the "utility of wealth" function developed by Daniel Bernoulli in 1738.

Figure 1.1 shows that as wealth increases, the value of the next increase in wealth becomes less important. This decrease in the marginal utility of wealth results in an investor being willing to accept less and less risk for additional expected gain. Bernoulli postulated that the relationship of additional wealth to existing wealth was logarithmic (scaled such that equal percentage moves appear equal).

FIGURE 1.1

Changes in Utility as a Function of Changes in Wealth

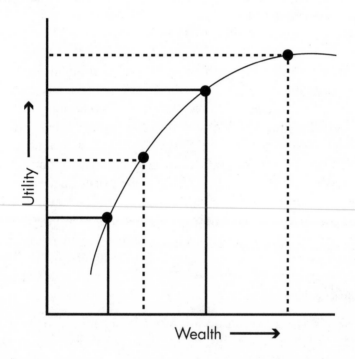

Modern portfolio theory in its basic form is a mean (average) standard deviation model of expected or historical returns. Please note also that, in modern portfolio theory or any portfolio approach to the market, the true risk of any asset is not its individual risk no matter how measured but how its addition impacts the risk of the entire portfolio.

It is possible for a risky asset (when measured separately) to reduce the risk of the portfolio when it is added. Note also that in discussions of returns in modern portfolio theory, "excess returns"—those above the riskless rate (T-bills)—are almost always used in the models. "Abnormal returns" refer to returns above those expected in an efficient market, and any process that leads to them is called an anomaly.

Diversification

In modern portfolio theory, risk is reduced through diversification. This is because part of the risk in any asset is unique to that asset (company-specific risk), and the more assets in the portfolio the more that unique risk is reduced.

Some risk is common to almost all investments in an asset class such as common stocks and cannot be diversified away by adding additional stocks. That risk is called "systematic risk," or market risk (and is often measured by beta). Consider the effect of a change in the taxes on capital gains. Such a change would affect the net returns of almost all common stocks and cannot be diversified away by adding more common stocks to a portfolio. Systematic risk will affect all or almost all stocks, but not necessarily equally.

The risk of a defect in a product caused by an engineering miscalculation at an assembly plant of Company X will primarily affect Company X. The more stocks in the portfolio, the more diffuse will be this unique or company risk, called "unsystematic risk." There are problems with this concept, which are discussed later.

Then it follows that within any market category such as common stocks, we can diversify away some but not all of the risk. Figure 1.2 shows the reduction in the unsystematic risk of a portfolio as the number of stocks increase. The risk level is reduced until it approaches the level of systematic risk, beyond which diversification no longer has an effect.

Research has shown that the effectiveness of diversification tapers off after the stock portfolio exceeds about 20 holdings. This assumes a random selection of assets. If a particular process is used in choosing assets, the diversification effect may be reduced. For example, if a portfolio had a large proportion of banking stocks, adding more banking stocks would likely not have as much risk reduction as adding a random stock.

This ability to eliminate much of the inherent risk of equity ownership by diversification has often been called the only "free lunch" in investing. Later I show why it is not a "free lunch" and why this can be one of the most significant misconceptions in investing.

FIGURE 1.2

Diversification and Risk

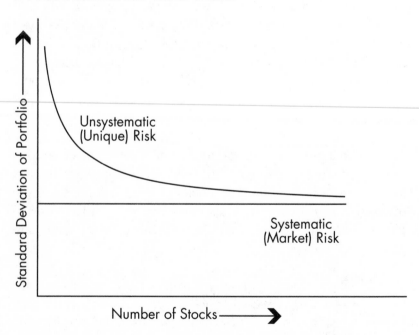

Two other characteristics of any market—and from here on we will concentrate on the equity market—are important.

First, while virtually all stocks are impacted by systematic risk, they are not impacted to the same degree. In the example above of an increase in the capital gains tax rate, we might expect market returns to drop 10% (i.e., from 10% per year to 9% per year), but we would not expect each and every stock's return to go down 10%.

The degree to which a stock moves with the market is measured by beta, which is the slope of the regression line from plotting the returns of the overall market (usually the S&P 500) versus the returns of any individual stock. Figure 1.3 shows a typical scatter diagram where the returns of both a stock and the market are plotted as dots on the graph for different time periods.

FIGURE 1.3

Dispersion of Returns

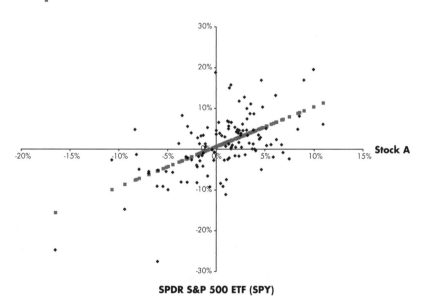

SPDR S&P 500 ETF (SPY)

The blue line is the least squares best fit through the joint observations, and the slope of the line (beta) indicates how much the stock will move relative to the market's move. If the returns move equally, then beta equals 1.0. A beta of 2.0 indicates a stock's return will change twice as much as the market and a beta of 0.5 indicates returns changing only half as much as the market.

The intersection of the regression line where the market return is zero indicates the "alpha" of the stock. That is the return on the portfolio when the market return is zero and also the return above the market return that the portfolio will have over any market return. The term "seeking alpha" assumes alpha is positive, but it doesn't have to be.

Correlation

Correlation is the degree to which two variables move together. For our purposes, the variables are individual stocks, a portfolio, or the entire market. The values of the two chosen variables are plotted over time, as was done in the calculation of beta in Figure 1.3. A line of least squares is plotted, and then the correlation coefficient is calculated based on the covariance and the two variances.

The result will be a number ranging between +1 (the variables move together exactly) and –1 (they move exactly opposite). A zero correlation means the variables move independently.

Correlation is important in risk reduction because as additional stocks are added to a portfolio, the volatility is generally reduced. The combined risk would be eliminated if two stocks had a correlation of –1, significantly reduced if the correlation is zero and not reduced at all if the correlation is +1. As we add stocks to a portfolio, there is generally a reduction in risk (volatility), but the reduction tapers off and becomes very slight after about 20 stocks are added randomly, as was shown in Figure 1.2.

This risk reduction is important for the various models in modern portfolio theory regardless of whether beta or standard deviation is used to measure volatility and risk.

Volatility/Risk

In modern portfolio theory, volatility is used as the measure of risk. Volatility is a measure of dispersion—how spread out from the average various data points are. The data points of interest are the portfolio returns over different time periods.

The starting point in modern portfolio theory, and sometimes the ending point, is that standard deviation (SD) is the proper measure of volatility and the normal curve is the way the dispersion of returns is best measured. Figure 1.4 shows a normal curve representation of the returns for a stock portfolio over time. The average return is 10% and the standard deviation is 20% for annual returns.

FIGURE 1.4

A Normal Distribution Curve

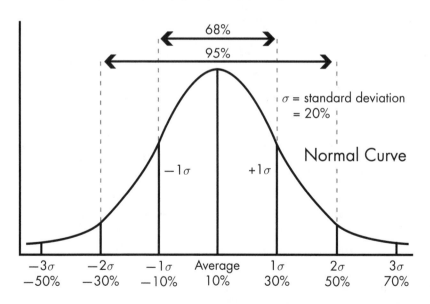

The normal curve has a known "probability density function." That means we know what the probabilities are that a return will be within a given number of standard deviations from the mean. This is illustrated in Figure 1.4 for one, two, and three standard deviations.

There is only a 4.56% (1.00 – 0.9544) chance that the next return will be beyond two standard deviations—or, in this example, 40% from the mean. Since we are generally only concerned with downside volatility, there is a 2.28% chance of a return 40% below the average of 10%, or –30%, in the coming year.

FIGURE 1.5

Skewness and Kurtosis in a Distribution Curve

Skewness	**Kurtosis**
The coefficient of skewness is a measure for the degree of symmetry in the variable distribution.	The coefficient of kurtosis is a measure for the degree of peakedness/flatness in the variable distribution.

A.

Negatively skewed distribution, or skewed to the left

D.

Platykurtic distribution, low degree of peakedness

B.

Normal distribution, symmetrical

E.

Mesokurtic distribution, normal distribution

C.

Positively skewed distribution, or skewed to the right

F.

Leptokurtic distribution, high degree of peakedness

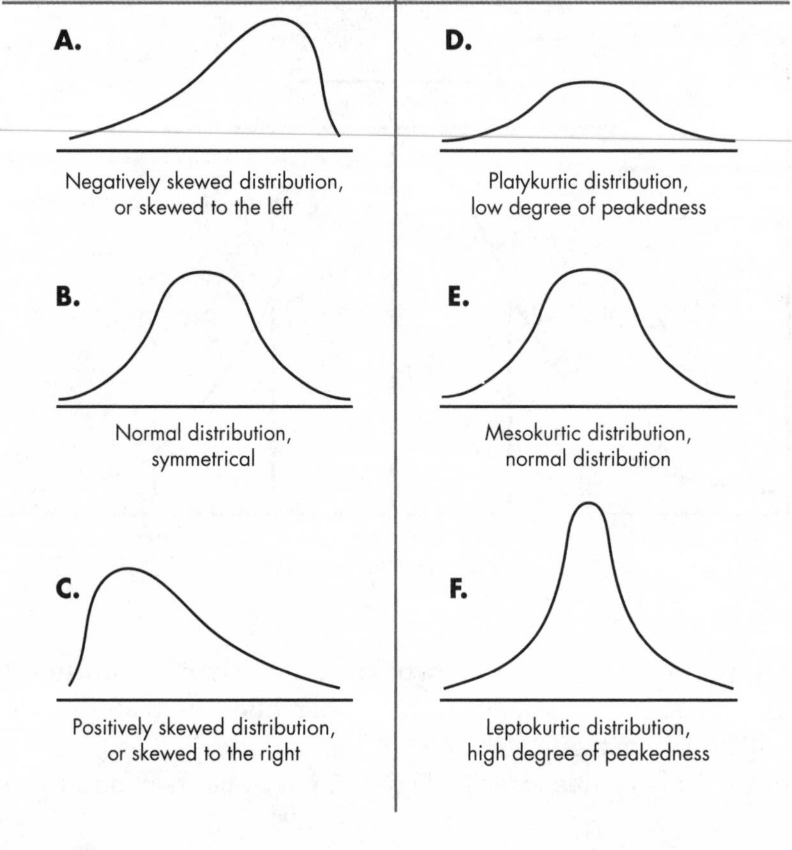

The standard deviation is not the only possible measure of volatility, but it is the one that is generally accepted and used.

While it is known that the normal curve does not exactly represent the distribution of portfolio returns, it is generally felt that it is close enough to be useful. If necessary, adjustments can be made to correct or allow for skewness (asymmetry) and kurtosis (peakedness). These characteristics are shown in Figure 1.5.

The distribution of returns must be skewed to the right, as in Figure 1.5(C). This is due to the fact that you cannot lose more than 100% of the amount invested, but you can gain more than 100%.

We have all witnessed markets where the losses and gains have been far greater than would be predicted by the normal distribution. This is explained by kurtosis, the fat tails of a distribution as illustrated in Figure 1.5(F). The problems of measuring volatility are discussed later in the chapter.

In general, skewness is either ignored based on the theory that most returns are close enough to the distribution mean or the lognormal distribution is used. It is the nature of skewness that the lognormal curve (the distribution of the logarithmic values) is normal even when there is skewness in the basic values.

Kurtosis is generally ignored or adjusted for by various approaches to measuring the tails of distributions. This is considered by many to be a very major problem, and we will be discussing it in more depth later in the chapter.

The Capital Asset Pricing Model

The capital asset pricing model (CAPM) is generally used to identify a basic model to explain asset (stock) prices. Significant variations and modifications have been made to it, so it is probably best thought of as a family of models. All of these models depend on the efficient market hypothesis.

The basic version is based on expected returns, risk as measured by the standard deviation of returns in a normal distribution, investor risk aversion, and the correlation of stocks in the portfolio. If unsystematic (company) risk can be diversified away, then beta can be used to measure risk. A rather elegant model is developed from this that shows the market portfolio, which is all the stocks in the market held in the proper proportion. This is theoretically the proportion that should exist in the market-place and in every investor's portfolio.

As I mentioned previously, there are problems with the capital asset pricing model in the real world. Some of these problems can be partially solved with variations on CAPM that consider other variables.

There are problems with the capital asset pricing model in the real world.

The most commonly cited are the Fama/ French three- and four-factor models. The researchers add capitalization size and value (measured by the book-to-price ratio) to volatility. Others have added momentum (extent and duration of upward price movements) to create a four-factor model, and Fama/French are currently developing a more generalized five-factor model. The rationale that keeps these variables as part of the core MPT belief is that somehow they are surrogates for volatility/risk.

What is being done here is to take what were the major anomalies creating (abnormal) returns that threaten belief in an efficient market and force them to fit the model. Once again, we see almost a religious approach. If you have faith in the efficient market, then all seeming contradictions must be explainable. As we go through various anomalies later in the chapter, you can see what a stretch it would be to say they are surrogates for volatility or risk.

THE BAD NEWS/GOOD NEWS

There are significant flaws in modern portfolio theory. In a way, this is bad news since the capital asset pricing model as developed by Markowitz and expanded by others is one of the most elegant, precise models imaginable, as are many of the variations on the basic version. It just doesn't accomplish the objective of maximizing return for a given level of risk in the real world.

As the chapter's opening quotation from John Tukey (an early student of the analysis of complex systems) indicates, it does little practical good to be precise in solving the wrong problem.

If we can understand the flaws of MPT, it will be a step toward more effective investing.

The good news is that if we can understand the flaws of MPT, it will be a step toward more effective investing. As Tukey suggests, while our solutions may not be precise, they will address the real objective—better investment performance.

Risk Measurement Weakness

Of all the weaknesses in the various aspects of modern portfolio theory that I discuss here, to me the most disturbing is the failure to measure risk in a way that makes sense to a real-world investor.

This failure is of particular importance because it is the aspect of modern portfolio theory that has gained the most acceptance—not only by adherents of the complete MPT model, but also by those who have partially accepted it, those who have advocated revisions of it, and even those who have rejected modern portfolio theory, such as advocates of technical and fundamental analysis who deny the efficient market hypothesis.

Every book and article on investing is telling you how to measure risk and the measures don't make sense in the real world.

Every book and article on investing is telling you how to measure risk and the measures don't make sense in the real world.

The problem lies with two concepts: "volatility" and "risk." In modern portfolio theory, volatility is considered the proper measure of risk and standard deviation is considered the best measure of volatility.

I strongly disagree with both of these contentions. I first examine why standard deviation is not the best or even an appropriate measure of volatility when dealing with investments. Then I consider if volatility, however measured, is a meaningful measure of risk for most investors.

STANDARD DEVIATION

Standard deviation is the square root of the deviations from the mean squared. For example, take three periods with returns of 8%, 10% and 12%.

Period	Return	Mean Return	Deviation From Mean	Deviation Squared
1	0.08	– 0.10 =	–0.02	0.0004
2	0.10	– 0.10 =	0.00	0.0000
3	0.12	– 0.10 =	0.02	0.0004
Sum of Returns	0.30			0.0008
Number of Returns	3			
Mean Return	0.10			

$$\frac{\text{Sum of Deviation Squared}}{\text{Number of Returns}} \quad \frac{0.0008}{3} = \text{Variance} \quad 0.00027$$

Standard Deviation = Square Root of Variance   0.01633, or 1.63%

Going forward, I do not use "volatility" and "risk" as if they were the same concept, as is done in most investment writing. While they have some relationship, particularly in very short-term investing, volatility has little to do with risk for the long-term individual investor.

The relevant definition of volatility is "the likelihood of shifting quickly and unpredictably." The relevant definition of risk is "the chance of injury, damage, or loss." To me, there is a significant difference. Risk and volatility may be kissing cousins but they are not the same. Since much of modern portfolio theory depends on viewing volatility as risk, the calculation of volatility is important to the theory. The accepted and generally used measure of volatility, or dispersion, is the standard deviation.

Since these concepts are at the root of the various measures used to describe the desirability of an investment or a portfolio of investments in the databases and reports you see every day, it is important that you know what they mean and, ultimately, how they are flawed.

There is nothing magic about standard deviation. It is just generally accepted as a good measure of dispersion. Squaring gets rid of the negative values, which is useful. However, we could also get rid of negatives by taking the absolute values of the original data. This measure is called the mean absolute deviation (MAD). It is sometimes used, but standard deviation is by far the most common measure. Using the squares of the deviations also gives more weight to far out values and makes standard deviation more sensitive to extreme values.

For example, a portfolio of $1,000 invested for six years with returns of:

> 12%, or 0.12
> 16%, or 0.16
> 8%, or 0.08
> 4%, or 0.04
> 11%, or 0.11
> 9%, or 0.09

would have a portfolio value of $1,766 after the six years (see top half of box on page 53). If you had received the average or mean return of 10% [(12% + 16% + 8% + 4% + 11% + 9%) ÷ 6] each year, you would have a terminal wealth of $1,771, not $1,766 (bottom half of box). The geometric mean or compound return, not the arithmetic mean, determines terminal wealth.

If each year's returns were equal, then the arithmetic mean and the geometric mean would be the same. Volatility in the returns reduces terminal wealth and this reduction is tied to the standard deviation of the returns. So volatility is important because it reduces terminal wealth. However, multi-period returns are generally expressed in terms of geometric (compound annual) returns, which already compensates for the volatility factor when making comparisons.

Probability Density Function

If we know the standard deviation of a portfolio and we know the nature of the distribution, then we can establish probabilities that returns of a certain size will occur.

A major assumption throughout modern portfolio theory is that the distribution of portfolio returns is described by the normal curve, or close enough to it so that we can use its probability density function, which tells us the probability that any specific deviation from the average return will occur in a given time period as measured by the standard deviation of the portfolio. The probability density function for the normal curve was shown in Figure 1.4.

Basically, the true volatility of stock returns is most likely a function with extreme kurtosis [Figure 1.5(F)], called a Levy or Pareto function, with an alpha of less than 2.0. If human heights were distributed this way around an average height of 5 feet, the next four people coming down the street might have heights of 1 foot, 13 feet, 3 feet and 11 feet. Most importantly, most forms of the Pareto function do not have a standard deviation or a probability density function, so little can be said about the probability of different values occurring.

This has been researched in the earliest work of Fama, which I have discussed, and the extensive work of Benoit Mandelbrot, covered in his book "The (Mis)Behavior of Markets (2004)." The concept is also explained in the popular "The Black Swan" (2007) by Nassim Nicholas Taleb and "The Myth of the Rational Market" (2009) by Justin Fox.

TERMINAL VALUE BASED ON GEOMETRIC MEAN

RETURN VALUE

Starting Amount				$1,000
Year 1	12%	$1,000 × 1.12	=	$1,120
Year 2	16%	$1,120 × 1.16	=	$1,299
Year 3	8%	$1,299 × 1.08	=	$1,403
Year 4	4%	$1,403 × 1.04	=	$1,459
Year 5	11%	$1,459 × 1.11	=	$1,620
Year 6	9%	$1,620 × 1.09	=	**$1,766**

TERMINAL VALUE BASED ON ARITHMETIC MEAN

RETURN VALUE

Starting Amount				$1,000
Year 1	10%	$1,000 × 1.10	=	$1,100
Year 2	10%	$1,100 × 1.10	=	$1,210
Year 3	10%	$1,210 × 1.10	=	$1,331
Year 4	10%	$1,331 × 1.10	=	$1,464
Year 5	10%	$1,464 × 1.10	=	$1,610
Year 6	10%	$1,610 × 1.10	=	**$1,771**

Although you would never know it from the popularity of normal curve assumptions in everyday investment literature, this highly leptokurtic (values far out from the mean) distribution of stock returns is generally accepted in academia, but at the same time it is largely ignored.

Although there would be agreement that extreme leptokurtosis exists in the distribution of stock returns, there would be disagreement on the extent and importance of it. Attitudes would differ among researchers. The attitudes can be divided into three groups.

1. The first group (quite large) would say that the degree of kurtosis is so slight that it can be ignored. So most models remain wedded to the assumption of distribution normality.

2. The second group believes that there is significant leptokurtosis and negative skewness, but that the appropriate approach is to use the extensive models that assume log normality and then make adjustments later.

   There are many approaches to making such adjustments, such as value at risk (VaR), conditional value at risk (CVaR), Bayesian analysis, scenario analysis, Monte Carlo simulation, chaos theory, fuzzy logic models, GARCH, Student's t-distribution and others. Many of these stem from research into floods, earthquakes and other rare but important occurrences.

   The Chicago Board of Options Exchange (CBOE) provides a "skew index" that measures negative skewness as determined by 30-day options. This may or may not show the likelihood of greater future downside volatility.

   In light of the discussion to follow, these approaches are not important to the long-term individual investor, but they are very important to those trying to measure short-term risk and compute the value of the complex "swaps" (a form of option) used for short-term portfolio insurance. The 2015 movie "The Big Short" illustrated this difficulty.

3. The third group believes that the real distribution of returns is so leptokurtic that virtually all contemporary investment models are not only useless but dangerous. That certainly appears to be the stance of Taleb and Mandelbrot and is used to explain the failure of defensive measures in

the 2007–2008 meltdowns.

It seems the distribution of investment returns is either an extremely leptokurtic distribution called a stable Paretian or Levy distribution with an alpha of less than 2.0, or an undefined distribution with extensive kurtosis.

My feeling is that there does not have to be a mathematical model that fits the complexity of market movements closely enough to be useful. I rather suspect that if there is such a model, it would be dynamic rather than static and would thus be changing through time, perhaps driven by both macroeconomic and geopolitical factors.

In practical terms, that means that any "true" model of volatility of asset returns, or the lack of a mathematical model:

- invalidates customary measures of risk, such as standard deviation, Sharpe ratio, beta, Treynor ratio, Sortino ratio and Jensen's alpha;

- eliminates the application of the basic capital asset pricing model as well as the effectiveness of the newer three-, four-, and five-factor versions; and

- reduces the effectiveness of measures of diversification and allocation.

In other words, while the empirical research that has come from academic endeavors may be useful in finding factors that influence investment success, the simplified models developed are basically useless in explaining overall market behavior.

While all of this may not be extremely important to the long-term investor following the approach of Level3 Investing, it may have some significance for two reasons.

1. To be comfortable in a new investing mode, it helps to understand why the old approach is unsatisfactory.

2. We are sometimes accidentally exposed to short-term investing even when we don't intend to be, and in short-term investing volatility is more closely related to risk.

While the empirical research that has come from academic endeavors may be useful in finding factors that influence investment success, the simplified models developed are basically useless in explaining overall market behavior.

What I find most distressing is that even though in the academic community the problems with basic modern portfolio theory are well-understood and very advanced research is taking place, the knowledge of the inadequacy of basic modern portfolio theory does not filter down.

Investment data providers, evaluation services, the financial press, analytical books aimed at individual investors, models provided on the internet and seminars given by brokerages and other organizations all still pretend that the normal distribution matters, that standard deviation and its offshoots, such as the Sharpe ratio, are useful in measuring risk, and that correlation-based portfolio optimization is state-of-the-art thinking.

More importantly, students of investing take this simplified but incorrect view of risk with them to their jobs as investment advisers and stockbrokers managing your money.

I have certainly been guilty of this myself. My rationalization has been the typical, "It's a start and is better than nothing." But it may not be better than nothing.

Even if we were to accept volatility as a measure of risk, we would find that we cannot model the volatility of the real-world asset markets. The only distributions that seem able to describe the volatility even reasonably well (Paretian), do not provide the ability to come up with a more realistic version of the capital asset pricing model. And, as previously pointed out, maybe the movement of stock prices is not explainable by any formal distribution.

A REAL-WORLD VIEW

Risk in the Real World

While most of the concepts discussed previously in this chapter have been written about in a multitude of books and research papers, some of which I have cited, the fundamental problem as I see it has been largely ignored in academic research. The larger problem is that volatility, no matter how measured, is not the same as risk in the real world. This is particularly so for the audience of our concern—the individual investor investing for the long term.

> *The larger problem is that volatility, no matter how measured, is not the same as risk in the real world.*

Let's start with a comparison of the two relevant definitions.

- **Volatility:** "the likelihood of (returns) shifting quickly and unpredictably. (I added "returns" to particularize the concept.)

- **Risk:** "the chance of (financial) injury, damage, or loss. (I added "financial" to relate it to investing.)

Just a commonsense look at the definitions indicates the difference. It is possible and often likely that a portfolio can be volatile but not lead to any financial loss. This will most often be the case for long-term investors.

On the other hand, a loss of 5% in each of multiple sequential periods will have no volatility but significant loss. Can we say that such an investment has no risk?

Now, as previously pointed out, less volatility is better because it will result in higher terminal wealth. We can take the terminal wealth impact of volatility out of comparisons by always using geometric or annualized returns.

We need to find measures of risk that look at the probability that particular portfolios, owned by particular individuals, in particular situations will lose some or all of their value at the time they are needed for consumption.

It is possible and often likely that a portfolio can be volatile but not lead to any financial loss. This will most often be the case for long-term investors.

Simply put: Volatility is a mathematical measure of market price behavior, while risk is a measure of potential investor losses and the consequences.

In this book, real risk is defined as the likelihood that when we must withdraw assets from our portfolio for consumption, they will have a lower value than we could reasonably expect based on our investment strategy.

The analysis and control of risk in individual wealth management will have to deal with a number of factors:

- **Investment horizon:** What is the general plan for the selling of portfolio assets for consumption, and what might interfere with that plan?

- **Risk aversion:** How risk averse is the investor, and how much unrealized loss can that individual tolerate without deviating from a program?

- **Portfolio volatility:** What is the likely maximum drop in portfolio value in any investment horizon? We don't escape volatility concerns completely, but we are only concerned about major downside moves in order to plan for them.

- **Returns on different asset classes:** What are reasonable expectations for different investments?

- **Relationships between different investment classes:** This is not correlation in the mathematical sense, but a look at relationships *at critical times*. Correlations between assets within a class (equities) and between asset classes are clearly dynamic, and static interpretations are misleading.

While estimation of future values is necessary in the approach, I take it as a more practical and less elegant route than that of modern portfolio theory. The MPT approach is to plot historical data and find the mathematical distribution model that comes closest to fitting the data—not necessarily close, but closest. That model is then used to predict future values or the probabilities of future values.

My approach is use the historical data more directly without bothering to formally define a mathematical model. My approach is much less elegant but deals with the real-world problems of individual investors and actual historical data.

In the real world, the MPT concept of systematic and unsystematic risk (really volatility) doesn't hold up if higher returns are our goal. And traditional modern portfolio theory approaches to diversification may lead to less volatility but not necessarily to less real-world risk nor to higher true risk-adjusted returns.

Traditional modern portfolio theory approaches to diversification may lead to less volatility but not necessarily to less real-world risk nor to higher true risk-adjusted returns.

Reducing Unsystematic Risk Is No Free Lunch

As explained, unsystematic risk is the risk (volatility) that is unique to each company. Diversification will reduce this risk in a portfolio until it approaches zero and only overall market (systematic) risk will remain. This is the "free lunch" in risk reduction. If risk can be reduced at no cost, why not do it? Consider the following statement, which is similar to those found in most investment textbooks:

"By diversifying across a number of stocks, we reduce the

impact of the unique *risk/volatility* of each individual stock."

While that statement may be true so is the following corollary:

"By diversifying across a number of stocks, we reduce the impact of the unique *return* possibility of each individual stock."

We reduce the possibility that a strike at ABC Company will hurt our portfolio, but we also reduce the possibility that a new product discovery at ABC will help the portfolio.

> ## In the real market, diversification can hurt returns.

In an efficient market where all stocks project equal risk-adjusted returns, diversification might be a free lunch. But in the real market, diversification can hurt returns.

For example, say you have six possible stock selections with expected returns of:

10%, 12%, 14%, 16%, 18% and 20%

If you invested only in the stock with the highest expected return, your expected return would be 20%. By adding the other stocks, your expected (or average) portfolio return would go down.

I am not saying that diversification is not wise, only that it is not necessarily without cost—it is not a free lunch.

But the evaluation of risk is not the only problem with modern portfolio theory.

QUESTIONS ABOUT RANDOM WALK THEORY

The theory of a random walk in security prices proposes that each change in price is random. It cannot be predicted based on previous changes. The previous discussion in this chapter should convince you that such movements are not normally distributed, but the random walk theory could still hold with other distributions. Unless those distributions are definable, random walk theory does not help us in portfolio management.

However, the random walk itself is suspect. There is considerable evidence that previous price changes do contain information that helps predict future changes. There are a significant number of studies showing that there is a short-term momentum effect lasting up to two years. As we will see later, momentum is one of the anomalies that is used in newer models of stock behavior.

> *There is considerable evidence that previous price changes do contain information that helps predict future changes.*

Adherents of the efficient market hypothesis believe that the random walk is still close enough to modeling reality that it is useful. Believers feel indications of slight trends do not provide sufficient information to provide excess returns after transaction costs and that such trends are of very short duration.

Mandelbrot, applying fractal geometry to asset price moves, believes there is repetition of price moves, particularly of large violent moves. He believes large moves cluster together. This is a belief in long-term dependence, not correlation. And it is only the size of moves that are dependent, so a large price change foretells another large price change, but not whether it will be up or down.

A model for predicting these clusters is still in its infancy, but the research in this area is certainly sufficient to raise additional questions about the randomness of asset price changes.

Arguments Against Efficient Market Hypothesis

In the earlier discussion of modern portfolio theory, I described the three levels of efficiency defined in the academic literature. The strong form says that all relevant information that would impact the price of the stock is already in the price. The semi-strong changes "all" information to "public" information, allowing that inside information could provide gains, as is clearly the case based on numerous U.S. government charges and convictions. The weak form says there is no information in past prices and volume that would allow for an excess profit. The semi-strong version is the one generally held by those who still hold with the efficient market hypothesis.

Based on the discussion of random walk above, it would seem that there are doubts about the validity of any of the three formal versions of the efficient market hypothesis. Clearly, if momentum works in obtaining abnormal returns, then there is information in historical prices that can lead to additional returns and not even the weak form of the efficient market hypothesis is valid.

There are other arguments against the existence of an efficient market. Let me point out that it is the academic definition of efficiency that is under fire. Everyone would agree that the market is extremely efficient in the general meaning of the word. It reacts to relevant information, but not instantly or completely. There is room for gains in excess of market averages.

Robert J. Shiller (1981) presented a strong empirical case against the efficient market in a long-term examination of the Dow Jones industrial average (1928–1979) and the S&P 500 (1871–1979). He found considerable difference between the market price of stocks and their theoretical value based on a dividend discount model. While there have been discussions about aspects of his modeled approach, the differences he found were so significant that they cast major doubt on the efficient market hypothesis.

Numerous stock characteristics do in fact lead to abnormal returns.

In addition, there are numerous anomalies in equity returns. Under the efficient market hypothesis, all information is in the current price and no selection process should provide risk-adjusted returns in excess of the market return. But numerous stock characteristics do in fact lead to abnormal returns. For some anomalies the effect is small and the evidence weak over time. For others, the evidence is strong and exists over long investment horizons. Here is a list of anomalies—rules that provide abnormal returns.

- **Low-priced stocks.** A very early anomaly from back before anyone was looking for anomalies in 1936. Later research indicates low price is a proxy for small cap.

- **Low price-earnings ratio (P/E).** Considerable research over time has established reasonable proof that stocks with low price-earnings ratios outperform.

- **Cash dividends.** There is some evidence that cash dividends are related to higher stock returns.

- **Low price-to-sales ratio (P/S).** Lower price-to-sales ratios provide higher returns. There is evidence that this is a strong effect, maybe stronger than low price-earnings ratios.

- **Low price-to-cash-flow ratio (P/CF).** Similar to price-earnings ratio but as the old saying goes, "earnings are an accountant's opinion, but cash is cash." So cash flow is often preferred, and there is evidence that there are positive anomaly earnings associated with high cash flow.

- **The owner/manager effect.** There is evidence that firms where management has significant ownership have positive anomaly returns.

- **The liquidity effect.** There is evidence that stocks with low liquidity have higher returns. The measurement of liquidity would involve both historical price information and the firm's balance sheet.

- **The earnings surprise effect.** When actual earnings deviate from anticipated earnings significantly, the stock price experiences abnormal gains if the earnings are above expectations and the stock price declines if earnings are

below expectations. This effect endures well beyond the
announcement date.

- **Calendar effects.** There are a number of aberrations that
  should not occur under the efficient market hypothesis.
  Stock prices tend to go up more in the first half of the
  month. They also tend to go up on Fridays more than
  other days. They go down the most on Monday mornings.
  Stocks, particularly small-capitalization stocks, tend to go
  up more in January than other months.

- **Relative strength—momentum.** As discussed previously,
  there is evidence that in the short term, up to two years,
  stock prices that have been going up tend to keep going
  up and that higher returns can be obtained by buying such
  stocks.

- **Capitalization size.** There is strong evidence that, as a
  group, smaller-capitalization stocks perform better than
  stocks with higher capitalizations. This is one of the stronger anomalies that I discuss in more detail in Chapter 6 as
  an investment strategy.

- **Low price-to book-value ratio (P/B).** Once again there is
  strong evidence that the lower the ratio of price to book
  value, the greater the return. This is also a strong anomaly
  that I discuss further here and in Chapter 6. Price-to-book-
  value ratio is the stock price divided by the firm's book
  value per share. For computational reasons, in much of
  academic research it is expressed as book-to-price (B/P), in
  which case higher is better.

- **Asset growth.** There are indications that companies that
  have low or negative growth in assets over time provide
  higher returns. The rationale for this is that effective management uses rather than accumulates assets.

- **Return on assets (ROA).** Research indicates that firms
  with higher returns on assets (net income divided by total
  assets) provide higher returns to investors. This anomaly
  would certainly relate to value investing.

- **Accruals.** In accounting, accruals are those income statement items that make earnings higher than cash flow. This is because current accounting practices attempt to match revenues to expenses at the time when the transaction occurs rather than when payment is made. The cash is spent on an item such as a new machine but only part of the payment is taken as an expense. The balance is accrued over a depreciation period. Accruals are negatively related to future earnings. This is a strong anomaly. It is the rationale for believing that cash flow is more important than earnings as a measure of a company's value.

- **Gross profit.** A recent anomaly is that of gross profit divided by assets. Gross profit is revenue less the cost of goods sold. This measure has shown to be a very strong predictor of future stock returns and much stronger than earnings.

While the effect of some of these anomalies has been contradicted by other research and other anomalies seem to exist during some time periods but not others, some of them are quite strong and enduring. There is certainly correlation between some of them. Here, I am only using them as evidence against the efficient market hypothesis, but they become more significant in the Chapter 6 discussion of effective investment strategies.

When I discuss the possible uses of these anomalies, I discuss their relationship to one another and their relative effectiveness as indicated by simulations. There is little history of their effectiveness in real-world investing except for capitalization size, price-to-book ratio and, more recently, momentum.

In recent evaluations of anomalies, most academic research has adopted a hedge portfolio approach. The variable is divided into quintiles (sometimes deciles) along the relevant dimension and then hedged portfolios are formed by being long the highest quintile in terms of effectiveness and short the lowest quintile. While this approach is effective in research, it does not have results that an investor, particularly an individual, could obtain.

Two of the anomalies, firm capitalization size and price-to-book ratio are so strong that Fama and French, who did extensive research on their impact (1992), used them to form a new model to replace the traditional capital asset pricing model (the Fama-French Model 1993, 1996). The same research indicates that beta is an inefficient measure of risk (volatility), which is not surprising given our discussion of volatility measures.

Momentum is sometimes added to make it a four-factor model and, as mentioned earlier, a five-factor model is in development. In this re-modeling of the capital asset pricing model, the inference is that these additional factors are measures of risk rather than anomalies. If this is true, then we have evidence that volatility is not risk, since we know the volatility of the stocks with the anomalies and it is not volatility alone that is enabling them to provide better returns. It must be some other factor—another dimension of risk. I can see how investors might feel that small-cap stocks are riskier, with whatever their own perception of risk is. I can't visualize investors perceiving low price to book or momentum as any form of risk, although there are some rationalizations.

With little justification for the efficient market hypothesis and the weakness of most of modern portfolio theory, it is time to revise some terminology. The word "anomaly" means a deviation from the general rule. Since there is no valid general rule like the capital asset pricing model, returns that are above average are not anomalies and their higher returns are not "abnormal." The use of those words supports the myth of modern portfolio theory. I use the term "above-market" to describe returns that are above those of the overall market and use "effective strategies" to describe decision models that provide above-market returns. I continue to use excess returns to mean returns above the risk-free rate.

Rethinking the Rational Investor

Underlying any theory of an efficient market is the belief that investors are rational in their investment decisions. There is substantial evidence that investors are less than rational in their decision-making and that behavioral factors diminish their ability to operate effectively in the marketplace. To the extent that this is true, prices will deviate from theoretical values.

Investors have been assumed to be risk averse. Risk aversion is based on the preference of an individual to hold on to what he has as opposed to gaining more. The assumption of this preference is based on the concept of decreasing marginal utility of wealth. As was shown in Figure 1.1 on page 40, each additional increment of wealth is worth less than the previous increment. At a specific point, investors are not willing to give up a unit of wealth for the chance to gain an additional unit. This theory developed by Daniel Bernoulli in 1738 has been widely held in general, if not in the precise logarithmic postulation of Bernoulli.

There is strong evidence that risk from the viewpoint of the investor is not based on Bernoulli's formulation but on an aversion to loss. Investors will take more risk to avoid a loss than to obtain a gain of equal amount. Daniel Kahneman and Amos Tversky in a number of publications starting with "Prospect Theory: An Analysis of Decision Under Risk" (1979) show that decision making is often not rational by traditional measures.

Investors will take more risk to avoid a loss than to obtain a gain of equal amount.

This aversion to loss explains the irrational behavior of investors when they refuse to sell losers and are too eager to sell winners. This behavior pattern explains why individual investors in mutual funds have returns lower than the funds themselves. It is not only poorly timed buying and selling, but also an inferior tax strategy.

There are a number of additional irrationalities in investor behavior. **Representativeness** is the tendency to believe some pattern of data is representative of a larger model. Commonly, investors will look at short-term stock behavior and generalize it to the long term. Kahneman and Tversky (1973) also studied this inability to deal with probability situations in a logical manner.

Framing is the tendency of individuals to respond to and interpret information depending on how it is presented. Pollsters know they can drive responses in the way they want by the way they frame the question. For example, take the question, "What was your return on your stock investments last year as compared to the 11.2% return for the S&P 500?" You will get a different set of responses if you reframe the question substituting 16.4% for 11.2%.

The *herd effect* can have a strong impact on the individual. It is interesting that a group as a whole can come up with average estimates on a variety of subjects that are extremely accurate and better than the estimates of individuals, but—a big but— only if they make their estimates on their own insulated from the estimates of others. Once discussion is out in the open, there will be leaders and followers and most people will follow the crowd. Numerous experiments range from getting people to say that an obviously shorter line is longer than a long line to getting individuals to administer severe painful (they believe) electric shocks to others because they believe others are doing it.

Overconfidence seems to be a persistent human trait. While in social situations it might prove useful and help in establishing a better place in the pecking order, in investment practice it is disastrous. It leads investors to take risks that are absolutely unnecessary; even if the risks are small, eventually they will lead to financial ruin.

The internet serves to illustrate how fast rumors, nonsense and falsehoods can spread in a viral fashion. While it has slowed recently, not long ago I must have received an urban legend email once a week. Educated people would forward complete fabrications believing they were true because they seemed to be reasonable or because they fit with their world view.

All day long the financial TV stations bombard the investor with opinions. In the evening the investment magazines take over. Opinions are expressed as if they were facts, and this "noise" influences investor behavior in an irrational way.

There are also everyday human frailties: pride, loss of face, decision-maker's remorse or regret, and the influence of past occurrences that sometimes are just chance. The Great Depression drove many people away from stocks for long enough to miss a great period of growth. Many finally returned just in time for the 1974 crash.

The impact of this kind of irrational behavior has been refuted with two primary arguments. First, erratic investor behavior is random and so the cumulative effects will even out. But the behavioral work cited should make it clear that irrational distortions follow a pattern in specific directions and are not random.

The second defense is that when some investors behave irrationally they create arbitrage opportunities for wiser investors who will then drive the prices back to the efficient level. Some of this occurs, but it is not easy to arbitrage all inefficiencies and there is often considerable risk involved in any attempt. We don't even get perfect arbitrage when the opportunities are obvious.

Individual investors aren't the only ones who deviate from what is theoretically rational behavior. Portfolio managers are very aware that "the long run" may never come for them if their two-year to four-year performance is poor. They are also often worried about relative rather than absolute performance. This can lead to taking too little risk when ahead of the pack and too much risk when behind. The long observed "window dressing" behavior to get rid of poor-performing stocks on the last day of a quarter so they don't appear in the portfolio's quarterly report has been well-established.

There are all kinds of pressures of a psychological nature on professional managers. Many portfolios are managed by a committee to avoid such problems, but this might well lead to other performance problems as well as closet indexing.

> *The lack of rational investment decision-making is one more indication that the pillars on which modern portfolio theory is built are rather weak.*

The lack of rational investment decision-making is one more indication that the pillars on which modern portfolio theory is built—the efficient market hypothesis, random walk theory, the capital asset pricing model, and rational investor behavior—are rather weak.

Here, I have mentioned the work of behavioral economics to show another flaw in the assumptions of modern portfolio theory. In Chapter 7, I discuss how you can protect yourself from behavioral impulses that can cripple your investment strategy.

CONSIDER OTHER OPINIONS

I do want to emphasize that there are any number of researchers in university finance and economics departments who would disagree vigorously with what I am saying. While they would acknowledge some of the problems I have discussed, they honestly feel that modern portfolio theory, with the changes we have previously discussed, still provides a workable structure that improves investment practice and provides a framework for future advancement.

I think any serious investor should be aware of the problems I discuss, but should also take some time to consider the other view since its advocates are often effective researchers. "A Random Walk Down Wall Street" (2015) by Burton G. Malkiel discusses and defends many of the problems I have pointed out—particularly the so-called anomalies. This popular and well-written book also covers some of the topics I discuss later.

In "Dissecting Anomalies" (2008) in the Journal of Finance,

Fama with French provide a mathematical analysis of different anomalies and the relative significance of them, and they provide new analysis whenever a new anomaly appears. Fama is among the most prolific of investment theoreticians and much of his work has been in the area of anomalies.

> *With discipline returns above market averages are possible and those profits are highly significant when compounded over an investing lifetime.*

The one area where I agree with modern portfolio theory is that it is not easy to exceed market returns. The pure MPT advocate would say there is no possible way to outperform without increasing risk. I feel it is difficult, but with discipline returns above market averages are possible and those profits are highly significant when compounded over an investing lifetime.

CHAPTER 2

THE LIMITS OF FUNDAMENTAL AND TECHNICAL ANALYSIS

"If the facts don't fit the theory, change the facts."

—Albert Einstein

Modern portfolio theory and its extensions are not the only organized approaches to stock selection and portfolio management. While there are all kinds of hit-or-miss, rumor-based, cocktail-inspired, brother-in-law-recommended, and phone-call-inspired motivations to buy and sell stocks, organized approaches beyond modern portfolio theory can be divided into two—*fundamental analysis* and *technical analysis.* A belief in the efficient market hypothesis would eliminate both of these approaches, which can be seen by examining each of them.

I should point out that many investors believe in using a combination of the two approaches.

TECHNICAL ANALYSIS

There are many different approaches to technical analysis. But the basis of this approach is the belief that the most significant information necessary for determining what assets to buy and sell and when to buy and sell them is in the historical price and trading volume data of the market itself. The rationality for this approach lies in the belief that when investors bought stock and what quantity they bought will determine at what price they will sell and thus influence the future price movement. Investors collect and analyze a wide array of trading data, such as the opening price, high price, low price, closing price and trading volume. This information is then plotted or used in various calculations.

Charts and Indicators

The approach started out with point & figure charting, which has become more sophisticated over time. In Asia, a different approach called Japanese candlesticks was developed and is now popular in the U.S. In these methods, certain formations of historical price and volume data are generated by buy/sell behavior and indicate the likely future path of prices.

There are other concepts that are used in conjunction with chart figures or by themselves that are quite popular and appear every hour on investment TV programs. These include a variety of moving averages, historical fixed-period cycles, determination of an established trend, and various approaches to determining resistance and support. Resistance is a price level that a stock will have difficulty surpassing, and support is a price lower than the current price that the stock will have difficulty going below. Changes in the direction of moving averages, the relationship of long- and short-term averages, and when current prices go through such moving averages, are believed to have significance.

One would expect that if patterns in price and volume existed and were useful in predicting future prices, then the science would have moved from the vagueness of graphical figures to the sophistication of mathematical systems that would provide very specific numerical indicators.

There are several computerized trading platforms, such as TradeStation, that permit investors to try out any conceivable rules based on price and volume, either to actually trade or test theories. There are numerous associations of technicians around the world, and individuals can take examinations leading to a chartered market technician (CMT) designation.

One would expect that if patterns in price and volume existed and were useful in predicting future prices, then the science would have moved from the vagueness of graphical figures to the sophistication of mathematical systems that would provide very specific numerical indicators.

And, in fact, this has been done. It is a form of artificial intelligence using artificial neural networks (ANN). These systems are based on the way biological networks operate and they search for the repetition of patterns and input/output relationships. Such programs involve very complex mathematical formulations requiring large computers. Published work is mostly academic, but I rather suspect that the Ph.D. scientists hired by hedge funds are at the leading edge of any meaningful progress. To date there are no consistent long-term results for such approaches, but if there is any information in past price and volume information that would help predict future price action, it would likely come from this type of analysis and not from funny pictures such as head-and-shoulders or cup-and-handle chart patterns.

Since modern portfolio theory and the efficient market hypothesis almost categorically deny the possibility of predicting prices based on past price and volume data, it is not surprising that research in this area is evolving not from economics and finance but from the hard sciences.

Since modern portfolio theory and the efficient market hypothesis almost categorically deny the possibility of predicting prices based on past price and volume data, it is not surprising that research in this area is evolving not from economics and finance but from the hard sciences.

Hedge funds looking for breakthroughs in investment approaches tend to hire from science and engineering graduate programs instead of MBAs. In fact, many universities have started programs in "financial engineering" that concentrate on the math of finance and risk rather than a broad business curriculum. Such programs exist at MIT, the University of Chicago, and Columbia University.

ArXiv, a clearinghouse for research papers in physics, has an entire section on quantitative finance.

If there has been any dramatic success in this area of technical analysis, it has not been reported. That would not come as a surprise, as no one would choose to share valuable secrets. However, it is unlikely that any really significant results could be kept hidden for long. Average hedge fund returns, over the long term, are not all that impressive.

There are even computer programs such as RIZM and Quantopian that will help you devise a complex system of your own.

Certainly technical analysts realize that external events can change price patterns. If the corporate treasurer takes off to Brazil with the assets or a company's product is suddenly found to be dangerous to consumers, these events would cause a shift in the meaningfulness of a stock's pattern. The technical analyst knows that things can become fuzzy, so any technical system only has a probability of success. But if the probability is high enough, then the system will outperform the overall market. Indeed most technicians would expect and accept a number of losses, but the gains would be expected to outweigh them.

Technical analysis does not eliminate rational portfolio management approaches such as diversification in the MPT sense or the impact of external economic events or the use of other loss-limiting techniques.

Technical analysis does not eliminate rational portfolio management approaches such as diversification in the MPT sense or the impact of external economic events or the use of other loss-limiting techniques.

When examining any explanation of historical data's ability to predict the future, a primary consideration is "does it make any sense." Over the years, there have been all kinds of discoveries about market behavior that are nonsensical and do not have a causal relationship. One that has been popular says that the market will have an up year when an original NFL football team beats an old AFL team in the Super Bowl. The length of women's skirts was another popular indicator.

Life is full of coincidences, and nonsensical relationships should be ignored. There should be some rational explanation for such analysis to be meaningful. For example, the market has had the highest returns in the years preceding a presidential election. It could be coincidence, but one can find a rationale for that behavior: Congress and the administration are willing to spend more money and promise more programs in order to influence votes in the following year's presidential election. Such spending then stimulates the economy.

> *Life is full of coincidences, and nonsensical relationships should be ignored. There should be some rational explanation for such analysis to be meaningful.*

A rationale does not prove a method, but without a rationale a method is likely meaningless. I am still mystified by a cycle I noticed 20 years ago because I cannot find a rationale. See "The Mystery Cycle" box on the next page.

The question then is whether there is some rational explanation for the validity of technical analysis in general and for the various interpretations within its different forms.

It is not unreasonable to believe that the purchase price and quantity of shares purchased by investors will influence the price at which they will sell. Behavioral science shows that this can be the case. It is also reasonable to assume that such influences might be detectable by some method of charting or, more likely, mathematical sensitivity analysis. In fact, it is this reasonableness that makes it so easy to promote and defend technical analysis.

But it simply doesn't work. It might work in a market where most of the participants are short-term price speculators, such

THE MYSTERY CYCLE

A widely discussed phenomenon in the news during 2015 was that the "election cycle" indicates an above-average return in the year prior to the U.S. national presidential election. Twenty years ago, I came across another cycle for which I can find no rationale, but that has been pervasive for the last 100 years. It is a 10-year cycle with a positive impact on the market of years ending in 5, and it is particularly important in those years when it coincides with the year before the election (year 3 of the election cycle). This occurs only every 20 years. The year 2015 was one of those unique years, but the string of high returns was broken rather dramatically with the S&P 500 index having a return close to zero.

I have always been suspicious of data like this that indicates a possible anomaly when I can't find a rationale for the behavior. In the election cycle, we have the rationale that government spending and talk of government spending prior to the election boosts expectations, but I cannot think of any cycle for years ending in 5, or any 10-year cycle, to explain this rather dramatic impact. With the poor performance in 2015, perhaps the cycle is demystified. Note that although the data covers a large number of years, the actual sample size is small. Here are the numbers.

Average annual returns since 1935, not including 2015:

11.0%   =   S&P 500 index
20.7%   =   year 3 of the election cycle
28.4%   =   years ending in 5
42.4%   =   year 3 + years ending in 5
   0   =   number of times year 3 was negative

as some commodities markets. But where such a vast quantity of stock purchasing and selling is done on an "as available" and "as needed basis" (pension funds and long-term personal portfolios) and more is done on a buy-and-forget approach, the impact of short-term traders becomes slight enough that even if discernible the impact would not overcome transaction costs.

That is an explanation of why technical analysis might fail even if the original justification makes sense. In a practical sense, technical analysis doesn't work because nobody seems to be able to make it work on a consistent basis over time.

There are stories about success, there are plenty of examples showing an accepted chart formation that led to what could have been a predicted move, but I have never seen or even heard of a portfolio driven solely by technical analysis that has a verifiable history of beating the market over a 10- or 20-year period.

> *In a practical sense, technical analysis doesn't work because nobody seems to be able to make it work on a consistent basis over time.*

It seems unreal to think that there are arbitrary cycles of a specific length unrelated to economic events—such as the Kondratieff cycle (50 years)—or that basic mathematical number series such as Fibonacci or the 1.618 "golden" ratio have anything to do with corporate earnings (since, ultimately, corporate earnings drive returns and prices).

Random number simulation programs generate all the formations, all the moving average variations, and all the "would be" resistance and support levels described in technical analysis— sometimes with the predicted market movement, more often without.

There are cycles, such as the business cycle, that do have fundamental significance on market behavior, but they are described by economic events and not by arbitrary numbers. Even with these, it is difficult to tell where you are in an economic cycle at a specific point in time.

I don't wish to insult serious technical analysts, but there are a significant number of astrologists predicting the market also. If the moon can impact ocean tides, why not stock prices—or is that lunacy? (pun intended)

While charting and various wave theories seem unproven, there are some attributes of a stock's price and volume history that have been shown to impact future returns. There is quite a bit of evidence that price momentum (sustained movement in one direction) can be used to provide above-average returns. In fact, of all the effective approaches, it seems next strongest to price-to-book-value ratio and market-capitalization size.

Related Concepts

There are other beliefs that are sometimes included with technical analysis but actually take a different approach. Many professional investors believe that the small individual investor is always wrong and you can predict the market by following their behavior and doing the opposite. An early approach to accomplishing this used "odd lot" analysis. Not too many years ago, trading was done only in lots of 100 shares. Individuals wishing to trade fewer than 100 shares went through an odd-lot broker who would combine such lots and tag them onto a round lot trade. Figures showing the number of odd lots traded were available. Odd lots were traded by small investors and so one could see whether small investors were buying or selling.

Those believing in this indicator would do the opposite of the small trader. The put/call ratio has been used that way in the past, but so much option activity involves hedging that it is probably not an effective measure of sentiment any more. The put/call ratio shows the relationship between the number of puts to calls trading on the options exchange. A put gives the option buyer the right (or option) to sell shares of a stock at given price. Conversely, a call gives the option buyer the right to purchase shares of stock at given price. If you listen to the commentary on CNBC, you still hear this concept being discussed as if it were gospel.

At AAII, we collect and distribute the market attitude of our members on a weekly basis in our Sentiment Survey. Results are available online at AAII.com and in Barron's every week and show the percentage of our members who are bullish, bearish, and neutral in their market outlook over the next six months. I gather that this information is used by institutional investors as a contrarian indicator. We also conduct an ongoing Asset Allocation Survey, which provides data on the portfolio allocation of our members' assets among stocks, bonds, and cash and monthly changes in that allocation. This also could be used as a contrarian indicator.

While I certainly agree that there are stupid investors and smart investors and that doing the opposite of the stupid investors might be beneficial, I don't know if one could work out the time delays and random aspects enough to take advantage of such information.

If institutions think that individual investors are sheep, that would suggest that they are followers. In that case, information from individual investors would be a lagging and not a leading indicator and not very useful for predictions.

I do know that "small" and "large" are not synonyms for "stupid" and "smart." AAII research shows that on average our 170,000 members outperform the market by a bit and institutions and mutual funds underperform the market by a bit. I examine some of the reasons for this in later chapters.

FUNDAMENTAL ANALYSIS

While often thrown together, here I separate what I define as fundamental analysis from macroeconomic analysis. Fundamental analysis is an effort to evaluate stocks (it can be used to evaluate other assets, but I concentrate on common stocks) based on characteristics within the firm. It can be—and I believe should be—expanded to include the firm's operational environment, which would encompass its markets and competitors.

Macroeconomic analysis examines what is happening in the general economy that impacts a particular company or sector. It would be a systematic impact similar to the systematic risk of modern portfolio theory.

While the emphasis has been on quantitative measures, qualitative measures can also be used in fundamental analysis. Qualitative measures would include items such as management ability, employee loyalty, product uniqueness, consumer loyalty and the relatively new concept of "moats" (something that makes the company's position invulnerable). But such qualities are most often reduced to a number, particularly if they become part of a report or rating system.

If Harry Markowitz is considered the father of modern portfolio theory, then Benjamin Graham (1934) would be the father of fundamental analysis. Fundamental analysis of securities as I defined it above has been going on for as long as securities have been traded. It was undoubtedly used prior to the beginning of organized trading when companies were sold on a total basis as complete entities and a potential buyer needed to look at available data on a company before deciding whether to make an offer to buy it and what price to offer.

Fundamental analysis of securities has been going on for as long as securities have been traded.

However, Graham presented an organized approach to stock analysis by looking at the data provided by companies in their various reports. Many professional investors, including Warren Buffett, credit Graham with providing the concepts that led them to success. While the organized approach provides a useful guide, Graham's specific rules, which have changed over time, do not always provide market-beating results. The concept of careful analysis of fundamental corporate data is his real contribution. Graham's focus has always been more on not paying too much when buying stocks as opposed to trying to find growth opportunities.

It has often been asserted that the decision to buy a stock should involve the same criteria you would use to buy the company. It sounds good, but many people buy companies with severe weaknesses at the right price so they can correct the weaknesses. Other investors buy companies to break them up into pieces and then sell some or all of the pieces. The fundamentals that are important will vary based on objectives.

The fundamental data appropriate for predicting future stock price behavior covers hundreds of variables, the change in these variables and the examination of them both on an absolute and comparative (compared to the average market values) bases. Generally they can be divided into two categories: Those that deal with a company's ability to survive adverse times without actions that hamper future earnings, and those that indicate future growth and profit potential.

> *The fundamentals that are important will vary based on objectives.*

Some of the most common of the former are: debt-to-equity ratio, level of cash and equivalents, quick ratio, book value, credit ratings, order backlogs, dividend ratio, cash flow, working capital and the changes in these metrics over time.

The indicators most used for predicting future growth opportunity relate to earnings and sales of the company and the price, dividend, gross profit, cash flow, and price-earnings ratio (P/E) of the company's stock and the changes in these over time.

Many of these appear in the strategies discussed in Chapter 6.

It would also expand into the immediate environment to examine market share, competitive strengths and the expansion/ contraction of the market. Of course, we want to know the future state of these measures, but future estimates are based on historical measures and estimated rates of change. This makes estimates of future stock performance very difficult, even on a

WHAT IS SUCCESS?

For this discussion of fundamental analysis—and the programs to be discussed in Chapter 6 of this book—I think it would be good to review the ways of measuring the success of any approach to investing.

First, to make any sense to individual investors, any system of stock and portfolio selection must provide better results than those of the market as a whole over the long term. The long term to me means at least 10 years; 20 years or more would be even better. It should outperform after considering risk, but not necessarily on a risk-adjusted basis as defined in modern portfolio theory because most of that risk is "ghost risk" for the long-term investor.

Second, the evaluation should be on a real portfolio managed through time. Simulations using backtesting are grossly misleading for numerous reasons. They are useful for eliminating possible approaches because if a system fails in backtesting, it will likely fail by an even larger margin in real-life applications.

Succeeding in simulations is no guarantee of success in real-life investing because transaction costs (the bid/ask spread as well as commissions) are generally understated significantly. There are also often other distortions, such as survivor bias (stocks or funds that have dropped out of a database may have had an influence).

As an example, I recently re-evaluated an approach to small-cap stock investing that seemed very effective. On closer examination, it turned out that transactions were based on last price; in real life, buys are transacted at the ask price and sells are transacted at the bid price.

In fact, for less-active stocks, the last price may have been based on a trade that took place hours (or days) previous to the close of trading, and the prevailing or actual bid and ask prices have moved on. In this case, I estimated that the adjustment for reality would have reduced simulated annual return by over 30% (the return was 10% instead of 40%)—rather significant. This "last price" bias is particularly pernicious when evaluating options and micro-cap stock strategies with simulations. And this impact compounds with strategies that require portfolio changes monthly or quarterly.

relative-to-market basis.

Even if I told you what the earnings of Stock ABC would be for the next 12 quarters, you would still have a difficult time predicting the stock price during that period. Most professional investors use a combination of different fundamental measures.

There are some measures that might be considered both technical and fundamental. For example, stock price momentum (continuing increase in price) is a technical indicator considered bullish. In fundamental analysis, it can be viewed as a prediction of the continuation of favorable fundamental factors that influence price.

Momentum is one measure that appears to effectively predict future price movement. Several studies show that short-term (under two years) momentum may be a strong indicator of future price increases.

Most professional investors use a combination of different fundamental measures.

The approach of virtually all professional investors would be a system that uses a combination of the various measures mentioned. Some combinations lead to popular concepts such as

GARP (growth at a reasonable price) or the PEG ratio (the price-to-earnings ratio divided by the earnings growth rate).

The AAII fundamental stock screening and research database program *Stock Investor Pro*, in addition to providing data and the ability to develop complex screens for stocks, also simulates the approaches of well-known investors such as John Templeton, Joseph Piotroski, James O'Shaughnessy, William O'Neil, John Neff, Peter Lynch, Benjamin Graham, and Warren Buffett to name a few. It allows you to try these approaches and also shows the fundamental approach used as AAII interprets it.

The bottom line is that fundamental research has had limited success but that success can be significant, as I show in Chapter 6.

The best proof of the limits of fundamental analysis is the inability of almost all, but not all, mutual funds to beat the market averages. I would expect that if fundamental analysis were completely useless, then on average the typical mutual fund would have a long-term (10 to 20 years) return of 1% to 2% per year less than the market average return because of the various operational and transaction costs. And that, with a few exceptions, is pretty much the case.

Fundamental research has had limited success but that success can be significant.

The reason for this, in my opinion, is that the market may not be efficient in the academic sense (as discussed in Chapter 1), but in the general sense of the word it is reasonably efficient. I would expect this to be the case because there are so many investors looking for inefficiencies that any such inefficiencies will be limited. This is particularly true in the U.S. markets, where information is readily available and secret dissemination of corporate information is proscribed by law.

There are, I believe, enough effective approaches to stock selection that they permit above-average profits, and some mutual funds and portfolios do excel over the longer term. When risk is examined in a more realistic way, the additional returns are not offset by risk.

I believe the majority of mutual funds fail to beat the market because:

- the obvious and hidden operational costs are too high;

- they are more concerned about beating the competition than the overall market;

- they don't stick to a rigidly defined selection process;

- they get mired down in factors that sound important but usually aren't—interviewing executives, attending corporate meetings, concern with corporate image, etc.; and

- they need to buy and sell to match the inflows and outflows of money to the fund—perhaps the most important detriment.

I examine mutual fund behavior in more detail in later chapters.

SUMMARY

If we consider all strategies that use historical price and volume data to be technical analysis, then technical analysis can help provide market-beating results because there is strong evidence that price momentum is an indicator of superior results.

There is also some evidence that moving averages can predict future price direction—especially for indexes—but it is not very strong. Price momentum, however, has proven predictive value.

On the other hand, there is little evidence that charting is more than an interesting game. Even if the underlying concept that buying and selling behavior in the past can predict buying and selling in the future, crude (by computer and artificial intelligence standards) charts are not likely to be very accurate. And, indeed, charting experts always seem to disagree on interpretations.

Fundamental analysis, on the other hand, can be useful. There are all kinds of research showing that various measures, alone or in combination, can lead to market-beating results. The various measures that I put into strategies in Chapter 6 are well-known. It is a mystery then as to why so many institutions attempting to use fundamental data don't beat the market.

I previously listed a number of institutional reasons for this, but I am still not convinced that those reasons and operational costs completely explain the underperformance.

CHAPTER 3

THE FINANCIAL SERVICES INDUSTRY: FRIEND OR FOE?

"Where are the customers' yachts?"

—Fred Schwed Jr.

When we finally arrive at an investment strategy that we feel is best for us, we must implement it. That requires working with the firms and individuals of the financial services industry. The degree of the interaction will depend on how much you can and want to do yourself, but some contact is always necessary.

You also need to utilize some of the many products that the financial services industry supplies, ranging from common stocks to options to hedge funds. In this chapter, I examine the various players and products to which investors may be exposed. My emphasis is on how these firms and products impact your success or lack of it. I don't want to imply that the financial service industry is out to harm us, although there are some outright crooks. But the objectives of many firms we deal with are not aligned with our objectives and, consciously or unconsciously, this conflict can lead to suboptimal performance in our portfolios. It is important to be aware of the conflicts with both firms and their products.

ASSET MANAGERS AND THEIR OBLIGATION

While all of the financial services industry is important to the individual investor, I am primarily interested in the impact of those individuals and institutions that make decisions as to which investments and how much of each are in the investor's portfolio. It is also necessary to examine the various products that have been created for us to invest in.

Except to say that investors should exercise normal caution by checking competency and fees, I am not going to discuss the role of attorneys, accountants and financial planners who are only giving advice about such issues as trusts, estates, wills, account designations, income and estate tax implications. The aspects of retirement planning outside the selection of specific investments or guidance on portfolio allocation are also not covered here.

The objectives of many firms we deal with are not aligned with our objectives, and this conflict can lead to suboptimal performance in our portfolios.

While all of these issues are important in developing an overall investment strategy and need to be considered, they are not the issues that concern Level3 investors.

Sometimes, the same individual or organization that carries out the above-mentioned consulting functions also provides advice on portfolio management or actually manages the portfolio. It is important to differentiate these functions. Attorneys and accountants will not typically be involved in portfolio management, but there are exceptions.

Financial planners generally perform both functions, but "fee-only" financial planners will typically advise on the issues without requiring you to let them manage your portfolio. A fee-only planner who also manages portfolios does not take commissions but charges a set fee, usually a percentage of assets managed. Any part of their services that involves portfolio management does concern us here.

Private banks generally want to be involved in every aspect of wealth management, but for high-net-worth individuals, arrangements are flexible.

For the purposes of this book, I have narrowed our area of

concern to those organizations or individuals who actually manage or provide guidance in managing your portfolio assets. I narrow it a bit further by eliminating small private group investments. These limited liability partnerships, or LLCs, include small real estate investments that might involve managing as well as owning property, angel investments (investing in start-up businesses and maybe providing guidance), and any small private group investments. Each one is unique and any evaluation would lack background facts. They can't even be discussed on a "general" or "average" basis, because there is no reliable source of average returns or fees.

> *For the purposes of this book, I have narrowed our area of concern to those organizations or individuals who actually manage or provide guidance in managing your portfolio assets.*

How well our interests as investors line up with the interests of those who serve us is important to understand. The relationship can run from the "boiler room" operator, such as shown in the 2013 movie "The Wolf of Wall Street," to highly effective money managers with only minimal conflicts. In examining all the members of the financial services industry with whom you are likely to have relationships, I look at the degree to which conflicts can reduce your portfolio returns.

The obligation that anyone in the investment arena has to us can range from no obligation—except to not break any ordinary laws—all the way to a fiduciary responsibility, which involves an obligation to put our interests as clients before their own. I look at what obligation each type of adviser has. Some of these obligations are in a state of flux because of current legislation and regulation changes.

CATEGORIES OF ADVISERS

There are several legal relationships with individuals or firms that may play a part in managing our assets.

Broker-Dealers

A broker-dealer is a firm registered with the Securities and Exchange Commission (SEC) and required to be a member of and be supervised by FINRA, the self-regulatory agency of the securities industry. The broker places trades of securities between parties and makes markets in securities. They are commonly called stockbrokers, and the individual employees with whom you do business are also commonly called brokers or registered representatives. They must pass various exams that relate primarily to state and federal law and regulations.

While brokers can be used simply to execute trades at your direction, they frequently provide information and advice about individual securities that can be expanded into advice about your entire portfolio. This can be done through consultations. Alternatively, the broker can be given discretion to manage your account independently, subject only to an agreement about objectives and limits.

Security law and regulation, until recently, only required that any advice or action be suitable for your financial situation as described to the broker (called the "suitability standard"). There was no fiduciary obligation to put your interests ahead of the firms. There are, however, some prohibited actions such as front running, which is using knowledge of your trades to gain extra profits in the broker's own trading, or churning, which is excessive trading.

Security law and regulation, until recently, only required that any advice or action be suitable for your financial situation as described to the broker.

The Dodd-Frank Wall Street Reform and Consumer Protection Act, passed in 2010 in the hope of preventing another stock market meltdown as occurred in 2007–2008, called for increased oversight and standards that had widespread impact on a multitude of financial areas. Among the provisions of the Dodd-Frank act was empowerment of the SEC to examine the current relationships between investors and broker-dealers and other financial advisers in respect to conflicts of interest. This allows the SEC to change the broker-dealer/client relationship, possibly even to change it to the full fiduciary relationship that applies to registered investment advisers (RIAs). Broker-dealers have managed to prevent that up to this time.

But the pressure grew enough to bring about a change in regard to retirement accounts: The U.S. Labor Department, which has authority over pensions, has issued a rule that brokers now must assume full fiduciary responsibility to put clients' needs first in regard to activities in retirement accounts. The old standard holds for other accounts, at least for the time being, and changes will have to be made at the SEC.

Broker-dealers claim they cannot provide the wide range of services to us if they have to put our interests first. That argument in itself is mighty worrisome.

The typical relationship is for the broker to receive commissions on your trades for the advice and support given. With an on-line execution-only broker (discount broker), you get no advice and you pay a minimal commission, usually $7 to $15 per trade regardless of size. Full-service brokers charge higher commissions that are based on both dollar value and number of shares, but average about 1% of the trade value for mid-sized trades.

Some brokers also will offer "wrap fees" for accounts they manage. Instead of higher commissions, they charge a percent of the portfolio value each year, which includes commissions. This would probably be the best managerial arrangement, if the fees were not too high. A fee below 1% would make sense, but fees tend to run 2% or more, which can rarely be justified by performance.

With the traditional broker relationship based on commissions, the broker makes more money with more trading. Severe over-trading (churning) is prohibited but not well defined. Over the long run, the more a portfolio turns over, the poorer the performance and the higher the taxes (gains are often short term).

So what is good for the broker is bad for the client, and this is a dangerous situation. It is moderated by the fact that the broker knows that if performance is poor clients will leave, so some control exists. But it would seem that even with the most ethical and client-oriented broker, there would be at least some unconscious rationalization justifying excess trading.

What is good for the broker is bad for the client, and this is a dangerous situation.

If the relationship is based on a wrap fee, overtrading is unlikely and undertrading (if there is such a thing) would be better for the broker. The wrap-fee approach aligns the interest of the client and broker as much as possible; if it were not for the high fees, it would be an excellent relationship for those who feel they need a money manager.

There are a few other significant factors with a full-service broker. They are also underwriters, market makers and firms that trade for their own accounts. Theoretically these activities do not influence the firm's research department recommendations to the individual brokers, but I suspect it does.

Investment Advisers

Investment advisers are individuals or firms in the business of giving advice about securities to clients but who are not broker-dealers. They must be registered with the SEC and/or with state securities departments. There are a few exemptions from registration for advisers that only have a few clients. Generally, the investment advisers you will be exposed to fall into three groups:

1. **Institutional advisers:** Advisers who advise mutual funds and other institutional portfolios.

2. **Portfolio managers:** Advisers who manage security portfolios, or portions of portfolios, for individuals and only have limited other involvement.

3. **Financial planners:** Advisers who provide advice about all aspects of a client's financial life. They provide help and advice on taxes, investments, insurance, retirement and estate planning. They help integrate all financial aspects of an investor's life into a strategic plan.

Institutional advisers

Large mutual fund families may have subadvisers who are generally paid a fee based on the dollar value of the funds managed. These advisers have no say about the overall fees charged by the fund. While these advisers are rarely paid as a percentage of their performance, their income is related to their performance both from their ability to negotiate their fee and the increasing size of the portfolio that should result from better performance. Their interests are almost completely aligned with those of the investor in the funds.

The efforts of a fund's primary adviser are also aligned with the investor, except for one very important and crucial consideration: how high are the fees paid to the adviser. This is a serious consideration, and I discuss it in detail later in the chapter when I cover mutual funds in the section on investment products.

Portfolio managers

Investment advisers who primarily manage assets for the individual are most commonly paid on a percentage of the assets managed. This is frequently segmented in that the fees for fixed income, equities and mutual funds (generally ETFs) are likely different. The fees start at the minimum amount the adviser will accept and are reduced for larger portfolios. Typical fees might be 1% for equities and 0.5% for bonds at the minimum investment requirement and go down to one half of that for large portfolios. Transactions might take place through an execution-only brokerage firm, and commission costs would be minimal. Often the assets are placed with a trustee, with the adviser able to manage but not access the assets.

Except for the fee structure, the interests of the adviser and client are pretty well aligned. Above-average performance will benefit both parties.

Financial planners

In most cases, financial planners are registered investment advisers (RIAs) but they expand their services beyond portfolio management into other areas of the client's financial concerns. Their investment advisory services come under the purview of the SEC, and they must pass exams that relate to those services. These exams, however, relate to laws and regulations and do not try to measure portfolio management capability.

Services provided that are not related to portfolio management are unregulated by the SEC. Proficiency in these areas—which include asset allocation, estate planning, insurance planning, retirement issues, risk management and tax planning—is not controlled or tested. Anyone is free to call themselves a financial planner or any other name they choose except broker-dealer and investment adviser.

Self-Imposed Restrictions

Except for tests about the law and regulations, the SEC does not impose any educational or competency requirements on broker-dealers or investment advisers and imposes no requirements on financial planners beyond their investment advisory activities. However, many firms and individuals choose to subject themselves to tests of competency and regulation of activities through voluntary membership in non-governmental professional organizations.

> *The SEC does not impose any educational or competency requirements on broker-dealers or investment advisers and no requirements on financial planners beyond their investment advisory activities.*

Competency in investment theory and practice can be shown through passing of a series of exams to earn the right to use the Chartered Financial Analyst (CFA) designation. While the three tests (or "levels") are complex and demanding, understanding the mathematics and theory of investing does not ensure superior investment results. It does, however, protect against damage that could occur due to adviser ignorance of how security markets work. CFA charterholders are required to adhere to a code of ethics (which includes adherence to a fiduciary standard) and commit to ongoing education.

Competency in financial planning can be shown by achieving the certified financial planner (CFP) designation from the CFP Board. Achievement of this designation requires passing of exams, financial education, experience, adherence to a code of ethics and continuing education. While it shows a level of proficiency and experience, it does not guarantee superior investment performance.

Influencers

There are other sources of influence and guidance that are available to you.

The oldest is the advisory letter. These services can have different degrees of influence. If you use their recommendations only as a starting point, to discover investments you wish to evaluate further, there is only moderate impact. If you religiously follow their model portfolios, their impact is similar to a mutual fund. Subscription costs are relatively low, so the main influence on your investment results will come from how good their advice is. The only way to get unbiased estimates of their success was from Mark Hulbert's Hulbert Financial Digest (HFD), which tracked long-term returns for the advisory letters and portfolios. Although Hulbert discontinued publication of his digest in 2016, **Level3investing.com** includes a list of advisory letters with superior results over the past 15 years as of December 31, 2015, as reported by the Hulbert Financial Digest.

Many magazines, newspapers and TV programs throw in stock recommendations with their stories, and these can be used as part of a gross list of prospects for additional processing. Magazine and TV recommendations with wide audiences can influence stock prices. The most common pattern is for the stock to move up immediately before the recommendation is made (somebody knows something), continue up for a while, and then retreat to its earlier level.

Robo-Advisers

A new approach to investment advice and portfolio management is somewhere between an advisory letter's model portfolio and an investment adviser. These online advisory services, called robo-advisers (a term they do not favor but is sticking), are an attempt to reduce advisory costs by automating or not providing all the services a financial planner/portfolio manager might provide. (for an overview of robo-advisory services and what to look for, see the *AAII Journal* article by Jaclyn McClellan "What Exactly Do Online Investment Advisory Services Offer?," (2015) available at AAII.com.

> *The major contribution of the robo-adviser is that you are less likely to deviate from the long-term strategy.*

Each of the current services is somewhat different. Generally, an initial analysis of the investor is needed to select the appropriate program, and re-evaluation is necessary in the event of a significant change in the investor's situation. Such plans tend to cost less than 0.5% a year when using mutual funds and ETFs, slightly more if individual stocks are used. These services can be utilized directly or through a defined-contribution plan if the plan sponsor agrees.

This is a new area and is changing fast, so current information is best obtained by searching the internet.

Since both Vanguard and Charles Schwab are moving into this area full force, we expect a significant new investment service to emerge soon. Vanguard is currently dominating the robo-advising field because of all of their contacts through management of 401(k) and 403(b) retirement accounts.

The Level3 investment approaches I discuss in the remainder of this book are much like a robo-adviser, except that you will be doing it yourself, saving the fees, and will be able to use a wider range of investments. The strategies robo-advisory services use are for the most part simple and you must provide the personal information that helps develop the strategy. The major contribution of the robo-adviser is that you are less likely to deviate from the long-term strategy.

Internal Revenue Service

The Internal Revenue Service (IRS) has a significant impact on our net returns. Different investments are taxed differently. Different types of accounts are taxed differently. Different holding periods are taxed differently. And, unfortunately, it is a rare year when there are not at least minor changes in the tax code. Changes to the tax laws are constantly being proposed.

We are often advised to concentrate on the profitability of our strategy and not worry about taxes. As the joke goes, the easy way to avoid investment taxes is to never make a profit or receive a dividend or interest payment.

Common sense says there is a compromise. If you can deviate slightly from your ordinary course to cut some taxes in half, it makes sense to do so. In some ways, good tax strategy is aligned with good investment practice. On the whole, it is better to sell losers and hold winners. It is also better to be a long-term investor, both from a tax and an investment standpoint as long as capital gains are taxed at lower rates and delayed until profits are realized. Overall, tax strategies need a book of their own, but it is wise to remember they can have a dramatic impact on net returns.

PRODUCTS AND THEIR PROBLEMS

The cost of using various investment products varies widely. These costs reduce our eventual return on investment. If they are high, they make it unlikely that we can realize returns above the average of a market index fund. The total costs are not always obvious, so I discuss the products here individually. I want to make it clear that it is not my intention to turn this into a general investment book. I am only concerned with pointing out aspects of the products that may reduce your returns. Let's start by defining a few terms.

The costs of using various investment products reduce our eventual return on investment.

Transaction costs involve both commissions and the bid/ask spread. The bid/ask spread is the difference between what you would pay to buy the security at a given point in time and what you would get for it if you were selling. For example, if the quote was 100 bid and 101 ask, the spread would be 1%. If you are looking at overall returns of 10% a year, paying 1% could be a significant amount, particularly if you turn your portfolio over several times a year. The spread will be lower for very active stocks and higher for less-active stocks. Also, the current spread will be for a certain number of shares. Larger orders will face widening spreads.

Many investors believe they can avoid the spread by placing an order somewhere between the current bid and ask—say, in our example above, placing a buy order at $100.50. When you do that, market makers react and the spread becomes 100.50/101.50. You will get a fill if the market weakens; you will not get a fill if the market strengthens. You may have paid the full spread even if you got a fill, you just wouldn't know it.

There are some exceptions, such as catching a sell for your buy from another individual who placed an order close to the time you placed yours at the same price and getting a matched execution.

Also, in thinly traded markets, market makers may set a very wide bid/ask spread because they don't want to be caught if some news or a big order suddenly emerges. They may be willing to buy or sell inside the quote but don't want it published.

Market makers set a wide spread regularly after the market close, so the bid/ask showing after the close is meaningless. The setting of wide spreads is particularly true in option markets.

Here are the major investment products and the potential impact on our portfolio returns.

Stocks

Obviously, the ultimate performance of the equities we choose will impact our returns. It is hoped that this book will help you select a portfolio of stocks that will surpass most index returns. In addition to performance, the main concern with stocks is controlling transaction costs and this will come from low commissions. Almost every online discount broker's commission charges are so low that for even moderate portfolios they are almost insignificant, particularly if you consider you are getting all kinds of data from them in addition to executions.

> *In addition to performance, the main concern with stocks is controlling transaction costs and this will come from low commissions.*

The difference between a $6.00 and $12.00 per trade commission will probably be a couple hundred dollars a year, so the online discount broker with the best website and data for your needs is likely the best choice. If you use a full-service broker, transactions will likely run 1% or more of the transaction value. If you turn your portfolio over frequently, the chances of investment success diminish rapidly.

Bonds

While government bonds and the limited number of bonds that are listed on the New York Stock Exchange (NYSE) trade much like stocks, most bonds including municipals trade through dealers. There is a real risk of wide spreads and great care is necessary. Most of us, if we need bonds at all, are better off with bond mutual funds, particularly exchange-traded funds (ETFs).

But individual bonds have the unique characteristic of having a date at which the face value will be reimbursed, and that is a desirable feature for many bond buyers. Tax-free municipal bonds appeal to many investors; with the current tax code, any strategy that reduces "adjusted gross income" may provide multiple favorable tax impacts.

Besides the dealer spreads, another area of caution to be aware of with bonds is the "call" feature.

Besides the dealer spreads, another area of caution to be aware of with bonds is the "call" feature. If interest rates go up your bond prices go down, but if interest rates go down the bond issuer can call your bond at a price below the theoretical market price. If you buy bonds for safety, it seems better to use government bonds, which do not have call features. Unfortunately, there are no government municipals. If you wish to use individual bonds, it is essential that you study the field.

Exchange-Traded Funds (ETFs)

Exchange-traded funds trade in a similar fashion to stocks. The additional danger is that you may pay too much in management fees. The area is very competitive, and at this point in time almost all ETFs are index funds. Unusual ETFs and those dealing in foreign securities will charge a higher management fee. Even complex ETFs should have fees well below 1%; those dealing with major indexes tend to be below 0.2%.

Trading commissions are the same as for stocks, which is almost trivial with online discount brokers and some trade commission-free because the sponsor reimburses the broker.

One weakness in ETFs is the possibility of mispricing in fast markets.

As we get more non-index ETFs, it will be harder to arbitrage the portfolios and there will be a greater difference between the true portfolio value and the market price. As in the case of closed-end funds, you will have to consider the impact of such differences.

Except for limits on the strategies that can be employed, ETFs seem superior to traditional mutual funds. I believe ETFs should be replacing most mutual funds gradually, but people are slow to change. One weakness in ETFs is the possibility of mispricing in fast markets (heavy trading and high volatility). Be very careful of market orders in fast markets. If there is an established index on which the ETF is based, check it when placing orders. In general, don't trade ETFs in fast markets.

Mutual Funds

Here we find a multitude of problems, each of which requires significant discussion. The problems can be:

1. Poor performance,

2. Ridiculously high fees and loads, and

3. Lack of truly independent directors.

Poor performance

I define poor performance generously as a return below that of the S&P 500 index. Over the long term (10 years), very few mutual funds have beat the index. Those that do are usually funds that have found a niche such as gold that often has long periods of up or down trends.

Health care mutual funds fit the bullish version of this model and have had a long bullish run. Technology had a long run until the year 2000, and then it collapsed with all the tech mutual funds and didn't recover until March of 2015 (using the tech-heavy NASDAQ Composite index as a measure).

If you are astute enough to find those funds that will excel during any period of time, you are astute enough to find an equivalent ETF with lower costs or be able to assemble your own portfolio.

Some funds follow the same approaches favored in this book and will perform above the S&P 500 over the long run if their fees, internal and external, don't exceed their investment advantage.

However, I believe if you are astute enough to find those funds that will excel during any period of time, you are astute enough to find an equivalent ETF with lower costs or be able to assemble your own portfolio.

High fees and loads

The mutual fund industry is rife with ridiculously high fees and loads. Any load is too high. You are not paying for better management of the fund. You are paying to reimburse the broker-dealer for selling you something that most likely isn't the best for you but that pays him the best commission or is sponsored by his firm.

Expense ratios for non-index mutual funds generally run about 1% and may go all the way to 2%. Fees include general expenses plus the advisory fee that is paid to the advisory firm and any subadvisers for managing the portfolios. In the past, fees generally went down as the fund grew in size, but that practice is disappearing. Economies of scale mostly wind up as extra revenue for the adviser, although very large funds (billions) often charge less than 1%.

The expense ratio is not the only impact on the realized returns. Funds generally pay commissions on transactions at a higher rate than you would pay an online broker. There is also the bid/ask spread, which goes up with the size of the transaction and down with the liquidity of the stock. A commonly used estimate of average transaction costs is 1.44%, but fund research firm Morningstar argues that such a level is not possible or index funds could not be able to track their indexes as closely as they do.

Regardless of the average, there is a wide range. Large-cap stocks will have smaller spreads even with large orders. Small-cap stocks will have larger spreads. My own experience with micro-cap stocks indicates that because of the wide spreads turnover must be kept to a minimum.

As a point of reference let's say that total fund expenses, advisory fees, and transaction costs total 2%. For this reduction in return, you have someone managing the equity part of your investment portfolio. For a little over half the total cost of investing in a mutual fund you can get a financial adviser who will pick stocks, ETFs and bonds for your portfolio; advise on asset allocation; and deal with numerous financial planning and tax issues.

For a little over half the total cost of investing in a mutual fund you can get a financial adviser who will pick stocks, ETFs and bonds for your portfolio; advise on asset allocation; and deal with numerous financial planning and tax issues.

Mutual funds simply do not make a lot of sense except in special areas of investment and the various index funds.

Lack of truly independent directors

The lack of truly independent directors for mutual funds is a large part of the disregard for stockholder welfare. The illusion that the directors are independent makes it worse because it offers a false sense of security. Rules imposed by securities law require that the majority of directors of a mutual fund be independent. Directors are considered independent if they have no interest in the advisory firm that serves the fund or any of its subsidiaries.

But true independence requires a lot more than that. Consider the relationship of the primary advisory firm serving the fund to the board of directors. The primary advisory firm:

- chooses the independent directors,

- determines director remuneration and expense policy,

- terminates directors,

- sets the meeting schedules (when, where, how long),

- chooses their legal representation, and

- determines the advisory fee, which the board members will rubber-stamp.

Has an independent board ever fired an adviser? Has an independent board ever even interviewed another adviser? When institutions hire investment advisory firms to manage their endowments, they interview numerous candidates and they replace advisers every six or seven years on average.

There are many funds that have dramatically underperformed the market for five, 10 or even 20 years, and their so-called independent boards have not tried to replace the advisers.

There are many funds that have dramatically underperformed the market for five, 10, or even 20 years and their so-called independent boards have not tried to replace the advisers.

As you can see, the boards of mutual funds are not independent in the real meaning of the word. It would be more honest and less confusing if the investment laws were changed so that advisory firms were permitted to openly control what a mutual fund does. It would also save money since a great deal is spent maintaining the illusion of independence. Eliminating fake independent boards is one of the real advantages of ETFs.

There is one final disadvantage to investing in most mutual funds, but it is not the mutual funds' fault. Stockholders in mutual funds are like stockholders everywhere—they trade too much. If you are a long-term holder in a fund with investors who panic and sell every time the market goes down, it will reduce the long-term return. This is particularly true of funds that choose less-liquid stocks. Those are often the funds that deal in market inefficiencies (such as small cap, high value, momentum, etc.) and have better returns. So the long-term investors in these funds lose potential returns because of the behavior of short-term-oriented investors.

Many funds try to offset this effect. One approach is charging penalties (which go back into the fund) of 1% to 2% for short-term trading, but these generally only apply to newly purchased shares. Limiting the amount of trading allowed in a fund is another approach. But if you have a market such as that in 2008, with losses in the 30% to 60% range, panicky sellers can cause the fund to incur significant transaction costs on the trades necessary to meet the redemption requests. Some mutual funds are considering special charges for trading during fast markets.

If you are a long-term holder in a fund with investors who panic and sell every time the market goes down, it will reduce the long-term return.

I believe that there can be a place for traditional mutual funds beyond just index funds, but only if the funds make some changes. The most significant improvement would be to cut the annual expense ratio to significantly less than 1%.

Hedge Funds

Much of what I have said about mutual funds applies to hedge funds. Like mutual funds, they are able to pass gains and losses on to the investor without double taxation because they are limited partnerships. Hedge funds differ from mutual funds in several ways:

- They can invest in a wide range of vehicles that are not generally open to mutual funds, such as swaps (complex options), commodities, unlisted securities and all forms of arbitrage. They can trade short term, which is not allowed or very limited for mutual funds.

- They can be long or short and even hedge. Despite their name, not many funds truly hedge, even though hedging was their original justification.

- Mutual funds can only charge profit-sharing fees if they participate both in gains and losses. Hedge funds can share in profits and not share in losses. The typical arrangement is for the fund manager to receive 2% of assets plus 20% of any profits. Many of the popular hedge funds can only be accessed through a fund of funds or through an investment adviser, both of which result in another level of fees.

- If a hedge fund is underwater (it has cumulative losses), the fund will waive its 20% until the portfolio is back in a profit mode. If the fund gets too far underwater and looks like it will not be collecting fees for a while, the fund can be closed and a new fund started that is not yet underwater and gets performance fees.

- Hedge funds can only sell to accredited investors, which currently means investors whose income is $200,000 or $300,000 jointly with a spouse or whose net worth is over $1 million. Typically the "hot" funds at the moment may require $1 million or higher minimum investment, which further restricts who can participate. High minimums also make investors feel special because they are allowed to participate.

- On average, hedge funds earn more than market returns on a gross basis because of the areas in which they can invest and the leverage they can use. But after the ridiculous fees, their net return over the long run is slightly less than the return on mutual funds and less than the market return. The average long-term (20 years) return for hedge funds based on the Hennessee Hedge Fund Index and the Dow Jones Credit Suisse Hedge Fund Index is 8.6% annualized.

Of course some hedge funds do better than average, at least over the short term. The very nature of some hedge fund strategies leads to extreme results. It is not unusual to see hedge funds with 100% gains in some years. Of course there are down years of the same magnitude, and hedge funds disappear at a significant rate.

Warren Buffett made his opinion of hedge funds clear by making a million dollar bet with Ted Seides of Protégé Partners that an S&P 500 index fund would outperform the average of a group of hedge funds of Seides' choosing over 10 years. The bet started in 2008, and with three years to go Fortune magazine reported that the index fund chosen (VFINX), is up 65.7% versus 21.9% for the fund of hedge funds selected by Seides (as of December 31, 2015). The year 2015 was a breakeven year for the S&P 500, but a weak year for most hedge funds.

There is certainly a chance of choosing a hedge fund that outperforms the market, but the odds are against finding it and even higher against getting into it. If you would like to read more on the interesting history of these funds and their approaches read Sebastian Mallaby's book, "More Money Than God: Hedge Funds and the Making of the New Elite" (2010).

Private Equity

Much of the discussion of hedge funds would also apply to private equity. It is organized in a similar way and the fee structure seems to be similar. Conceptually, private equity partnerships are formed to invest in the securities of non-listed companies. However "invest in" does not mean the passive investment of a mutual fund. Private equity can and does influence and control private companies, often selling them in whole or piece by piece.

For an investor lucky enough to find a partnership that has provided a long-term return of 14% to 17% who felt that the risky investment required an equal amount in safe investments, the net effect might be a total portfolio that underperforms the overall market.

Even though private equity entities try even more than hedge funds to maintain secrecy about their activities and their fee structures, some information does leak out. Mitt Romney's run for president in 2012 exposed his connection with and the activities of Bain Capital and by inference other private capital partnerships.

Because most readers will not be exposed to private capital, I don't want to devote much space to it. For those interested, there was insightful coverage by Gretchen Morgenson in the New York Times on October 19, 2014, and by James Surowiecki in The New Yorker on January 30, 2012. More recently, in the March 23, 2015, issue of Bloomberg Businessweek, Neil Weinberg and Darrell Preston describe how private equity entities seem able to get away with anything and are truly expert at doing what's best for the managing partners. All of these articles are available online (see Bibliography).

It appears that through well-written partnership agreements and skillful use of the tax laws, the managing partners will be the dominant beneficiary of any gains from the $3.5 trillion invested in these entities.

A very important consideration in evaluating the returns from either hedge funds or private equity is the proportion of your wealth you want them to manage. Most individuals investing in hedge funds and private equity feel that they must also have savings in safe investments. For an investor lucky enough to find a partnership that has provided a long-term return of 14% to 17% who felt that the risky investment required an equal amount in safe investments, the net effect might be a total portfolio that underperforms the overall market.

Options

I don't want to devote a lot of space to options because, in my opinion, very few individual investors should be using them except for special reasons. However, there is continual promotion of option usage aimed at the individual investor, so I think it's important to review some of the problems.

If you have little familiarity with stock options and haven't been tempted to participate, just continue to stay away from options.

As a reminder: A call option gives the buyer the right (but not the obligation) to purchase from the option seller an asset at a specified price (exercise price) on or before a specified date (expiration date). A put option gives the buyer the right to sell to the option seller an asset at a specified price (exercise price) on or before a specified date (expiration date).

The reason option use is promoted, of course, is that commissions are like the old stock commissions: They are very high. On top of that, the bid/ask spreads are extremely wide for all but the options on the most liquid individual stocks, popular indexes and ETFs. Options also expire, so owners continue to periodically execute the strategy. All of these phenomena make fees a major source of income for the options industry. That profit comes out of the value of your portfolio and/or significantly reduces the effectiveness of any potentially useful option strategy.

The reason option use is promoted of course is that commissions are like the old stock commissions: They are very high.

Since option values are derived from stock values, they can be used as a substitute for it or in combination with it to modify the gain/loss and risk possibilities.

To understand the rationale of option investing and the discussion of its pitfalls to follow, it is important to understand the basic stock/option relationship.

At expiration with the same exercise prices, owning 100 shares of a stock is the equivalent of being long a call and short a put. That relationship and the five equivalent relationships can be expressed in equation form where a minus sign means being short. Thus:

1. Stock = Call − Put
2. −Stock = Put − Call
3. Call = Stock + Put
4. −Call = −Stock − Put
5. Put = Call − Stock
6. −Put = Stock − Call

There are generally four reasons that options might be used:

1) Arbitrage/conversion

Conversion is arbitrage between puts and calls. Conversion profit comes from taking advantage of mispricing the theoretical relationships of different puts and calls on same stock (i.e., different exercise prices or expiration dates). Doing this effectively requires computer analysis—preferably high speed—and minimal transaction costs, so this strategy is not open to individual investors.

2) Leveraging

If you feel very, very sure that a stock or index is going up or down, you can get more leverage by using options than by using margin. Leverage works both ways, however, and I have nothing more to say about this strategy except—you'd better be right.

3) Trading off risk and return

Most of the combination of calls, puts, and stock you see in articles or on CNBC are designed to limit risk when seeking gains from predicted stock movement. Doing so also limits the gain, and whether you get the gain or the loss depends on which way the market goes and when. But the strategy is to limit loss by sacrificing potential gain.

Covered call writing fits into this category. You maintain a portfolio of stocks or an ETF. You then write (sell) calls against the holdings, adding the proceeds of the option price to your results and giving up profit on growth of the stock beyond the exercise price.

You will note from our list of equalities above that equation 6 indicates that covered call writing is the same as selling a naked (unhedged) put. Selling the put involves fewer trades and less cash tied up, so the price will be a bit less than that of the call to reflect this.

This is a good example of option "hype." Covered call writing is described as the safest approach and suitable for conservative investors. You are also told that selling options where you do not own the underlying stock (naked option) is the most dangerous investment and not suitable for most individuals. Yet selling a put and writing a covered call are the same thing and have the same risk. Either way, if the stock goes down you lose the amount of dollars it went down less the amount you received for the option.

In my opinion, you can reduce risk (if you feel you should) more effectively by reducing your stock holding than by selling a covered call or a naked put.

4) Hedging your portfolio

Another highly promoted use of options is to hedge your portfolio. Fondly called "portfolio insurance," you are advised to spend some money to protect your holdings by buying puts so your loss is limited. The limit is determined by the exercise price of the put you use.

Now take a look at equation 5 above. Buying a put to protect a stock is the same as selling the stock and buying a call or simply not buying the stock but just buying calls to start with—not leveraging, just buying calls to match the number of shares of the stock you were going to buy originally.

Your loss is limited to the price you pay for the calls and your upside is reduced by that price. There will be differences depending on the exercise price of the option you choose. Once again, "smart hedging" is the same as risky call buying.

Under the right market conditions and with very liquid ETFs, the use of puts or calls for portfolio insurance can make sense in principal.

Theoretically, if options were perfectly priced they would reflect all the trade-offs in these various strategies, and over the long run they would provide the same result—except that the option approaches would have the outcomes reduced by transaction costs, which can be considerable.

The mutual funds that use covered call writing have average returns over the past five years of approximately 6.9% compared to the S&P 500 index at 16.0% (as of December 31, 2015). The standard deviation of the funds was lower, at approximately 6.2% compared to 9.5% for the index. [The funds are Madison Covered Call & Equity Income A (MENAX) and Russell Strategic Call Overwriting S (ROWAX; no longer available) and the ETFs are PowerShares S&P 500 BuyWrite ETF (PBP), Horizons S&P 500 Covered Call ETF (HSPX), and iPath CBOE S&P 500 BuyWrite ETN (BWV).]

Most of the calls sold were slightly out of the money, and I estimate that volatility was reduced by one-third. That means that you could have reduced the volatility of the stock holdings by putting one-third of the equity value of the index into Treasury bills to obtain the same lower volatility and gotten an annual return of about 11% versus 6.9%. So 4% a year of risk-adjusted return was lost to transaction costs and fund expenses.

Save yourself time, money and aggravation. Forget options. I say this knowing that for the investor who really understands them there will be occasions that justify their use.

One final thought to connect some dots. The smart money has always said that sellers of options made money and buyers were suckers. Remember the discussion in Chapter 2 indicating that the market was more volatile than indicated by the normal (lognormal) curve.

I can think of no other lawful industry where so many people get paid so much for contributing so little.

The Black Scholes (B/S) model, which is the most-used pricing model, uses the lognormal distribution and most certainly undervalues options. Theoretically then, options, if priced at or below the

B/S price, could provide an excess return to the buyer. But, then again, there are those ridiculous transaction costs, including wide bid/ask spreads for all but the most liquid stocks and ETFs and even then only for the shorter expiration periods.

SUMMARY

In addition to the expected challenge of designing a strategy, our implementation of that strategy is going to face all kinds of roadblocks set up by those who want a piece of our action.

All kinds of intermediaries have their hand out. It may be necessary or even desirable to give a small piece to a deserving hand, but many would-be helpers have two hands and a bushel basket out there trying to get rich on what should be our retirement. I can think of no other lawful industry where so many people get paid so much for contributing so little.

And the saddest part of it is that the advice we are paying too much for may be bad advice. So it is essential to know the competence of our advisers and make sure their fees are competitive. Please don't "tip the whipper."

Many products have such high usage costs that it is virtually impossible to beat or even match the market using them.

We must also be concerned with the products we use for investment. Too many of them have built-in inefficiencies that cost us money. Many products have such high usage costs that it is virtually impossible to beat or even match the market using them.

I hope this chapter has provided some insight into the nature of the financial services industry—its services and its products—and we can now turn to developing the strategy for successfully "Investing at Level3."

PART II
Where We Should Be: Investing at Level3

The next three chapters explain the Level3 approach to improving return and dealing with risk over the long term as well as during periods when you must withdraw savings for expenditures.

The final chapter provides guidance for setting up a program to efficiently apply the precepts of the Level3 Investing approach and avoid the strong behavioral impulses that will try to lead you astray.

CHAPTER 4

THE NATURE OF REAL INVESTMENT RISK

*"I would rather have a $2 million portfolio that could lose 50%
than a $1 million portfolio that could only lose 30%."*

—Level3 Investor

Perhaps the single most significant aspect of the Level3 Investing approach is redefining risk for long-term investors. While volatility, if it can be properly measured, may be a satisfactory measure of risk for short-term investing, it is rather meaningless for long-term investors.

A primary message of Level3 Investing is that individual investors who are investing for the long term belong to a subset of investors that is entitled to higher returns than the returns of the overall market because:

- they can invest in areas not open to larger investors and that have higher returns, and

- they can ignore much of the risk faced by institutions and other short-term investors. Their basic return is already risk-adjusted.

Chapter 6 expands on the former of these two concepts, and this chapter expands on the latter.

As I have pointed out, real risk properly means the chance of investment loss. My formal definition is:

Risk is the likelihood that when we must withdraw assets from our portfolio for consumption, they will have a lower value than we could reasonably expect based on our investment strategy.

Volatility is somewhat related to the chance of loss in the short term but has only limited relationship to it in the long run. How to measure the chance of investment loss is not a simple problem and much of this chapter is devoted to developing approaches that provide insight into understanding and controlling real investment risk.

This approach to risk requires the assumption that no matter how much the equity market collapses, it will always exceed its previous high.

This approach to risk requires the assumption that no matter how much the equity market collapses, it will always exceed its previous high. One can imagine events that would make this assumption not hold up, and I discuss this later.

LEVEL 2 RISK CONCEPTS

Let's review some concepts from Level 2 thinking that will help us move to a "real risk" orientation. Level 2 investing as I describe it would be considered "best practices" in investment management today.

Volatility describes how stock returns vary up and down through time. Level 2 thinking says that volatility measures risk for all investing, long term or short term. It also holds that standard deviation and the normal distribution curve describe the probability of losses at least well enough for everyday use.

Earlier I indicated that the normal curve is not a satisfactory measure of the volatility of returns and that volatility is not a satisfactory measure of risk for the long-term investor.

Real risk is the chance of investment loss, and there are better ways to measure that risk than to turn to the "ghost risk" of volatility. Measuring risk is not easy, and the approaches used in this book are not mathematically elegant. Although they are a bit uncertain at times, I believe they attack the real problem.

I use historical data directly rather than trying to squeeze the data into a mathematical distribution and then using that inadequate distribution to predict volatility.

The important consideration is what happened to our portfolio during those few but significant deep downturns. That can be examined directly from price changes at critical times. Considering volatility during up markets or slightly weak markets detracts from the importance of market movement at the critical times. It is only during those bad times that volatility counts and in fact it is only at those times that correlation and diversification matter.

The wonderful thing about volatility is that all the short-term investors who are trying to avoid it push up returns for those who know it doesn't matter in the long run and don't have to "risk adjust" their expected returns.

To paraphrase the guidance of John Tukey quoted earlier: Better to have a less elegant model of the real investment world than an elegant model of an imaginary investment world.

The wonderful thing about volatility is that all the short-term investors who are trying to avoid it push up returns for those who know it doesn't matter in the long run and don't have to "risk adjust" their expected returns. The CBOE Volatility Index (VIX), based on prices of short-term puts and calls on the S&P 500 index (approximately the one-year standard deviation), is called the "fear index." For long-term investors, it is really the "opportunity index," because high volatility leads to greater long-term returns.

RISK CONCERNS FOR THE LONG-TERM INVESTOR

For the long-term investor, then, it would seem that there is no need to be concerned with volatility/risk. To a large extent that is true, but there are three aspects of volatility that require consideration:

- the possible reintroduction of significant risk where there should be none,

- the need for an operational definition of "loss," and

- the need to define "long term" more specifically.

How Risk Might Be Reintroduced

The possible reintroduction of risk can come from failure to follow the rules of long-term investing. The most likely reason for a departure from the long-term path is panic in the face of a significant bear market. This is the one aspect of volatility in the real world that does contribute to risk because of human nature.

> The possible reintroduction of risk can come from failure to follow the rules of long-term investing.

Downside volatility is frightening to most of us and it increases the chances of non-optimal behavior, primarily selling out at cycle lows. The "fear index" can't become the "opportunity index" if investors panic at market lows.

I discuss this at greater length in Chapter 7 when I discuss behavioral impulses that impede our arrival at Level3 and how we can endeavor to neutralize them.

Another way that the long-term approach can be disrupted is if the investment approach used would lose all or most of its value during a negative market period. Our long-term return, or terminal wealth, is the geometric mean (compound return) of the various period returns. It is the nature of a geometric return, since it starts with the product of the period returns, that if you ever go to zero you stay at zero. That means that if your portfolio loses all its value, you won't benefit if the market goes up 100% in the next period.

Even getting close to zero may make the recovery period so long that it goes beyond your operational definition of long term.

I discuss various investment strategies in Chapter 6 and none of them are likely to devastate your portfolio disastrously, even during a significant bear market. But there are additional steps that can and should be taken to protect against such a disaster.

Three steps that I believe should be taken are:

- limit leverage,

- moderately diversify assets and

- time diversify new large investments.

Limit leverage

In Chapter 6, I explain that not only should the long-term investor be invested completely in equities and equity-like investments, but also that a case can be made for leveraging the holdings. However, the individual investor should never leverage so much that a severe bear market would result in having to sell equities to meet margin calls at the market low or risk too much in leveraged exchange-traded funds (ETFs).

Moderately diversify assets

Diversification is an almost sacred approach in Level 2 investing because, we are told, it reduces risk at no cost. As I pointed out, however, it is not a free lunch. It reduces unsystematic (company specific) risk, but it equally reduces unsystematic gain. You reduce the impact on your portfolio of negative news for one of your holdings—for example, if a company's product must be recalled. But you also reduce the impact of positive news—say, when a company discovers a new energy source.

If you have four potential investments with expected returns of 30%, 25%, 20% and 15%, diversifying and buying all four will give you a portfolio with an average expected return of 22.5%, whereas buying just the highest would give an expected return of 30%. Diversifying might be the better choice because of the risk reduction, but it is not a free lunch.

I believe that some diversification is desirable, but for the long-term investor, the commonly suggested amount of diversification is probably overdone. I am talking about diversification for risk reduction. There can be other reasons to have more holdings, such as not wanting to impact the market too much in any one micro-cap holding if you have a sizeable portfolio. In any event, unless all your intended investments have an equal expected return, diversification is not free.

For the long-term investor the commonly suggested amount of diversification is probably overdone.

For the long-term investor with a specific strategy and a rational expected return, the significant risk along the way is that they might lose all or a large percentage of their portfolio value such that even the long term will not help them recover.

To avoid this kind of terminal risk, some diversification is necessary, because if you are out of the game no amount of time will help you come back. Generally, any of the investment approaches discussed in Chapter 6 will lead to sufficient diversification, but it will be necessary to avoid being in only one or two investment sectors.

The perfect example of this is the history of tech and internet stocks. Investments in such stocks were wildly successful in the late 1990s—so much so that companies could get their stock price to increase just by changing their name to one with a tech or internet sound. But it was a bubble, and in the year 2000 it burst. More importantly, it did not recover quickly and in fact did not recover until 13 or 15 years later, depending on how you measure.

Figure 4.1 shows the price chart since 2000 for the NASDAQ Composite index, which is a good proxy for tech stocks before and after the bubble. It is to avoid the devastation that can come from such a collapse of a single sector that some level of diversification is essential. It could happen again. I am a fan of the health care sector. It has been leading the pack for years, and most analysts expect it to continue to grow even more with an aging population. But what if the U.S. Congress changed the current law, which requires Medicare to pay whatever the health care industry asks, and permitted negotiation as they do in Europe?

FIGURE 4.1

NASDAQ Composite Index After the Tech Bubble

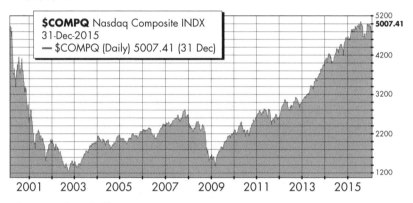

Source: StockCharts.com

In Chapter 6, after looking at strategies that provide higher returns than the overall market, I consider how you might diversify among them, at least enough to limit downside movement and shorten the recovery period.

Time diversify new large investments

Time diversification means adding assets to your portfolio gradually over time. Generally such an approach is suboptimal from a return point of view. Even the much-loved dollar cost averaging is suboptimal. From a maximum return point of view, the most effective strategy is to invest assets as soon as you receive them because the long-term trend of the stock market is up.

However, sometimes it is worth giving up a bit of return for safety. Some special circumstances that would justify deferring investing in equities when assets have become available are:

- The amount that has become available is large relative to your total invested assets. This is a situation that might occur in the event of an inheritance or a major lottery win.

- The stock market is at or near a high.

The situation you want to avoid, even though it doesn't happen often, is investing a large portion of new assets at a market high just before a major pullback. The portfolio will come back but it might take so much time that it goes beyond the time you are able to be in long-term mode.

This is illustrated in Figure 4.2, which extends the NASDAQ Composite index price chart back to 1986. While everyone may think in terms of the loss from the 2000 high, in actuality most investors were investing before the peak, some long enough to have a cost basis below where the sector hit bottom. The only investors hurt really badly were those who came to the tech sector just before the bubble burst.

FIGURE 4.2

NASDAQ Composite Index Leading Up to the Tech Bubble

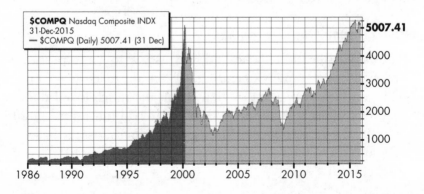

Source: StockCharts.com

It is to avoid such a situation that a limited time diversification strategy should be employed, but only if the market is near (maybe within 5% of) the high. Even then, the investment only needs to be spread over a maximum of 18 months if the market continues up, and for a shorter period if it is going down. These figures are just suggestions. You will have to think specific rules through for yourself because there is a risk/reward trade-off. But you need to understand the concept and how it can limit extreme portfolio value drops and anxiety.

So how can we measure risk in a meaningful way for long-term investors? Actually we don't have to measure it, we just have to avoid it as much as possible. Still, it is worthwhile to study risk concepts to give us confidence in our approach and place it in context with other approaches.

Overall, I view the avoidance of risk as an insurance process. The natural approach to maximizing investment return would be to pick that investment with the highest expected return. But that would involve a significant risk of losing everything, so we take steps to reduce that risk. Those steps—asset allocation, strategic diversification and time diversification—are viewed as insurance policies. Various degrees of them provide different degrees of protection and, like insurance policies, additional protection has additional cost.

I discuss this in detail in Chapter 6, but in general I feel the Level 2 approach is way over insured at a very significant cost.

There is no way to avoid all risk in investing except to not invest at all. The following advice is attributed to Warren Buffett: "The first rule is not to lose. The second rule is not to forget the first rule." Certainly it was meant tongue-in-cheek, but it has become a frequently quoted saying. If he did indeed say this, he probably regrets it. Buffett knows more than most that taking risks is an essential part of investing. It is the evaluation of the risk/reward trade-off that separates those who win from those who lose.

We also have to consider the possibility of panic or some unexpected event driving us to sell. While I want to concentrate on the most likely scenarios, rare occurrences cannot be completely ignored, and I show how we adjust strategies to compensate in Chapter 6.

Most importantly, we have to look at market movements to obtain an operational definition of long term. I consider long term to be a period long enough for us to ignore volatility. To operate at Level3, a specific period needs to be selected. Such a period may be different for different investors. Specific definitions for long term and short term are discussed more in-depth below.

Developing an Operational Definition of Loss

I believe real risk to be the chance of losing invested assets when we need them. But, as mentioned, it is not clear how to define and measure even short term or potential loss. Figure 4.3 shows the growth of $100,000 for AAII's Model Shadow Stock Portfolio, a real portfolio begun in 1993 that concentrates on micro-cap value stocks. There are three different possible measures of the short-term shock that could be a loss if you sold at the bottom. They are discussed below as answers to the question of how to measure a potential loss in this portfolio. As you can see from the chart, any time you are looking at a rate of return over a significant period, the compounding effect makes it appear as if all the gain is toward the end of the period. This is a pitfall of using an arithmetic scale.

In order to be able to compare periods easily, it is instead necessary to use a log scale, as shown in Figure 4.4. With a log scale, a constant rate of return over the time horizon is a straight line and the volatility becomes easier to compare throughout the overall time period. From this point on, I usually use figures with a log scale for charts with long periods of time.

The chart shows the actual returns of the Model Shadow Stock Portfolio based on $100,000 initial investment and no money added or withdrawn over 23 years (to year-end 2015). The portfolio grew at an annualized overall rate of 15.4% a year and the terminal value is $2.7 million. At the bottom of the major decline (point D), the portfolio is worth about $600,000. At the 2007 peak (point A), it was worth approximately $1.2 million.

FIGURE 4.3

Model Shadow Stock Portfolio

Growth of $100,000

Source: AAII

The chart could be adjusted for aftertax returns and for additional investment through the years and converted to real vs. nominal returns (allowing for inflation), but for the time being I just want to illustrate an approach and develop some nomenclature for the Level3 approach to risk.

The question to ask here is: If I sold at the bottom of the decline in 2009, how much was lost?

Answer 1

I haven't lost. I started with $100,000 and now have $600,000. There may have been a crash, but it didn't hurt me. I'm nicely ahead by $500,000.

This, by the way, is what the tax man is going to say if I sell out. It is almost certain that any reasonable approach to the equity market will typically lead to a positive return after about five years, so this approach really doesn't represent a real-world understanding of investment markets or inflation.

Answer 2

I am out $600,000 because I would have had $1.2 million.

This is the response I heard most in 2008 and 1974. If, if, if. For long-term investors with any awareness of how markets behave, this is not rational thinking. In most cases, not only will typical investors curse themselves and the part of the system they blame (the damn Fed, the damn politicians), but their view of their wealth will change and they may cut back on spending, thus helping to prolong any macroeconomic problem.

This attitude is wrong, but so was the attitude that their portfolio was really worth $1.2 million a year earlier—back when they thought their new car should be a Lexus instead of a Ford and they helped inflate the bubble.

Answer 3

Our view of our portfolio as long-term investors should be based on reasonable expectations, not just about the final outcome but about what will happen along the way. Based on how we are investing, we should have a feel for an expected return and for the volatility that we might see along the way. That is a critical part of Level3 Investing.

Our view of our portfolio as long-term investors should be based on reasonable expectations not just about the final outcome but about what will happen along the way.

That volatility should be based on a view of market history where the value comes from looking at the actual market behavior at significant points in time. This differs from the academic approach that simply measures the deviations, averages them out and comes up with a number (the standard deviation) that is just an average deviation. An average deviation is not going to provide much wisdom.

"The Flaw of Averages," by Sam L. Savage (2009), is an excellent book showing how "averages" distort reality; standard deviation and all the measures derived from it have this problem. While the standard deviation certainly gives a better picture of a set of values than the mean alone, it is still an insufficient picture. Knowing the standard deviation does not provide clarity on the deviations themselves.

FIGURE 4.4

Model Shadow Stock Portfolio on Log Scale

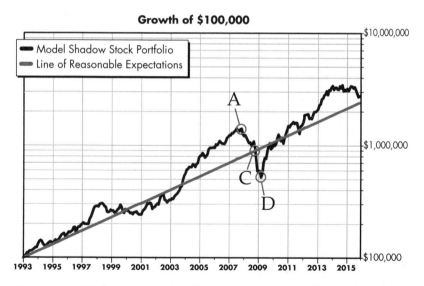

Source: AAII

When discussing the limits of averages as a measure, the often-used example is how you can drown in a river with an average depth of one foot. It is important to note that with exactly the same standard deviation, you could have a river with a maximum depth of two feet as well as one with a maximum depth of eight feet. Standard deviation as just another average does not show us the extremes of river depth. In investing, it does not show us the extremes of losses.

If we examine the 20-year annual return history of a particular portfolio, we have 20 returns and 20 dates. If we sacrifice all this data for two measures, a mean and a standard deviation, we may well have thrown away the most important insights. Without dates, we have lost the sequence of returns, which destroys evidence of momentum. We have also given weight to positive changes and to minor negative changes, neither of which should be important to the long-term investor.

We need a feel, an insight, into what the market will look like in bad times. Looking at historical occurrences of the bad times, I believe, is the only way to understand the nature of real-world risk, the real chance of losing our assets—our retirement.

Looking at historical occurrences of the bad times is the only way to understand the nature of real-world risk.

As long-term investors, we don't need to be deeply concerned about what might happen in the short run. We should be able to stand and cheer for the wild rides of the market because the wilder the ride, the more the short-term investors (most institutions as well as undisciplined individuals) are going to have to pay us to accept that meaningless (to us) risk. But there are two reasons to pay attention to short-term market moves.

First, constantly reminding ourselves of what we are doing and why makes it easier to get through dramatic times without doing anything foolish. So an awareness of possible market drops based on history is desirable. Extreme bull markets as well as bear markets can distort our long-term vision and be damaging in the long run.

In Level3 Investing, there should be recognition that high

volatility can occur; it is the very reason that equity investments have returns significantly higher than risk-free investments such as T-bills and CDs. This additional return is so high that it creates what is known as the "equity premium puzzle"—the contention that the additional return to equities is far greater than the additional risk would justify. This is really the investor's free lunch.

Second, as we approach the time when we will need to spend proceeds from our portfolio, we need a feel for the measures of short-term market moves to adjust to the investment changes. We need a feeling for when we can transition from the risk-free independence of the long-term investor to the risk-sensitive retiree. Chapter 5 goes into more detail on handling risk during the transition to the withdrawal stage of retirement.

With this viewpoint of risk, we can now go back to Figure 4.4 and answer the question of how much is lost at the portfolio's bottom. I believe the best way to view the pullback is as going from what I should have expected to have at the beginning of the pullback to the actual bottom—$900,000 (Point C) minus $600,000 (Point D), or $300,000. This is how far the portfolio is from where it should have been based on a long-term expectation of 15% a year.

The straight line on the chart shows this estimate and is what I call the line of reasonable expectations (LRE). An idea of its development was given in the Introduction with the description of how different strategies impacted the retirement assets of the Smith family. How the line of reasonable expectations might be estimated is covered more completely in Chapter 6.

When the Model Shadow Stock Portfolio began, a conservative estimate of the annualized return for a micro-cap value portfolio such as this would have been 15%. This was based on the long-term study of small-cap stocks by Ibbotson's SBBI and the work of Fama and French (1992). The estimate included adjustment for the impact of equal weighting, use of a price-to-sales ratio (P/S) requirement and the potential elimination of stocks on the way to bankruptcy, by missing earnings requirements and, very importantly, based on rules to reduce expensive turnover.

I refer to the drop that the portfolio experienced of $300,000 below the line of reasonable expectations (LRE) as the potential portfolio shortfall (PPS). As long-term investors, this should concern us only as we approach the time when we will be withdrawing funds. Otherwise, the potential portfolio shortfall is

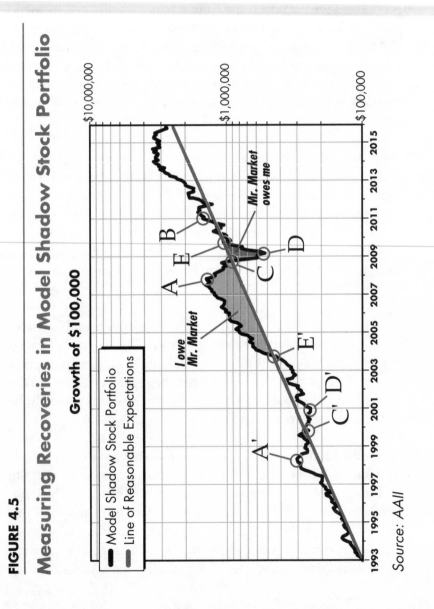

FIGURE 4.5

Measuring Recoveries in Model Shadow Stock Portfolio

Growth of $100,000

Model Shadow Stock Portfolio
Line of Reasonable Expectations

Source: AAII

only important to the extent that it causes distress or promotes panic, behavioral issues that are covered more fully in Chapter 7.

The next aspect of risk that will impact our strategy as we approach the time we must withdraw money I call the true recovery period (TRP). Just as there were several ways to view potential loss during a market pullback, there are different ways to measure how long it is until the market and our portfolio have recovered from any collapse.

Analyzing the length of this period provides the necessary insight required to determine when we need to be concerned about short-term volatility because we will be withdrawing funds. Once again, we face a trade-off. Do we require a complete return to an expected level at a cost to our expected return, or do we only require some "satisficing" level that allows some risk?

In this chapter, I am only concerned with any recovery period a few years prior to the time of the first withdrawal period, perhaps retirement day. In Chapter 5, I use the estimates of the recovery period to plan through the withdrawal period.

Looking at Figure 4.5, which is the same basic situation as in Figure 4.4, you can see that there are several ways to measure a recovery period. The commonly used measurement is based on the historical portfolio value and how long it is between the previous high and a return to that level. In the chart, it is the time between points A and B. The high at point A before the pullback was $1.2 million, and it was reached again at point B in about three years.

The Level3 approach concentrates on where the portfolio should have been in terms of our long-term view when the pullback impacted it and how long it took to get back to where it should have been—not where it was. For this portfolio, it is point E on the chart. The true recovery period (TRP) is the time it took for the market to return to the line of reasonable expectations after having gone below it. In this case, the true recovery period (from C to E) was about a year and a half.

For this pullback, the true recovery period was less than the conventional recovery measure. However, the true recovery period after the 1998 pullback was much longer, about four years (C' to E' on the chart), even though the potential portfolio shortfall was much less than in 2007 (from C' to D').

The Level3 approach concentrates on where the portfolio should have been in terms of our long-term view when the pullback impacted it and how long it took to get back to where it should have been.

It shouldn't even be thought of as a downturn until the portfolio goes below where it should be from a long-term perspective. Likewise, I don't feel the portfolio is where it should be until it returns to the line of reasonable expectations (LRE). Generally, the true recovery period will begin later and end later than other cycle measures. In many cases, a moderate downturn won't even trigger a bear period because the upturn comes before our portfolio goes below the line of reasonable expectations.

I have added a quip in Figure 4.5 to the spaces where the portfolio value goes above and below the line of reasonable expectations. The labels of "I owe Mr. Market" and "Mr. Market owes me" are intended to be humorous, but they embody the necessary attitude of the true long-term investor.

If you can maintain an attitude that this is a temporary short-term movement when your portfolio pulls way above the line of reasonable expectations, then you will be better able to handle the natural gloom that comes when it falls beneath the line. If your expectations are reasonable, in the long run your debt to Mr. Market will always be paid, as will his debt to you.

The accuracy of the Level3 approach depends on setting an accurate growth estimate for the line of reasonable expectations. While extreme accuracy is not necessary (or possible), there may be need for adjustments over the years. Alternatively, you can set the LRE growth rate to be a slightly reduced 10-year moving average based on your experience.

For psychological and practical reasons, the line of reasonable expectations should be conservatively set. Overall, based on the approaches I discuss in Chapter 6, a reasonable first estimate of your line of reasonable expectations could be compound growth of 10% to 12% a year. For a Level 2 investor, it would be 10% less estimated transaction and advisory costs.

The accuracy of the Level3 approach depends on setting an accurate growth estimate for the line of reasonable expectations.

This explains the definition of risk as thought of in Level3 Investing and how it should be viewed by long-term investors. As stated at the beginning of this chapter, investment risk is the likelihood that when we must withdraw assets from our portfolio for consumption, they will have a lower value than could be reasonably expected based on our investment strategy.

In terms of the examples in this chapter, risk means the likelihood that when we need to withdraw funds, the current portfolio value is below the line of reasonable expectations (LRE).

I use the word "likelihood" rather than "probability" because the chance of occurrence is not based on any formal probability distribution but rather on what has happened in the past. I believe it is possible to view a historical price chart carefully and get a more meaningful comprehension of volatility directly than you can get from calculating the standard deviation or other volatility measures.

Defining the Long Term

Since the major downside moves don't really have to be of concern if we act as long-term investors, but do concern us if we are short-term investors, it is important to determine where we draw the line between short term and long term in terms of our strategy.

The strategy in Level3 Investing is to treat short-term funds differently than the long-term approach we have been generally discussing.

Based on the discussion in this chapter, I make a case for using four years as the length that divides short term from long term. Funds needed in four years or less will be treated as short-term funds; the Level3 strategy for these funds is discussed in Chapter 5. Funds not needed in the next four years are invested without regard to risk; the investment approaches discussed in Chapter 6 are oriented toward maximum return over the long term.

There is no absolute cutoff point. There are some possible market occurrences where even a portfolio managed under the Level3 strategy might be hurt because a bear market lasted longer than four years.

Over the past 50 years, there have been two occasions (1973–1974 and 2007–2008) where the bear market was severe enough that the downturn lasted over five years, using the S&P 500 index as our portfolio. However, the recommended Level3 portfolios in Chapter 6 use equal weighting of holdings. If we use the equal-weighted Wilshire 5000 index as our comparison, the maximum bear market duration was four years. Protecting a portfolio for five years is not cost-effective (as I show in Chapter 5), but risk-sensitive individuals can use five years if it makes them more comfortable. More aggressive investors can use three years as the safe period.

The longer the safe period, the more the overall return on investment will be reduced.

The longer the safe period, the more the overall return on investment will be reduced.

The duration of the downturns discussed above would be reduced under the Level3 strategies. Portfolio diversification into small-cap stocks would have reduced the duration of the typical downturn significantly.

There is also the reality that stocks were not all bought at the peak and that the drop from the maximum value of the portfolio is much more likely than the drop from the portfolio cost or the line of reasonable expectations. This point was illustrated in Figures 4.1 and 4.2 when describing the year 2000 tech collapse.

Also mitigating the maximum pullback and the recovery time is the fact that the trough is usually fairly soon after the beginning of the fall and recovery is often well on its way prior to the time of complete recovery. Even in the long 1972 bear market, the S&P 500 had mostly recovered long before the complete recovery.

It is also important, and reconfirming of the long-term view of the Level3 approach, that the horrifying potential loss figures for a market pullback that are bandied about are based on the market level of a single record high day. If we look at quarterly or annual charts, the pullback appears to be significantly less. We would all probably be better long-term investors if we checked the market only quarterly or, at most, monthly.

It seems likely that each of us will see two or three severe stock market collapses of 40% or more in our investing lifetime. Expecting them will make them easier to endure.

REAL-WORLD EXAMPLES

Figures 4.6 and 4.7 show examples of two portfolios that have market-beating returns. They represent my estimate of the lowest and highest return you might expect under the Level3 approach.

There are many approaches in combination that will provide returns in between these two extremes, and I discuss many of them in Chapter 6. Returns will be somewhat lower when we are withdrawing money, as we will see in Chapter 5.

Guggenheim S&P 500 Equal Weight ETF (RSP)

In looking at possible approaches and returns for the Smith family in the Introduction to this book, Level3 Plan Z was introduced and suggested for those who do not have the time or interest to study and develop superior approaches. Plan Z is simply to invest one's entire portfolio in the Guggenheim S&P 500 Equal Weight ETF (RSP), an exchange-traded fund (ETF) that invests in the S&P 500 index but equally weights each stock.

> *Guggenheim S&P 500 Equal Weight fund had more volatility than the benchmark portfolio but not enough to justify sacrificing so much wealth to reduce it even for a short-term investor.*

The Guggenheim S&P 500 Equal Weight ETF has only been around for 12 years, but analysis of theoretical equal-weighted portfolios (discussed in Chapter 6) indicates it should do as well or better over longer periods. It is shown in Figure 4.6 with a line of reasonable expectations (LRE) of 12%. We also include a "best practices" benchmark based on a 60% stock/40% bond portfolio. Stocks are represented by the S&P 500 with a 10% return and bonds are represented by long-term Treasuries with a 6.0% return for an annualized return for the benchmark of 8.4% [(0.60 × 10%) + (0.40 × 6%)], which is shown as LRE @ 8.4% on the chart.

As you can see in Figure 4.6, the Guggenheim S&P 500 Equal Weight fund had more volatility than the benchmark portfolio but not enough to justify sacrificing so much wealth to reduce it even for a short-term investor. With a little effort, you can not only add to the return of the Guggenheim S&P 500 Equal Weight fund but also provide some diversification to reduce the shock of extreme bear market moves.

The Model Shadow Stock Portfolio

The Model Shadow Stock Portfolio was started in 1993 at AAII. This is a real portfolio. It invests in micro-cap value stocks and has some rules that reduce turnover. A complete description and history is in the Appendix.

FIGURE 4.6

Guggenheim S&P 500 Equal Weight ETF vs. 60% Stock/40% Bond Portfolio

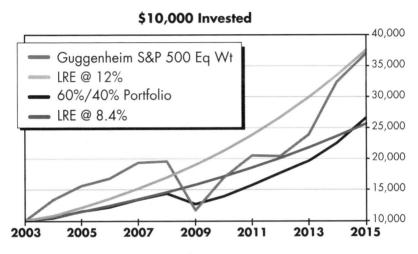

$10,000 Invested

Source: AAII

Figure 4.7 shows the portfolio value over the years 1993–2015. The portfolio grew at 15.4% year and has existed through several major downturns. I anticipated about a 15% annualized rate of return, which is used as the line of reasonable expectations (LRE) in Figure 4.7. The chart also shows the Vanguard 500 Index fund (VFINX). Its annualized rate of return over the same period was 8.9%, below its long-term expected average of 9.5% (shown in the chart as LRE @ 9.5%).

> *When it really counts, small-cap stocks not only have higher returns but less real risk than large-cap stocks.*

The major pullback was in 2009. As you can see, the portfolio did not drop through the line reasonable expectations (LRE @ 15%) until October of 2008 (point C) and came back to the line in September 2009 (E), so the true recovery period (TRP) was 11 months.

FIGURE 4.7

Model Shadow Stock Portfolio vs. Vanguard 500 Index Fund

Growth of $100,000

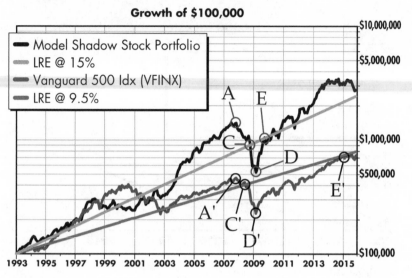

Source: AAII

While the percentage drop of the Vanguard 500 Index fund was slightly less than that of the Model Shadow Stock Portfolio (points A' to D' versus points A to D), the index fund took much longer to recover (E'). This highlights an important fact: Not only do small-cap stocks provide higher long-term returns, but they often recover faster after severe downturns in the market. This means that when it really counts, small-cap stocks not only have higher returns but may have less real risk than large-cap stocks.

Figure 4.7 shows, once again, how the higher return portfolio gradually overcomes the impact of even severe downturns. Even though the Model Shadow Stock Portfolio fell more than the market during the Great Recession, over the long term it was still significantly ahead of the market.

Possible Returns

Long-term returns for the Guggenheim S&P 500 Equal Weight fund and the Model Shadow Stock Portfolio represent approximate boundaries for the returns you might expect from the Level3 approaches. As the Guggenheim S&P 500 Equal Weight fund shows, potential returns range from 12% to 13% with almost no effort or involvement to 15% to 16% following a more complex approach that involves time and effort.

> *Potential Level3 returns range from 12% to 13% with almost no effort or involvement to 15% to 16% following a more complex approach that involves time and effort.*

I look at some of these possible approaches in Chapter 6, but there is a shortage of long-term actual investment results since most of the possible approaches are newly discovered and there are only simulated portfolio results for past periods.

A LOOK AT PAST CRASHES

Over the past 50 years there have been a number of significant pullbacks, as shown in Table 4.1. This table shows the maximum decline and the recovery time in the traditional way. Maximum decline is the percent reduction in value from the high to the low. Recovery time is measured from the prior peak to the re-establishing of that peak value. The S&P 500 index is used as the market proxy, although portfolios suggested in Chapter 6 moved from recovery more quickly.

The 2007–2009 Great Recession was the worst since the Great Depression of the early thirties, but each major pullback has its own characteristics, and over the very long term the nature of the economic system changes. For this reason, I am only looking at stock market recessions since 1965.

I don't believe that 1929 could happen again because of significant changes in regulation, social attitudes and political viewpoint. I can't imagine a future scenario similar to the one in Washington, D.C., in 1932 when Douglas MacArthur and George Patton charged 40,000 protesting World War I veterans and their families on horseback with sabers drawn and backed by tanks. And I also can't imagine a government that would let the financial situation deteriorate to such an extent as prior to the 1929 crash. Allowing 90% of a stock's price to be bought on margin and unregulated puts and calls are not likely to be permitted again.

TABLE 4.1

Major Market (S&P 500) Pullbacks Since 1970

Begin Date	End Date	Max Decline (%)	Recovery Time
Oct 2007	Mar 2013	49	5 yrs 5 mos
Aug 2000	Sep 2007	54	7 yrs 1 mo
Aug 1987	Jul 1989	30	1 yr 11 mos
Dec 1972	Jun 1980	52	7 yrs 6 mos
Nov 1968	Nov 1972	35	4yrs 0 mos

Source: Ibbotson SBBI 2015 Yearbook: Market Results for Stocks, Bonds, Bills and Inflation, 1926–2014.

Although there are certainly other scenarios that could lead to bear markets of significance, I believe they either would be less severe than 1929 or so severe that no investing approach would help.

The 1968 and 1987 pullbacks were of such short duration that they should not have impacted any long-term approach to the market.

The dot-com or tech collapse of 2000 was certainly severe as measured by the S&P 500 and even more severe for the NASDAQ Composite. Some analysts would argue that we had not recovered by the time the 2008 pullback started and that the bear market lasted almost 13 years and had a maximum retreat of 54%.

In viewing the 2000 collapse, it must be pointed out that the extreme losses were taken only by investors heavily in tech stocks or index investors who chose market-cap-weighted indexes that were heavily weighted in tech stocks. Everyone thinks of the S&P 500 as being diversified, but because it is market-cap-weighted it is impacted dramatically by the largest companies; after the tech run up prior to 2002, these stocks dominated the index.

No investor following any of the approaches of Level3 would have been down for more than four years. The Model Shadow Stock Portfolio was down for three years (in the 1998 pullback, small stocks started down earlier than the market).

The Guggenheim S&P 500 Equal Weight fund (RSP) did not exist during the tech collapse, but we can see how the equal-weighted version of the Wilshire 5000 and NASDAQ Composite indexes compare to their cap-weighted versions.

For the three-year period 2000–2002:

- The cap-weighted Wilshire 5000 was down 14.4% per year, about the same as the S&P 500 (–14.6%). Cumulatively, it was down 37.2%.

- The equal-weighted Wilshire 5000 was up 2.3% per year. Cumulatively, it was up 7.1%.

- The cap-weighted NASDAQ Composite was down 30.5% per year. Cumulatively, it was down 66.5%.

- The equal-weighted NASDAQ Composite was up 50.3% per year. Cumulatively, it was up 240%.

Basically, what was a very bad period for the cap-weighted indexes was not bad for most public companies, and the 2000 tech bubble collapse would have largely missed investors who followed a Level3 type of approach.

Actually, it probably missed most investors who invest in their own stock portfolios, except psychologically. It did hit most investors in index funds or large-cap funds.

It is only the 1972 and 2007 bear markets that could pose problems for the long-term investor. How much of a problem they may pose revolves around the definition of long term and how much short-term risk we are willing to assume for increased returns. Let us examine these two periods more carefully.

1972–1980

In the very significant collapse of 1972, not much meaningful research had been done on specific investment approaches, and there were no model portfolios or active mutual funds following a clearly defined process. There were various vague approaches and there has been extensive after-the-fact research for all investment periods, but there were no actual defined index portfolios operating at the time.

The mutual funds all had their own investment philosophies but nothing very specific or research oriented. Later, concepts such as the small-stock effect, the low price-to-book-value ratio (P/B) effect and others have been simulated through this period, but there was not much being done contemporaneously.

At the time, this bear market was the most severe since the 1929 crash. In some ways it was more severe than the Great Recession of 2008, if we use the S&P 500 as the guide for the 1973–1974 collapse. As shown in Table 4.1, the S&P 500 took 7½ years to return to its previous high.

However, if we use the year-end Wilshire 5000 index, which includes small- and medium-cap stocks, the time to recovery was only four years; if we use the equal-weighted Wilshire 5000, the recovery time was only 3½ years.

2007–2013

The Great Recession was much more than a stock market crash. Real estate mortgage foreclosures, high unemployment, and severe weakness in the entire financial system made this a very scary time. Table 4.1 shows the S&P 500 dropping 49%, and small-cap stocks fell even more. The recovery took nearly 5½ years, although small-cap stocks recovered more quickly. The Wilshire 5000 with its small and medium caps took approximately the same time to recover, but the equal-weighted Wilshire 5000 took only four years to recover.

ACCOUNTING FOR UNKNOWN RISKS

When I speak of risk free, I always mean "almost risk free." There are always unknown risks. Economic disasters that have never happened in the United States have happened elsewhere. Losing a war on one's own ground has caused many a crisis around the world. Severe natural disasters are always possible.

The Japanese Nikkei index hit an all-time high closing value of 38,916 on December 29, 1989, and then went well below 10,000 and is not yet halfway back to that 26-year-old high.

Dystopian (the opposite of utopian) movies and books are extremely popular these days and cite a variety of causes for the collapse of political and economic systems. Many of these are of the nature that what happens to the stock market would be of little consequence.

But there are always new possibilities that would impact different investments differently and change the nature of returns. The high returns on equities have been with us a long time but are not guaranteed. In fact, if every investor accepted my point of view and forgot about ghost risk, the return on equities would go down significantly. There are also unforeseen possibilities of events in your life and the life of all investors that might require selling at a portfolio low point, so we should give some consideration to short-term risk.

However, even if you are a short-term investor or are just very nervous about short-term volatility because you believe the worst could always happen, I don't believe the conventional risk measures are the best approach.

Rather than take historical data and force it into an inappropriate model and then use the model to predict the probability of different outcomes, why not use the historical data directly and see what the worst is that could have happened to a particular portfolio in the past?

OTHER VIEWS

My view that real risk almost disappears for the long-term investor would be challenged by many believers in traditional modern portfolio theory. In fact, there are those who believe risk increases with the length of the holding period. In the late 1990s, the relationship of holding period to risk was a major topic and almost all the leading academics weighed in—often emotionally. The differences were largely based on definitions and assumptions.

Fundamentally, however, according to Jeremy Siegel in "Stocks for the Long Run" (2014) over the last 45 years (through 2012) and even back into the 1800s, the longer the holding period the less the chance of a real loss and the closer the market portfolio return will be to the 45-year average of 10.3% for the cap-weighted S&P 500, 10.5% for the cap-weighted Wilshire 5000, and 17.1% for the equal-weighted Wilshire 5000.

SUMMARY

The objective of this chapter was to revisit the concept of investment risk for the long-term investor. The first step was to show that volatility and real risk are not the same. In fact, because volatility can add to the return on investment, it can actually reduce real risk.

This is because over time additional return will continually increase the value of the portfolio until even in the worst-case scenario the portfolio will be able to maintain a higher value than its lower-return alternative. This is real risk reduction.

Next, I defined real risk as the possibility of investment loss over the investment period. For long-term investors, there is virtually no risk unless they panic and sell. I examined potential portfolio shortfall to reinforce our understanding of bear markets and to provide a reason not to panic.

In short, the long-term investor has almost no risk.

I showed that loss, or potential loss, may be defined in different ways. Present portfolio value can be compared to:

- The highest it ever was, or

- What we expected it to be at that time, or

- What we actually paid for the portfolio, or

- What the value would be if we had invested it differently, for example in T-bills.

I also looked at how long bear markets last. I did this partly to build a familiarity with how long we need to be patient, but primarily to develop an operational meaning of "long term" to build the investment strategy of Level3.

Once again, there are several different approaches to the measurement of downturns in the market or our portfolios. Looking backward, we needed to use the common measure of the time from a peak level to a return to the level. Going forward, I suggested using a line of reasonable expectations for your portfolio and measuring the true recovery period as the time between when your portfolio value fell below that level until the time it recovers to it.

Reviewing the history of bear markets, I made the case for using four years as the operational definition of long term. That means that the basic investment strategy that ignores volatility can be used for the investing of all funds that will not be needed for expenditures in the next four years. Funds that will be needed for expenditures should be invested differently, and the next chapter covers that approach. It was noted that conservative investors could use five years instead of four and that more aggressive among us could use three or less.

In short, the long-term investor has *almost* no risk. We can never have no risk because things can happen that we can't foresee and that might require selling our portfolio in the short term. The loss of employment for an extended term might require selling the portfolio when the market is down, or the next downturn might run even longer than history suggests. In the following chapter, I discuss how to control risk in the short term.

CHAPTER 5

REAL RISK IN THE WITHDRAWAL STAGE

"When contemplating a particularly harsh winter, I prefer a program of gathering more nuts to one of training myself to subsist on fewer calories."

—J. C. Squirrel

For most of us, there will come a time when it is necessary to withdraw funds for expenditures. The primary time that this will happen is at retirement, which is the focus of this chapter.

There are other withdrawal occasions that may occur prior to retirement, typically for shorter periods. The most common are saving for future educational expenses and saving to accumulate the down payment for a house or condo. The principles suggested here for controlling short-term risk in retirement can be applied to such other occasions, as explained later in the chapter.

Our major concern in Level3 when it comes to facing short-term risk is to find an operational definition of "short term" that balances the two bad things that can happen:

- not earning enough return on our portfolio, and

- losing too much in down markets.

We lose capital in down markets if we have to withdraw funds while the market is down and has not had sufficient time to recover.

Unfortunately, the risk of too little return and the risk of loss are linked and we can't avoid both. The superior long-term return of the equity market comes about as compensation for being exposed to volatile short-term market moves. Our task is to find an approach that balances risk and return in a rational way. The approach of Level3 Investing is to protect the assets needed in the near future from market downturns. To do this, I take a very different approach to asset allocation than is customary.

> *The asset allocation that is appropriate for short-term investments is between risky and safe investments.*

I believe in asset allocation among different risky assets as a partial solution to the problem of reducing the length of portfolio downturns during bear markets. The asset allocation that is appropriate for short-term investments, however, is between risky and safe investments.

The problem then is how to allocate assets between very risky and very safe assets. I have argued in Chapter 4 that for the long-term investor, the portfolio should be 100% in risky assets. But what should the allocation be when funds need to be withdrawn for consumption?

As before, we follow the insurance metaphor: What is the risk and how much should we be willing to pay to insure against it?

THE LEVEL3 APPROACH TO SHORT-TERM ASSET ALLOCATION

I take a significant departure from the conventional approaches. Typically you have heard advice such as:

- 100 minus your age should be in equities and the rest in bonds, or

- You should have 60% in equities, 40% in bonds, or

- Your allocation should be 50% equities and 50% bonds.

None of it makes sense to the Level3 investor. Except in some sense of an overall population average, what does age have to do with it? Some of us will be leaving a significant portion of our wealth to our descendants; others will need to consume it all. Your investment horizon for your portfolio may have nothing to do with your age.

The criteria for determining asset allocation should not be age or some uniform arbitrary percentage. It should be based on how much you need to withdraw from the portfolio in the short term. In fact, you should approach it as an insurance problem.

To develop a strategy, you must answer three questions:

- What is the appropriate operating definition of short term for the protection period?

- How much do you need to withdraw from the portfolio over the defined short term?

- What investment strategy will accomplish this?

The criteria for determining asset allocation should be based on how much you need to withdraw from the portfolio in the short term.

Determining the Protection Period

The objective here is to protect the funds you will need to withdraw over a given period from all or most of the impact of a significant downturn. Your overall approach to investing in the long run is based on the assumption that a diversified portfolio of equities may lose value temporarily, but it will always return to new highs.

This assumption is based on the history of U.S. markets. While I only look back 45 years because I feel there are some fundamental changes in the world over time, the assumption has always been true in the United States.

If we look at the last 45 years, the two worst bear markets (1973–1974 and 2007–2008) took the S&P 500 index 5½ and 7½ years to completely recover from the previous high (Table 4.1).

The S&P 500 represents the average of almost all equity gains or losses, but more diverse portfolios would have had a shorter recovery period.

You would have had a shorter recovery period of 3½ years with the equal-weighted Wilshire 5000 index. This index is similar to the various suggested portfolios in Chapter 6. Based on this, I believe using a safe period of four years is sufficient.

There would be nothing wrong with using five years to be more conservative, but I feel the added safety is not worth the cost. A better case could be made for three years, but I am pushing conventional wisdom as it is. I discuss this again after reviewing some data later in the chapter.

Any risk in using a four-year safe period is offset by:

- The diversification discussed in the next chapter,

- The realization that most of a typical portfolio is not purchased at the exact high, and that high may not have been a reasonably expected high but a temporary overshoot.

What I mean by a safe period is the number of years of necessary withdrawals put aside with the intention of using these funds and not selling stocks whenever the stock market is significantly below its previous high.

A safe period is the number of years of necessary withdrawals put aside with the intention of using these funds and not selling stocks whenever the stock market is significantly below its previous high.

Throughout this and the following chapters, I use the word "equities" and "stocks" to refer to equity-like investments. Many real estate investments, partnerships, and even some distressed debt would be included—almost anything with equity-level returns.

How Much Should Be Withdrawn?

The quick answer to the question of how much to withdraw is: Only what you need to fund your estimated living expenses after subtracting income from pensions, Social Security and any other such sources. This rule is also appropriate when planning on funding any major purchases or outlays in the next four years.

The calculations are a financial planning process that are not covered in this book. But I would remind you that everyday expenses during retirement may not decrease as much as many financial planning guides suggest. Medical expenses will most likely increase—significantly, if your employer was funding much of your health insurance prior to retirement.

There are probably a number of expenses that may decrease during retirement a bit, but the major savings will result from not having to save for retirement.

There are probably a number of expenses that may decrease during retirement a bit, but the major savings will result from not having to save for retirement. This savings, plus your escape from Social Security and Medicare taxes, should be quite significant, particularly if you were saving significantly for retirement.

Whatever the amount you feel you need to withdraw from your investment portfolio, the program described here suggests that your withdrawals should not exceed 5% of your investment portfolio each year, unless you wish to consume your portfolio.

I know that the most common figure suggested is 4%, and that is with the gradual depletion of the portfolio. I believe 5% is possible using just the earnings of the portfolio with no depletion. The capital can stay there to protect against a market worse than we have seen in 45 years, for personal emergencies or to pass on to heirs.

I suggest that a higher percentage amount can be withdrawn than conventional wisdom partly because I feel that it is very possible to exceed the average 10% return of the S&P 500 and partly because almost all the investment advice out there would spend way too much capital insuring against possible losses.

Another reason that the often-suggested 4% might be wrong is that it is usually based on simulations. Simulations follow the same reasoning as modern portfolio theory: Take real data and try to arrive at a mathematical model that will fit it, and then use the model to give new data about probabilities of volatility. As I have pointed out, there is no satisfactory model. Simulations use a mathematical model, usually the normal curve density function, and run it countless times to see what percentage of the time you get which outcome.

A much more sensible approach is to simply see what would have happened if you used a specific approach in bad times with the actual historical data.

I want you to view diversification and allocation as insurance policies to protect against the short-term risk that even an effective portfolio must face. That and the actual creation of an effective equity portfolio are the heart of Level3 Investing.

The Level3 Short-Term Strategy

To put the strategy into perspective, let's review the fundamental beliefs of Level3 Investing. These principles underlie the short-term strategy that follows as well as the approach to long-term portfolio building developed in Chapter 6.

> *View diversification and allocation as insurance policies to protect against the short-term risk that even an effective portfolio must face.*

Equities and equity-like products should comprise the entire portfolio of the long-term investor except for funds needed for expenditure in the next four years.

The stock market may go down significantly, but it will always rebound and exceed previous levels unless something so extreme occurs that all investments are suspect.

Volatility is not related to risk except in the short term and may actually reduce real risk through higher long-term returns.

Higher long-term returns ultimately are the best protection against bear markets.

Figure 5.1 shows the growth of $100,000 invested in the Model Shadow Stock Portfolio compared to that of the Vanguard 500 Index fund (VFINX) since 1993 (through 2015). In just over 11 years, the Model Shadow Stock Portfolio reached a level where a 50% downturn would still put it ahead of Vanguard 500 Index fund. In 2008–9 when it does drop by about 50%, it is still significantly ahead of the market (as represented by Vanguard 500 Index fund). It would be ahead even if the market-based VFINX did not go down at all.

FIGURE 5.1

Model Shadow Stock Portfolio vs. Vanguard 500 Index Fund

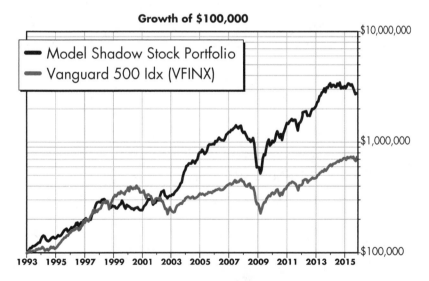

Source: AAII

In Chapter 4, "real risk" was defined as the likelihood that when we must withdraw invested assets from our portfolio for consumption they will have a lower value than could reasonably be expected based on our investment strategy.

Looking at Figure 5.1 again: If you are a lifelong investor saving for retirement, which portfolio presents the greater risk of not having sufficient funds?

Shown another way, Table 5.1 presents hypothetical accumulated wealth at retirement for a traditional Level 2 strategy of 60% stocks/40% bonds compared to two Level3 approaches: one that is 100% in Level3 equities and the other that adjusts for a safe period.

TABLE 5.1

Accumulated Wealth at Retirement for Level 2 Versus Level3

$250,000 invested, on average, for 18 years

Level3 Basic Strategy (100% in Level3 stocks)	$1,922,000
Level3 Adjusted for Short-Term Risk*	$1,862,000
Level 2 (60% stocks, 40% long-term bonds)	$1,068,000

Average Returns Used

Level3 stocks	12.0%
Stocks (S&P 500 index)	10.0%
Long-term bonds	6.0%
Safe investments**	4.0%
60% S&P 500/40% long-term bonds	8.4%

*Safe investments added in last four years prior to retirement.

**Can include short-term bonds, insured CDs and savings account.

While we accept that volatility is related to real risk as defined in the short term, it is important to point out that only the part of the portfolio we actually withdraw in the short term is impacted by short-term volatility. The balance of the portfolio is still long-term and free of real risk.

Table 5.2 presents the average annual cost of insuring our portfolio against the probability of a loss in the retirement stage with different approaches. Note that regularly recommended non-equity investments have already cost the portfolio a considerable amount prior to retirement, as shown in Table 5.1.

THE COST OF RISK REDUCTION

Using the Level3 approach, the starting point for any portfolio should be 100% in equities or their equivalents, since that is the highest return class of assets.

Any deviation from an all-equity portfolio is an effort to reduce risk. It is, in effect, a method of insuring the equity portfolio. Like all insurance, it has a cost that must be justified.

Only the part of the portfolio we actually withdraw in the short term is impacted by short-term volatility.

Table 5.2 shows the calculation of those costs as a reduction in the expected returns over the long term depending on the insurance package chosen.

As the benchmark, a long-term annualized return of 12% is assumed possible for the Level3 approach, based on the portfolio strategies described in Chapter 6. Until retirement (or some other withdrawal program), Level3 Investing requires 100% in stocks.

As shown in Table 5.2, a Level3 approach that is 100% stocks provides a 12% annual return and 0% risk reduction. The second and third columns show the expected annual return of each strategy and how much less it is each year than the 100% in equities strategy. This is the insurance cost. The table also provides dollar figures for a $1 million portfolio as a reference.

The last column shows how long the assets in bonds would last if the portfolio was managed in accordance with Level3 requirements. The Level3 approach is to use rainy day funds when it rains. That means that in down markets, equities are not sold until any assets in bonds have been completely used up.

In Level3 to meet withdrawal needs, equities are sold when the market is steady or up and bonds are sold when the equity market goes down.

Many advisers who advocate that significant assets should be in bonds maintain that you should rebalance regularly whether the market goes up or down. To meet withdrawal needs in Level3, equities are sold when the market is steady or up and safe investments are sold when the equity market goes down.

In Table 5.2, the cost of various degrees

TABLE 5.2

Annual Cost of Risk Reduction During Retirement

$1 million portfolio

Strategy	Expected Average Annual Return	Return Loss Due to Risk Reduction
Level3 Passive Strategy (100% stocks)	12.0%	0.0%
100% Safe Investments	4.0%	8.0%
30% Stocks/70% Safe Investments*	5.8%	6.2%
60% Stocks/40% Safe Investments	7.6%	4.4%
60% Level3/40% Safe Investments	8.8%	3.2%
80% Level3/20% Safe Investments**	10.4%	1.6%

Average Returns Used:

Safe Investments	4.0%
Stocks (S&P 500 index)	10.0%
Passive Level3 portfolio	12.0%

*Stock portion based on 100 minus age (70).
**Four-year safe withdrawal period.

of safety runs from 8% of portfolio value per year for an all-safe investments portfolio to 1.6% for the Level3 approach to portfolio selection with four-year withdrawal protection (80% Level3/20% safe investments). Once again, these are calculations only for the time that withdrawals are taking place.

As you can see, the cost of protection is quite high—too high in most cases for the limited value of the protection.

LEVEL3 RULES FOR WITHDRAWAL STAGE

Here are the basic strategy rules for the Level3 withdrawal

Average Annual Dollar Gain in Portfolio Value	Average Annual Dollar Amount Cost of Risk Reduction	Number of Years of Protection From Equity Sales
$120,000	–	0
$40,000	$80,000	all
$58,000	$62,000	14
$76,000	$44,000	8
$88,000	$32,000	8
$104,000	$16,000	4

stage. Remember that until this point the portfolio is 100% in equities.

1. Beginning four years before your retirement date, estimate the annual dollar amount you will need to withdraw with a maximum of 5% of your portfolio and move that amount of assets into safe investments (the nature of safe investments is discussed later).

2. Transfer the same amount in each of the next three years so that when you reach retirement you have four years of necessary portfolio income in safe investments.

3. Decisions will generally be made once a year. There may have to be exceptions to this if your requirements change significantly, but acting only once a year will reduce short-term volatility and risk as well as simplify activity and record-keeping. Making a strategic process as simple as possible greatly increases the chances that it will be followed.

    If you don't retire at the exact end of a year, make a one-time adjustment so that your decisions are always near year end. This makes all kinds of market data easily available and, more importantly, gives you a chance to act just before or just after the calendar year based on income tax considerations.

4. At decision day each year (December 31), check the level of the S&P 500 index at that time and compare it to the all-time highest level of the S&P 500. If the current level is more than 5% below the all-time high of the S&P 500, put your portfolio in defensive mode. Your withdrawal in the year you determine as a down year will be taken from the safe investment part of your portfolio.

    Your withdrawal in the year you determine as a down year will be taken from the safe investment part of your portfolio.

    Please note that using 5% is arbitrary. You could use 1%, 10% or even 20%, which is the usual definition of a bear market. The higher the criteria, the less activity there will be. It's your choice, but pick one and stick to it. Consistency will reduce the chance of mistakes coming from behavioral pressures.

5. Continue withdrawing from the safe portion each year until on a decision day the S&P 500 is above the level that you used to choose defensive mode. At this point, you not only resume annual withdrawals from the equity holdings of your portfolio but you immediately begin to restore the four-year withdrawal level to the safe investment segment. I recommend doing this over two years, restoring half of the deficit (the amount below four years of withdrawal) each year. Any restoration would stop if a new down year occurred and withdrawals would revert to the safe portion.

If the defensive mode lasts long enough that the safe investment part of the portfolio is depleted, you would have to withdraw from the equity part, but based on the recommended portfolios of Chapter 6, this has not happened since the Great Depression of 1929.

If a down market occurs at decision time while you are in the process of building the safe investment portion of the portfolio (one to four years before retirement), don't put the one-year withdrawal amount into the safe investment portion of the portfolio until your definition of the end of defensive mode applies. If the down market continues into the actual withdrawal period, withdraw from any safe assets until they are used up and then sell equities. Build the safe investment portion up again after the market recovers.

Build the safe investment portion up again after the market recovers.

There are choices in determining how to measure market highs. The market could be measured by a number of indexes or by your own portfolio. I have chosen the S&P 500 because it is generally accepted as the primary market measure. The performance of the S&P 500 is used to represent the weighted average of all portfolios. This is not quite true since there are considerably more than 500 stocks, but the totality of all the remaining stocks is minuscule compared to the 500. In addition, data on the S&P 500 is readily available. However, I have and will also continue to refer to the Wilshire 5000 and the equal-weight Wilshire 5000 because they more closely represent the type of portfolios recommended here.

Since we are much more concerned with our own portfolio than with the overall market, why not use our own portfolio as the market indicator? We could, but this involves extensive record-keeping and we would have to make adjustments for withdrawals and additions. Rule simplicity avoids rule violation.

An additional problem involves assigning market highs. We can use intraday levels, closing daily levels or closing levels of the week, month or even year. Looking at the market only once a year would likely be the wisest thing any of us could do, but in the real world it is unrealistic to think that the vast majority of investors can ignore market behavior in the short run.

Rule simplicity avoids rule violation.

I would prefer to just look at monthly levels in making decisions, but most of the market highs quoted will be based on daily closing and that will work. Don't use intraday highs in your decision-making. Based on the type of equity investments suggested, the Guggenheim S&P 500 Equal Weight ETF (RSP) will be a better market indicator than the cap-weighted S&P 500 itself or an exchange-traded fund investing in it.

TABLE 5.3

Establishing a Defensive Strategy

Retirement Date: January 1, 2020

Date	Market Condition
Pre-Retirement Stage	
1/1/2016	OK
1/1/2017	OK
1/1/2018	OK
1/1/2019	OK
Start of Retirement	
1/1/2020	OK
1/1/2021	DOWN
1/1/2022	DOWN
1/1/2023	DOWN
1/1/2024	UP
1/1/2025	UP

The process described in moving into retirement mode is shown in Table 5.3.

As you can see, based on a retirement date of January 1, 2020, money begins to be shifted into the safe portion of the portfolio at one year's withdrawal rate during the four years prior to retirement. Withdrawals are made from the equity portion of the portfolio while the market is in a flat or up mode.

When on January 1, 2021, the market is 5% below its previous all-time high, we switch to defensive mode. Annual withdrawals are taken from the safe portion of the portfolio until the market returns to within 5% of its previous high. At that time,

Withdrawal/ Transfer Amount	Location of Withdrawal/ Transfer	Withdrawal for Year	Total Amount in Safe Fund
$50,000	transfer from Equity to Safe	2020	$50,000
$50,000	transfer from Equity to Safe	2021	$100,000
$50,000	transfer from Equity to Safe	2022	$150,000
$50,000	transfer from Equity to Safe	2023	$200,000
$50,000	withdraw from Equity for expenses		$200,000
$50,000	withdraw from Safe for expenses		$150,000
$50,000	withdraw from Safe for expenses		$100,000
$50,000	withdraw from Safe for expenses		$50,000
$50,000	withdraw from Equity for expenses		$50,000
$75,000	transfer from Equity to Safe		$125,000
$50,000	withdraw from Equity for expenses		$125,000
$75,000	transfer from Equity to Safe		$200,000

annual withdrawals once again are taken from the equity portion of the portfolio. Any deficit is restored to the safe portfolio in annual transfers spaced equally over a two-year period.

THE STRATEGY IN DOWN MARKETS

The key to the strategy is to use the funds put aside for rainy days when it rains. As stated, if the market has not fully recovered in four years then the safe funds may have run out and

TABLE 5.4

Application of Defensive Strategy During Great Recession

$1 million portfolio

Decision Date	S&P 500 Current	High	Strategy Mode	Beginning-of-Year Value/Activity Equity	Safe
1/1/2008	1424	1468	Normal	$800,000 − $50,000 = $750,000	$200,000
1/1/2009	866	1468	Defensive	$473,000	$208,000 − $50,000 = $158,000
1/1/2010	1124	1468	Defensive	$598,000	$164,000 − $50,000 = $114,000
1/1/2011	1283	1468	Defensive	$688,000	$119,000 − $50,000 = $69,000
1/1/2012	1301	1468	Defensive	$702,000	$72,000 − $50,000 = $22,000
1/1/2013	1827	1827	Normal	$814,000 − $139,000 = $675,000	$23,000 + $89,000 = $112,000

*Safe investments return.

you may have to liquidate some stock. But with the strategic approach developed in Chapter 6, this scenario would not have occurred in the last 50 years.

Table 5.4 traces the Level3 defensive strategy through the Great Recession until the recovery. Actual S&P 500 returns are used rather than the advanced Level3 portfolio strategies to illustrate how the defensive approach would have worked during that time. Four percent is used as the return on the safe investment

Full-Year Gain/Loss (%)		End-of-Year Value		
Equity	Safe*	Equity	Safe	Total
–37.0%	4.0%	$473,000	$208,000	$681,000
26.5%	4.0%	$598,000	$164,000	$762,000
15.1%	4.0%	$688,000	$119,000	$817,000
2.1%	4.0%	$702,000	$72,000	$775,000
16.0%	4.0%	$814,000	$23,000	$837,000
32.4%	4.0%	$894,000	$116,000	$1,010,000

portion of the portfolio, which could be a blend of short-term Treasuries and other very safe investments.

The key to the strategy is to use the funds put aside for rainy days when it rains.

The impact of inflation is ignored on the $50,000 annual withdrawal in order to simplify the example; inflation was not very significant over this short period and would not have impacted any decisions. The 5% withdrawal rate, however, is inflation-adjusted.

It is important to note that the withdrawal amount is in dollars, not in percentage of the portfolio. If the market drops 10%, your mortgage payment doesn't. You would still need $50,000 a year, even though that is now 5.56% rather than 5% of your portfolio.

In Table 5.4, the portfolio had $1 million on January 1, 2008, and an annual withdrawal rate of $50,000. The market was not lower than the previous January and so the normal withdrawal process was used, taking the funds from the equity portfolio.

The portfolio took a 37% hit that year, and so at January 2009 the portfolio was put in defensive mode and the $50,000 withdrawal was taken from the safe portion of the portfolio. The table shows the results of the strategy and the returns for each year.

At January 1, 2013, the market was above the old high and the strategy reverted to normal mode, taking the $50,000 withdrawal from the equity part of the portfolio along with restoring half ($89,000) of the existing shortfall in the safe portion.

Going into 2014, there was $897,000 in equities and $116,000 in bonds (if you allow the bond to grow at 4% during 2013). The portfolio was back above its original value even after taking $300,000 out in cumulative withdrawals.

Despite the severe downturn, the four-year reserve of $200,000 in the safe portion of the portfolio was enough to handle all the withdrawals. However, one more down year would have required going into the equity holdings.

A MORE GENERALIZED DEFENSIVE APPROACH

The very specific defensive approach illustrated in this example was taken for two reasons:

- First, if you have a very specific approach with defined rules, it is easier to avoid deviating randomly and substituting guesses about market direction at various points in time. Certainly, withdrawing a full year's needs at one time or acting only on the first of the year is not a requirement for the Level3 defensive approach.

- Second, a specific version of the Level3 approach was needed to illustrate its application. Different variations of the general approach will give different results depending on the actual market behavior over time.

A more generalized version of the rules would be:

1. In the safe portion of your portfolio, keep four years of living expenses.

2. Make withdrawals as you need them.

3. When you make a withdrawal, see if the market is above or within 5% of its all-time high. If it is, take the withdrawal from the equity segment. Otherwise take it from the safe segment.

4. Whenever the market is back above its previous high after a pullback, return to taking withdrawals from the equity segment and also begin to gradually restore the safe portion from the equity portion.

DO YOU NEED A DEFENSIVE STRATEGY?

I confess to a somewhat dirty little secret: If I were writing this book for a computer, I would say to forget the defensive strategy and just follow the long-term Level3 strategy of being 100% in stocks in the portfolios suggested in Chapter 6.

Look at Table 5.2 again. While better than alternative examples, the Level3 defensive strategy costs $16,000 a year if an all-stock Level3 portfolio would provide a gross return of $120,000. The actual net payout would be reduced by taxes and inflation would impact your purchasing power over time, but those factors also impact the defensive strategy. If we assume an average tax rate of 20% during retirement and an average annual long-term inflation rate of 3%, the gross annual income of $120,000 is reduced to around $66,000. The defensive strategy (80% Level3, 20% safe investments) would see its gross annual income

> *If I were writing this book for a computer, I would say to forget the defensive strategy and just follow the long-term Level3 strategy of being 100% in stocks.*

TABLE 5.5

100% Equity Strategy During Great Recession

$1 million portfolio

Decision Date	S&P 500 Current	High	Strategy Mode	Beginning-of-Year Value/Activity
1/1/2008	1424	1468	Normal	$1,000,000 – $50,000 = $950,000
1/1/2009	866	1468	Defensive	$599,000 – $50,000 = $549,000
1/1/2010	1124	1468	Defensive	$694,000 – $50,000 = $644,000
1/1/2011	1283	1468	Defensive	$741,000 – $50,000 = $691,000
1/1/2012	1301	1468	Defensive	$706,000 – $50,000 = $656,000
1/1/2013	1827	1827	Normal	$761,000 – $50,000 = $711,000

of $104,000 reduced to $53,000 when adjusting for taxes and inflation. (The calculation of net returns after taxes and inflation is shown in Chapter 6).

So the safety offered by the defensive strategy (80% Level3, 20% safe investments) would reduce the $66,000 a year net income to $53,000. Giving up 20% of your potential income for safety is a big decision.

Table 5.5 takes the same Great Recession period shown in Table 5.4 but keeps the portfolio all in equities. The six years ends with $941,000 instead of $1,010,000, after making all withdrawals. So the defensive strategy would protect $69,000 ($1,010,000 – $941,000) during a once-every-30-years market storm at a cost of $16,000 a year (see Table 5.2), on average, for all of our retirement period—maybe 25 years.

Now, there are a lot of estimates in that description. We don't know when the next serious market crash will come. We don't know how long it will last. But we should be aware of how much being safer might cost.

I believe for most investors the defensive approach is best for three reasons.

Equity Gain/ Loss	End-of- Year Value
–37.0%	$599,000
26.5%	$694,000
15.1%	$741,000
2.1%	$706,000
16.0%	$761,000
32.4%	$941,000

First, the behavioral research discussed in Chapter 7 indicates that it will be very difficult for an individual to take severe losses and do nothing. Even with all the examples of 50% market drops with quick recoveries to reassure us, it is still somewhere between difficult and impossible to ignore such pullbacks.

Second, and more of a real risk, is the chance that the severe pullback comes at the beginning of retirement and the early withdrawals are made while the market is down severely. In investing without withdrawals, the order of bull and bear moves doesn't matter if the moves are the same. However, if you are withdrawing during each period, the order makes a difference.

The extreme of this is shown in AAII editor Charles Rotblut's article in the *AAII Journal* where annual returns with withdrawals were examined with all the worst years of the S&P 500 occurring first as opposed to all the best years first ("The Sequence in Which Returns Occur Affects Your Wealth," *AAII Journal* May 2015).

The extreme of having all the bad years first is unlikely to happen, and in fact in the last 45 years the market has only been down three years in a row twice. However, being down 37% as happened in the Great Recession period is a significant hit and would have an impact if it occurred at the beginning of retirement.

The extreme of having all the bad years first is unlikely to happen, and in fact in the last 45 years the market has only been down three years in a row twice.

While this impact is another reason to employ a defensive strategy and I use it to justify the four-year reserves recommended, it is not as severe as most articles and research have suggested. The Monte Carlo simulation approaches used to illustrate the impact of bear markets on withdrawals show significant reductions in how long your retirement savings will last if down years occur in the first years of retirement.

Part of this comes from the bear market impact on the early withdrawals. But much of the supposed bad impact occurs because the simulation portfolios that didn't get hit in the first few years had the chance of never being hit at all. Since horrendous markets only occur every 30 years or so, a retiree might never encounter one.

Also, if a portfolio faces a bear market early in the withdrawal stage, there is an increased chance that it will see another one during a long retirement period.

Let's take a worst-case example of what could happen if one was 100% in stocks. Retirement comes and the retiree needs to withdraw $50,000 a year from a $1 million portfolio. The stock market goes down 25% in the first year and 25% more in the second year before turning up.

Withdrawing $50,000 at a 25% loss costs $12,500 ($50,000 × 0.25) the first year and $21,875 [$50,000 × ((0.75 × 0.75) − 1)] the second year, for a permanent loss of $34,375 (this amount won't be recovered when the market turns up). When you consider there is a very small chance of a major turndown coming exactly at the beginning of your retirement, it once again raises the question of how much you give up to protect against a rare $34,375 loss and whether anything but 100% stocks all the time makes sense.

The third reason for using a defensive strategy is that the success of a strategy that is 100% in equities all the time is largely dependent on having done that from the beginning of your investment career. If you have used a 60% stocks/40% bonds strategy through the years, you probably will not have built up the higher portfolio value to see you through any major downturn during the withdrawal stage. In this case, a defensive strategy may be best even if you have exceptional discipline. The significant difference was shown in Table 5.1.

In the illustrations here, the cap-weighted S&P 500 has been used as a measure of the market to be conservative. I believe that the strategies discussed in this book, even the passive index strategies, will outperform the cap-weighted S&P 500, and that provides even more safety. Chapter 6 examines the possibility of being even more aggressive after looking at possible returns.

WHAT SHOULD BE IN THE DEFENSIVE PORTFOLIO?

I refer to the defensive portfolio as the safe portion. What kinds of investments belong in this portfolio?

The safe portion doesn't have to be Treasuries or insured assets, but it should be very safe in the default sense and also safe from significant price volatility in the short term. The best, of course, would be short-term Treasuries or insured CDs. Depending on the exact form of the defensive strategy, immediate liquidity might be required.

For example, in the defensive strategy used in Table 5.4, you only need to be able to withdraw once a year for perhaps four years. In this case, CDs of up to four years or Treasuries maturing on the dates when withdrawals would take place (a bond ladder) would be appropriate.

With so many appropriate ETFs in existence and the ease of making changes as well as the ability to sell whatever quantity is necessary, they become an ideal investment for the safe portfolio.

If the timing of withdrawals is definitely set then Treasury STRIPS can be effectively used. (See "A Pseudo-Life Annuity: Guaranteed Annual Income for 35 Years," by Robert Muksian, June 2012 *AAII Journal*.)

If withdrawals are on an "as needed" basis, then an insured savings account or an exchange-traded fund of safe short-term securities would be better.

Actually, with so many appropriate ETFs in existence and the ease of making changes as well as the ability to sell whatever quantity is necessary, ETFs become ideal investments for the safe portfolio.

WITHDRAWALS FOR OTHER OBJECTIVES

There are other long- and medium-term savings objectives besides retirement. The primary ones would be saving for a down payment on a home, future educational expense and, in some cases, saving to start a business.

Separate funds and strategies should be set up for each objective. Different accounts aren't necessary; you only need to keep a record of the value committed to each purpose.

The rules for each invested segment should follow the same approach as that for retirement. For example, money for college would require putting the planned contribution for freshman year into the safe portfolio four years before college and expenses for sophomore year into the safe portfolio the following year, and so forth. If you are using a more aggressive or more conservative approach than our basic plan, then continue with that approach.

SUMMARY

This chapter refined the way that Level3 Investing approaches risk. I don't equate risk with volatility. Volatility may increase real risk or it may decrease it. It certainly has little importance for long-term investors. Even in the short term, volatility is not necessarily in sync with my concept of risk as the chance that our assets will be below reasonable expectations when we must withdraw them from the portfolio for expenditures.

As we reach the time when we must regularly withdraw assets from the investment portfolio, we must be concerned about the likelihood that we will face a severe bear market as we withdraw funds. I believe that in the long run the market will always come back to new highs. But when withdrawing in a bear market, the withdrawn assets are gone and never have a chance to recover. However, it is only the withdrawn assets that suffer the permanent downturn loss, not the entire portfolio.

We can reduce the risk of a permanent downturn loss occurring by investing some of our portfolio in assets that are unlikely to lose value in the short term.

We can reduce the risk of a permanent downturn loss occurring by investing some of our portfolio in assets that are unlikely to lose value in the short term. There are a number of traditional approaches to doing this that advocate an asset mix that will be less impacted by a bear market. These approaches use a mix of stocks and safe investments of various durations.

In most of these traditional approaches, the portion of the portfolio in equities is reduced as the investor approaches and enters retirement. We have seen that we can assign an insurance cost to such approaches, but the cost of the risk reduction in most cases is higher than the benefit of the risk reduction.

Instead, the Level3 approach proposes a defensive strategy that focuses the use of safe investments not on some arbitrary percentage but on protecting the assets needed for withdrawal in the short term. The recommended approach is to protect four years' worth of estimated withdrawals.

The Level3 approach proposes a defensive strategy that focuses the use of safe investments not on some arbitrary percentage but on protecting the assets needed for withdrawal in the short term.

When a bear market occurs, the safe part of the portfolio is used to fund withdrawals and equities are not sold. This protects withdrawals for up to four years, which has been enough time to cover down periods over the past 45 years.

While this withdrawal strategy is efficient compared to other approaches, it still is expensive in terms of sacrificed returns. The case can be made for never being defensive and staying 100% in equities from our first investment through retirement until our assets pass to our heirs. This approach is expanded on in Chapter 6, but I believe for most investors the Level3 defensive strategy is appropriate because of behavioral problems discussed in Chapter 7 and because we want to avoid the possibility of a major bear market in the first years of retirement.

For those of us who have not been 100% in equities in the past, there is also the problem that we have missed the early portfolio growth that could make the lifetime 100% equity strategy work.

I now move on to discussing investment strategies that can provide a return above the market (S&P 500) return with a more efficient approach to diversification. A significant part of Level3 Investing hinges on the belief that higher returns are the single most effective weapon in reducing real risk.

For most investors the Level3 defensive strategy is appropriate because of behavioral problems and because we want to avoid the possibility of a major bear market in the first years of retirement.

CHAPTER 6

OBTAINING HIGHER-THAN-MARKET RETURNS

"Experts argue that the best offense is a good defense. If so, why are quarterbacks paid 10 times as much as safeties?"

—James Cloonan

Equity and equity-like holdings are the highest returning investments an individual can make. Given that, it is my position that a long-term investor should always be 100% (at least) in equities. Even when you become a short-term investor for part of your portfolio because of withdrawals, equities should still dominate your holdings.

The basic position of Level3 Investing is that only the part of your portfolio that needs to be withdrawn in the next four years should be in other investments, and these should be short-term, extremely safe holdings.

Being less than 100% in equities has been compared in this book to buying an insurance policy to reduce occasional losses. As I have said, I feel the premium paid in reduced earnings is in most cases way too high for the reduction in real risk.

The first of the two major objectives of this book was to dispel the current belief that safety requires allocation of significant holdings to fixed-income investments.

Only the part of your portfolio that needs to be withdrawn in the next four years should be in investments other than equities and these should be short-term, extremely safe holdings.

The other objective is to show investors that equity portfolios can attain higher returns than the average 10% obtained from the market portfolio (S&P 500 index). This second precept is the subject of this chapter.

SETTING THE STAGE

I begin by defining some terms as used here. (More formal definitions can be found in the Glossary.)

Bonds: Fixed-income securities with more than five years to maturity.

Equities: Stocks, stock mutual funds, stock exchange-traded funds (ETFs), equity real estate investment trusts (REITs), some master limited partnerships (MLPs), and special investments such as distressed bonds or any investment with equity-like expected returns.

Safe investments: Short-term (less than five years) debt either insured (CDs, savings accounts), U.S. government or very highly rated.

Investment returns: The returns we receive from managing the securities in our portfolios. For the typical individual investor, investment returns consist of the gains or losses from holding our securities coupled with the reinvestment of any income that the securities produce. (Other ways to generate returns from the market—such as market making, high-speed/high-frequency trading, arbitrage, risk arbitrage, conversion and others—are not considered here.)

There are opportunities for buying large proportions of firms and creating managerial change or buying, altering and selling all or part of the firm. However, these opportunities are not generally available to most investors, except through private equity funds.

While I have emphasized that long-term investors can largely ignore short-term volatility and risk, they shouldn't be ignored altogether, for the psychological and practical reasons discussed.

We want to avoid drops in portfolio value that will continue for several years, and we want to avoid drops that will cause too much investor anxiety. We want to avoid anxiety so it doesn't push us to make mistakes and also because anxiety is bad in itself. But if we want to obtain significantly higher-than-market returns, we will have to deal with some anxiety and experience some short-term losses.

Two steps were suggested in the previous chapter to lessen extreme reductions in portfolio value—time diversification and portfolio diversification. However, portfolio diversification in the Level3 approach means diversifying among equity investments, not among other asset forms. These steps are suggested on a limited basis even though in the long run they might reduce expected returns a bit.

Asset Classes Absent From Level3

Before we begin to examine the possible strategies and their return, I feel I should expand a bit on why two of the most advocated asset classes for diversification are absent from all of the Level3 approaches: long-term bonds and international equities.

The primary reason I avoid long-term bonds is that they have lower returns over the long run and they provide no significant risk reduction for the long-term investor because of any diversification effect.

In addition, over the long run bonds may be more risky than equities. The Level3 view of risk is not based on mathematical measures of volatility, but on the likelihood that we will have fewer assets than we need when we need them.

Bonds, even over the long run, may in real (after-inflation) terms have a negative return even after 30 years. As Jeremy Siegel points out in his book "Stocks for the Long Run" (2014), stocks provided a return of 2.6% above inflation during their worst 30-year period. Bonds had returns 2% less than inflation in their worst 30 years, resulting in an actual loss when measured by real (inflation-adjusted) dollars.

Over the long run, bonds may be more risky than equities.

Because bonds are of no use to the Level3 investor, target date mutual funds are also useless. Target date mutual funds follow traditional convention and invest a greater proportion of their holdings in bonds as you approach your target retirement date. The average "in retirement" target date fund has around 34% of its assets invested in domestic and foreign stocks, 53% allocated to domestic and foreign bonds, 10% allocated to cash and the remaining 3% invested in preferred stock, convertible bonds and other investments.

Over the long term, diversifying into international stocks provides little reduction in volatility and reduces the expected return, which by itself increases risk as viewed by the Level3 approach. Figure 6.1 compares the performance of a mutual funds covering the U.S. market and foreign markets, as measured by the Vanguard 500 Index fund (VFINX) and the Vanguard Total International Stock Index fund (VGTSX), respectively.

I am not opposed to foreign stocks per se. If you have a process for selecting stocks and a foreign stock meets your criteria, buy it. I only reject buying foreign stocks simply for diversification. Short-term differences in the performance of various foreign markets are greatly impacted by currency movements that tend to wash out over time. It is another example of paying too much for unnecessary insurance against ghost risk.

The Market Return

The long-term annualized return of the overall stock market is approximately 10%, using the S&P 500 index as an adequate proxy for the market. Since the market has more than 500 stocks, the broader-market Russell 3000 or Wilshire 5000 indexes would

FIGURE 6.1

Comparing Domestic and Foreign Stock Performance

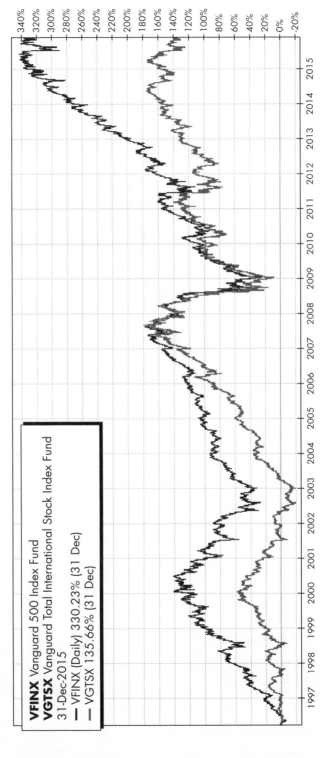

VFINX Vanguard 500 Index Fund
VGTSX Vanguard Total International Stock Index Fund
31-Dec-2015
— VFINX (Daily) 330.23% (31 Dec)
— VGTSX 135.66% (31 Dec)

be more accurate and have a slightly higher return. The S&P 500 is the usual market proxy because it accounts for almost all the market value, and information about it is readily available.

The S&P 500 is capitalization weighted—that is, the dollar value of each holding is proportionate to the market value of the issue based on number of shares outstanding (sometimes the freely traded shares, the float) multiplied by the current share price.

So, if Company A has one billion shares at $20/share and Company B has two billion shares at $30/share, then:

- Company A's market cap is $20 billion ($20 share price times one billion shares), and

- Company B's market cap is $60 billion ($30 share price times 2 billion shares), and

Company B would be given three times the weight of Company A in the composition of the S&P 500 index and when tracking the change in the index.

With cap-weighting of the shares, the S&P 500 represents the total value of all equity holdings and the performance return on the S&P 500 is the weighted average of all returns (before transaction costs).

While the stock market is not a zero-sum gain (theoretically everyone can win), it is true that for all returns higher than the return on the S&P 500 there have to be equal returns that are lower. The market is a zero-plus-10% sum game, less transaction costs of course.

Long-term investors should average returns above the market return, because volatility risk disappears over a long-term horizon and returns don't have to be reduced to avoid it.

The Level3 philosophy holds that short-term investors should have average returns that are less than the market because they must avoid/reduce volatility risk. Long-term investors should average returns above the market return, because volatility risk disappears over a long-term horizon and returns don't have to be reduced to avoid it.

Possible Rates of Return

What are reasonable return expectations? It depends, of course, on the investment process used and the amount of time and effort expended on research and management.

Previous chapters of this book have discussed why "the efficient market" as defined academically does not hold in the real world. However, in the usual sense the market is quite efficient. There are many bright investors out there looking for opportunities to excel, so there is certainly a limit to reasonable expectations for the returns on stock portfolios.

The figures used here in estimates of possible returns assume 100% in equity investments. When it is appropriate to have money set aside for short-term needs, the return will be less. If we choose to use leverage (discussed later in this chapter) the return will be more.

When trying to determine possible achievable return rates, the starting point is the long-term market return of 10%. This can be obtained through the various S&P 500 index mutual funds or ETFs. Fees are very low, transactions infrequent and, with additional income from lending stocks for a fee, the funds can deliver the same return as the index itself, and sometimes a hair better. As a bonus, these index funds tend to be very tax-efficient as well, producing very little in the way of ongoing capital gains taxes that often impact the owners of actively managed mutual funds.

It is more difficult to estimate the potential upside for other portfolios over the long run. Long-term simulations of different approaches deviate from what real results would have been, and bad results often don't get reported. Here are some other indexes for comparison.

Since 1970, which includes the two greatest bear markets since the Great Depression—1972 and 2008—the following indexes had these annualized returns (through 2015):

Cap-weighted S&P 500	10.3%
Cap-weighted Wilshire 5000	10.5%
Equal-weighted Wilshire 5000	17.1%

Long-term results for the best hedge funds and private equity funds are not readily available. On average, hedge funds return a little less than an index fund to investors, according to the Credit Suisse Hedge Fund Index (www.hedgefundindex.com), but the more successful ones do much better. I would be surprised if any hedge fund returned over 16% to investors over the long run, since to do that they would have to gross 22% before typical fees. However, hedge funds and private equity funds can invest in areas not open to individual investors and can use more leverage.

While private equity and hedge funds' long-term results have been hard to come by, recently there have been some insights due to actions by The California Public Employees Retirement System (CalPERS).

According to a Wall Street Journal article (November 25, 2015) CalPERS indicated that their private equity holdings yielded 12.3% a year over 20 years. This was from a gross return of 19.3%, with the specialist firms keeping 7% in fees. Considering the clout of CalPERS, I feel that these are among the best-performing firms and the lowest fees. Remember that private equity funds can make investments not available to individual investors.

The 12.3% net return is sufficient enough that CalPERS is keeping its private equity program. According to a Bloomberg Businessweek article (September 15, 2014), CalPERS gave up most of its hedge fund program because its long-term (10-year) net return on hedge funds was only 4.8%. In fairness, the last 10 years were a below-average period in the equity market.

So while I feel it is possible to beat the 10% return of the S&P 500, it is unlikely that long-term returns of over 18% are possible without leverage, even though some of the Level3 approaches discussed here suggest that returns over 20% are possible.

The 17.1% return of the equal-weighted Wilshire 5000 index is outstanding, but it is not possible for a fund of any size to invest in such a portfolio. The smallest stock will have a capitalization of $1 million. With a limit of 5% of the company equity, or $50,000 per company (since they must have same value), and about 3,800 companies (the Wilshire started with 5,000 stocks in 1974, but has ranged from 3,000 to 7,500), less than $200 million could be invested. This is much too small for an index fund. In addition, there would be very high transaction costs, and large purchases would drive the stock prices of the smaller companies up to unreasonable levels.

Sampling the Wilshire 5000 could be used, but I feel it wouldn't work well because of the impact of very small companies. An individual could not effectively maintain a portfolio of 3,800 stocks and rebalance with any frequency because so many of the smaller companies are poorly covered and because of the costs.

I believe it is quite easy to increase the 10% long-term stock market average return to the range of 12% to 13% without extensive active involvement.

Equal-weighted index funds of larger-capitalization stocks will increase expected return, but not by 6.6%. This approach is one of the Level3 strategies.

In his book, "Excess Returns" (2014), Frederik Vanhaverbeke shows 50 professional investors who have beaten the market for over 15 years. Many of these have beaten it by very significant amounts, but many involved the daily trading of commodities or used significant leverage. A summary of Vanhaverbeke's work can be found in his article in the *AAII Journal* ("Investment Wisdom From Wall Street's Legends," November 2014). The use of leverage is discussed later in this chapter.

Even a 10% return would be a great improvement, if we only convinced long-term investors to be 100% in equities. The common 60% stock/40% bond mix recommended by most advisers reduces long-term annual returns to about 8% using indexes. This assumes that you can earn the 6% long-term average annual rate of return of a mixed-maturity bond portfolio. But I believe it is quite easy to increase the 10% long-term stock market average return to the range of 12% to 13% without extensive active involvement.

PASSIVE APPROACHES

Three levels of investor involvement are considered here: passive, intermediate, and active. But it is really a continuum where investors can find a level of involvement that matches their interests, time availability and abilities.

The passive Level3 approach primarily uses a variety of index mutual funds and ETFs. The active approach involves developing strategies from guru approaches, from academic and institutional research, from advisory services, and possibly from one's own original research. The intermediate approach would combine some active approach elements with some passive approaches.

Plan Z

The Introduction gave the hypothetical portfolio of John and Mary Smith using a Level3 approach called Plan Z. Plan Z entails simply putting 100% of your portfolio in the Guggenheim S&P 500 Equal Weight ETF (RSP), an exchange-traded fund that invests in the S&P 500 index but equally weights each stock. As discussed, over the long run such a portfolio should return 2% to 3% above a cap-weighted index, based on its real performance since 2004 as compared to the cap-weighted S&P 500 (shown in Figure 6.2).

Plan Z entails putting 100% of your portfolio in the Guggenheim S&P 500 Equal Weight ETF (RSP).

FIGURE 6.2

Equal-Weighted vs. Cap-Weighted Market ETFs

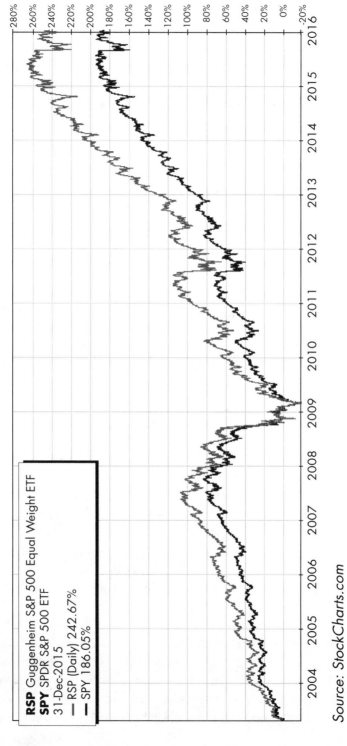

RSP Guggenheim S&P 500 Equal Weight ETF
SPY SPDR S&P 500 ETF
31-Dec-2015
— RSP (Daily) 242.67%
— SPY 186.05%

Source: StockCharts.com

The equal-weighted Wilshire 5000 index has returned 17.1% a year over the last 45 years compared to 10.5% for the cap-weighted Wilshire 5000 index holding the same stocks. That means a dart-throwing investor equally weighting selections could have averaged a return of 17.1% a year over the long term. Of course, depending on the number of darts, the returns could have ranged widely around that average.

While investing the entire portfolio in Guggenheim S&P 500 Equal Weight ETF would beat the vast majority of portfolios and mutual funds, I feel Plan Z can be improved on by some diversification.

I have argued that while diversification may reduce volatility, it does not necessarily reduce real risk. Real risk is the likelihood that our portfolio will have a lower dollar value than expected when we need to withdraw money from the portfolio. Diversification is not a free lunch and it is typically overdone.

Plan Z can be improved on by some diversification.

However, some diversification can reduce real risk indirectly because it can reduce the chance of an extreme pullback in the portfolio and it can reduce the duration of a pullback so that in the withdrawal stage we need to invest less in lower-returning safe investments.

Most investors believe the stock diversification provided by the S&P 500, or broader indexes like the various Russell and Wilshire indexes, is as broad as necessary. But because these portfolios are cap-weighted, they greatly favor large corporations, and large corporations are largely clustered in several industries.

As a result, if one of the dominant sectors is hard hit, the cap-weighted indexes will also be disproportionately hard hit. The 2000 tech "bubble burst" is an example: The technology sector took 15 years to recover and pulled the entire NASDAQ Composite index down with it. Several of the heavier-weighted sectors such as health care and financials are highly regulated and thus subject to legislative and administrative impacts, which could be severe, in addition to the usual sector risks.

Improvements on Plan Z

While the use of the Guggenheim S&P 500 Equal Weight ETF will provide some allocation of assets to real estate, it is still underrepresented in term of its significance in the economy. Equity REITs have outperformed the S&P 500 over the past 40 years by 1.7%, according to Ibbotson's SBBI 2015 Yearbook, and they provided some useful diversification. I would allocate 20% of the passive portfolio to Vanguard REIT ETF (VNQ). This would give us a passive portfolio of:

> *Equity REITs have outperformed the S&P 500 over the past 50 years by about 1%.*

> 80% Guggenheim S&P 500 Equal Weight ETF (RSP)
> 20% Vanguard REIT ETF (VNQ)

However, there are some new ETFs that might replace both of these funds in the future. PowerShares Russell 1000 Equal Weight Portfolio (EQAL) includes some mid-cap stocks, so it could provide a higher return (and may be a better investment) than Guggenheim S&P 500 Equal Weight. However, it is relatively new, has higher costs, and is more thinly traded, which might offset better performance.

I believe the PowerShares Russell 1000 Equal Weight Portfolio is far enough along at this time to use it as a partial substitute for the Guggenheim S&P 500 Equal Weight ETF. It has an interesting feature in that it equally weights in two stages. It first equally weights the nine investment sectors and then equally weights the stocks in each sector. The fund managers feel that approach gives better diversification and I agree, but it is likely to reduce the return a bit.

Using PowerShares Russell 1000 Equal Weight Portfolio for part of the passive portfolio provides an opportunity to compare it to Guggenheim S&P 500 Equal Weight ETF. If enough investors start using it, the liquidity will improve.

Even though the Guggenheim S&P 500 Equal Weight ETF increases the emphasis on value stocks beyond that of the cap-weighted S&P 500 and the PowerShares Russell 1000 Equal Weight Portfolio gives some weight to value and mid-cap stocks, since the value and mid-cap segments are superior performers they should be given additional weight. For that reason, the Vanguard Mid-Cap Value (VOE) is added to the suggested passive portfolio. There are several other ETFs similar to Vanguard Mid-Cap Value that could be used, but this fund's very low expense ratio (0.09%) makes it likely that it will continue to outperform in this category.

Since the value and mid-cap segments are superior performers they should be given additional weight.

This leads to a passive portfolio of:

> 40% Guggenheim S&P 500 Equal Weight ETF (RSP)
> 20% PowerShares Russell 1000 Equal Weight Portfolio (EQAL)
> 20% Vanguard REIT ETF (VNQ)
> 20% Vanguard Mid-Cap Value (VOE)

If in withdrawal mode, a safe portion of fixed income would be added:

> 32% Guggenheim S&P 500 Equal Weight ETF (RSP)
> 16% PowerShares Russell 1000 Equal Weight Portfolio (EQAL)
> 16% Vanguard REIT ETF (VNQ)
> 16% Vanguard Mid-Cap Value (VOE)
> 20% iShares 1-3 Year Treasury Bond ETF (SHY), or insured CDs or other short-term fixed income

A couple of alternatives for the Level3 passive approach are worth watching. There is now an equal-weight portfolio for the Russell 2000 index, which captures the next 2,000 stocks in size after the largest stocks in the Russell 1000. Historically, these smaller-cap stocks have provided higher returns than the Russell 1000. But I don't believe it will be possible to create and maintain such a portfolio except by sampling approaches, and I would question how well this will work.

There is also the new Guggenheim S&P 500 Equal Weight Real Estate ETF (EWRE), which may turn out to be better than the Vanguard REIT ETF, but I would not suggest it until it has a longer track record.

Funds will be monitored to evaluate possible changes to the suggested passive portfolio at Level3investing.com.

These funds will be monitored to evaluate possible changes to the suggested passive portfolio at **Level3investing.com**. I will also review the Level3 Passive Portfolio periodically in my Model Portfolios column in the *AAII Journal*.

What to Expect From the Passive Portfolio

There are two important things to notice about the Level3 Passive Portfolio (consisting of the four equity ETFs). First, it provides diversification, but the diversification does not sacrifice return since all of the additions to the Guggenheim S&P 500 Equal Weight (RSP) have expected returns equal to or better than RSP.

Second, it has no exposure to the higher expected returns of small-capitalization stocks, particularly micro caps. I believe that it is very difficult for a fund to specialize in micro-cap stocks. Bid/ask spreads are wide and micro-cap funds get hit extra hard in a downturn because some of their investors panic, driving the losses deeper when the fund has to sell to honor withdrawal requests.

If you wish to be partially active, micro- and small-cap stocks are the most rewarding segments. You can do this following the selection strategies outlined in the next section either by using someone else's model or by developing your own.

While there is no history of portfolios with the make-up of the Level3 Passive Portfolio, estimates can be made based on the history of other similar indexes and research. I believe a reason-able—conservative—expected long-term return for the Passive Portfolio that is 100% equities would be 12% annualized in the accumulation stage.

A reasonable expected long-term return for the Passive Portfolio would be 12% annualized in the accrual stage.

In the withdrawal stage—where four year's needs are kept in safe short-term investments—a reasonable expected long-term return for the Passive Portfolio would be 10% annualized. That should permit an annual with-drawal of 5% of portfolio value each year with no reduction in portfolio value over the years, although there will be fluctua-tions. The calculation of withdrawal rates for different expected returns is discussed at the end of the chapter.

ACTIVE APPROACHES

Active approaches involve creating the equivalent of your own mutual fund or funds. You must select one or more approaches that you feel will exceed the 12% to 13% return of a passive ap-proach and then implement it. Some of the approaches examined here require a frequent revision of holdings, and others would have very gradual changes.

Active approaches involve creating the equivalent of your own mutual fund or funds.

They all involve serious continual moni-toring and a rigid discipline. Just a little carelessness will offset whatever advan-tage your approach has. It is so easy to get careless, particularly in up markets. Up 31% instead of up 34% seems im-material, but it is the same as down 2%

instead of up 1% in long-term calculations.

It would be nice to be able to lay out a dozen well-defined approaches that have provably beaten the market by 5% to 7% over the long term. Unfortunately "provably" is a hard nut to crack. There are many approaches with different levels of proof, but none without some limitations on the certainty that they were not biased in some way.

There are three sources of strategies that may outperform the market: model portfolios with defined rules, enhanced advisory services, and academic and other historical research.

Model Portfolios

We have mentioned AAII's Model Shadow Stock Portfolio several times. It comes close to meeting the criteria of Level3 Investing in order to have confidence in the returns. At a long-term return of 15.4% annualized, the Model Shadow Stock Portfolio has a return that is meaningfully better than passive approaches. It is a real portfolio with the costs and problems that entails. It has 23 years of history behind it. However, as an estimate of how well you would have done or will do in the future, following its approach has some limitations:

At a return of 15.4% annualized, the Model Shadow Stock Portfolio has a return meaningfully better than passive approaches.

1. Since the portfolio and any variations of it are real portfolios, the money invested is finite. When the portfolio is out of excess cash, new stocks, no matter how appealing, cannot be bought until there are sales. It is likely that no two portfolios will be exactly the same—even though they are following the same rules—since different investors may run out of excess cash or find new funds at different times. This bias should be neutral on average but indicates that individuals may not achieve equal results.

2.   Since stocks are bought for the Model Shadow Stock Portfolio prior to the actions being announced, the impact of others buying the same stocks later should be beneficial to the model portfolio. This is a positive bias to the portfolio and makes its returns higher than they might otherwise be.

3.   Since the portfolio rules are spelled out in detail and always followed, anyone is free to take positions prior to the portfolio announcement. It could be a day ahead or a month ahead. This bias is negative and makes the model portfolio returns less than they might otherwise be.

Another well-defined strategy that has been monitored through time is Joel Greenblatt's "The Little Book That Still Beats the Market" (2010). His Magic Formula strategy can be used to provide recommended stocks at different capitalization levels and is available for use by all investors at **magicformulainvesting.com**.

There are not very many model portfolios maintained in real time and followed over the long run. Active mutual funds could be considered such portfolios if the precise rules for portfolio decisions were spelled out and maintained over the long run. But funds jealously hide their rules and they tend to vary their decision processes as well as their managers over time.

Enhanced Advisory Services

Advisory services generally make buy and sell recommendations and maintain a list of their recommendations. Very few show what an actual portfolio based on their recommendations would look like and what the actual return would be over time. Over the years, the Hulbert Financial Digest (HFD) has turned most advisory letters into model portfolios and tracked their performance.

Unfortunately, HFD stopped publishing in early 2016. The last data published showed John Buckingham's The Prudent Speculator has produced a long-term (35-year) average return of 15.8%.

In his 2016 Honor Roll, Hulbert showed several advisory letters that have significantly outperformed the market over the long term. These include:

- Bob Brinker's Marketimer
- The Buyback Letter
- Fidelity Investor
- Investment Quality Trends
- Investor Advisory Serivce
- Morningstar StockInvestor
- Outstanding Investments
- The Oxford Club
- Sound Advice
- Zacks Premium

These are only a few of many advisories that have outperformed the market for 15 years or more.

In most cases, advisory letter portfolios, or HFD's interpretation of them, equally weight the selected stocks. This in itself should account for 1% to 2% of the return, so to beat Guggenheim S&P 500 Equal Weight ETF or other equally weighted indexes, I would suggest that an effective advisory must beat the market by 3% over the past 15 years.

An effective advisory must beat the market by 3% over the past 15 years.

While the Hulbert Financial Digest is gone, the results for the long-term winners will be valid for quite some time. A list of stock advisory letters that outperformed the S&P 500 by 3% or more for at least 15 years as of December 31, 2015, and met the other recommendations of Level3 Investing can be found at **Level3investing.com**.

Academic Research

To uncover other approaches, we must rely on simulations used over historical periods. Voluminous academic research has been done on the so called anomalies. Unfortunately, much academic research is aimed at explaining stock behavior rather than developing effective investment strategies.

Typically the research shows that a particular investment strategy makes a positive difference, but it is difficult to translate the findings into return estimates. The list of stock characteristics that increase returns over the market return introduced in Chapter 1 have all been supported by academic research, but in most cases long-term estimates of the actual returns are not easily inferred.

While all of the strategies listed in Chapter 1 have shown some improvement over market returns, many have only slight impact or there is contradicting research.

The following are the factors that seem to provide the most significant impact on returns, but even these sometimes must be used in combination in order to make a significant improvement over passive strategies.

- Price-to-cash-flow ratio (P/CF): Cash flow seems to be more important than earnings. Earnings are calculated through the principles of accrual accounting, which attempts to match expenses to revenues when the revenues can be expected or recognized. Accrual accounting introduces many interpretations and estimates by management into the financial statements. Decisions regarding the capitalization of expenses, the recognition of revenues, the creation of reserves against losses, and the write-off of assets are just a few of the factors that may vary from firm to firm. Cash flow can be measured directly from the cash flow statement or adjustments can be made to the income statement. When adjusting the income statement, non-cash expenses are added back to net income after dividend payments are subtracted. Non-cash expenses such as depreciation, depletion and amortization are expenses that appear on the income statement but require no cash outlays. They represent the accountant's attempt to measure the reduction of the book value of assets as these assets are depleted. While dividends are a discretionary item, they are a real cash outlay that is not tax deductible and is not reflected in net income. There is evidence that there are positive anomaly earnings associated with high cash flow; therefore, low price-to-cash-flow ratios are favored.

- Price-to-sales ratio (P/S): Usually used to eliminate stocks with high price-to-sales values, but may require adjustments for typical industry profitability. Unlike earnings and book value, sales are less subject to management assumptions and more difficult to manipulate. Furthermore, all companies that are going concerns have sales and positive ones at that. Therefore, the vast majority of companies will have meaningful price-to-sales values. Lastly, sales tend to be less volatile than earnings, making the price-to-sales ratio a more reliable means of valuation. However, price-to-sales ratios do not generally work well for financial firms such as banks, where sales are not a driving force. Furthermore, the price-to-sales level is driven by profit margins, which tend to vary from industry to industry. Companies in industries with low profit margins, such as supermarkets, tend to sell with very low price-to-sales ratios. For this reason, it is best to compare price-to-sales ratios across companies in similar industries or lines of business.

- Shareholder yield: The combination of dividend yield and stock buyback yield seems better than either figure alone. A shareholder yield shows what percentage of total cash the company is paying out to shareholders, either in the form of a cash dividend or as cash spent to repurchase its shares in the open market and reduce the number outstanding shares. While there are a couple of ways to calculate the buyback yield, the easiest is to look at the change in the number of outstanding shares. A stock's buyback yield is determined by comparing the average shares outstanding for one fiscal period with the average shares outstanding for another fiscal period. If a company is paying a 5% dividend yield and has a buyback yield of 10%, its shareholder yield would be 15%.

- Earnings surprises: Reported earnings above expectations have a positive impact, and earnings below expectations have a negative impact that lasts into the future. Not an easy approach to use without close monitoring, but it appears to be very effective.

- Relative strength/momentum: Stocks going up tend to keep going up. If a stock has displayed significant positive relative strength against the market, it tends to continue to display positive relative strength into the future. Improving relative strength or momentum may signal that the market recognizes that a stock is attractive and help pull in other investors that continue to bid the stock price up. While relative strength is a worthwhile analytical technique on its own, its usefulness increases when combined with other stock selection criteria. Notably, requiring low valuations or strong earnings growth with high relative price strength ranks tends to lead to better stock price performance than when the factors are used independently.

- Company capitalization size: The smaller the capitalization, the better. A strong factor, but it can have long periods (two to three years) of underperformance.

- Price-to-book-value ratio (P/B): Lower values are a strong predictor of excess returns. Works best with factors that provide confidence in stated book value. The price-to-book ratio provides a relatively stable measure of value, which can be compared to the market price. It is a valuation metric that can be used even if a company has negative earnings, which renders the price-earnings ratio not meaningful. However, over the history of the firm, many events occur that can distort the book value figure to where it bears little resemblance to current economic values. For example, inflation may leave the replacement cost of capital goods within the firm far from their stated book value, or the purchase of a firm may lead to the establishment of goodwill, an intangible asset, boosting the level of book value. Different accounting practices across industries may also come into play.

- Return on assets (ROA): A higher ROA is a strong value factor. In the earnings-to-assets ratio, earnings before interest, taxes, depreciating and amortization (EBITDA) can be substituted for earnings and enterprise value can be substituted for assets. EBITDA is used to analyze and compare profitability between companies and industries, since the effects of financing and accounting decisions are eliminated. EBITDA is a good metric to evaluate profitability, but not cash flow. Enterprise value (EV) is a measure of a company's value and is thought by some to be a more accurate measure than market capitalization because it includes debt in its calculation. Enterprise value is often calculated as the sum of market cap (historical), short-term debt, long-term debt, minority interest and preferred equity less cash. Enterprise value is sometimes referred to as a company's theoretical takeover price. In the event of a buyout, an acquirer would have to take on the company's debt, but would pocket its cash. Whereas multiples that use the stock price look only at the equity side of a stock, enterprise value includes a company's debt, cash and minority interests and therefore gives the total value of a company.

- Gross profit-to-assets ratio: A newer anomaly finds gross profit (revenue minus cost of goods sold) more predictive than earnings. Gross profit is revenue less the cost of goods sold and reflects the pricing decisions of a company as well as the costs of the materials needed to produce their goods and services. A higher relative or absolute ratio is attractive.

Combinations of these factors, particularly value factors paired with accounting measures, provide a strong interactive effect. This is because firms headed for disaster posess attractive value measures as the value inputs are lagging in time, so an added check on financial strength helps to eliminate these weak stocks.

Because Fama and French have been so deeply involved in the study of so-called anomalies and have provided a framework for the study of anomalies that most researchers follow, I should point out again that they have introduced a new five-factor model to explain stock price movements. In addition to risk, capitalization size, and book to price, they are adding a measure of profitability and one of investment pattern.

Many researchers feel that price momentum is an essential ingredient for a successful model, but a belief in momentum would be a sacrilege for true believers in the efficient market hypothesis. Price momentum looks for stocks that are performing better than a market index or better than stocks as a whole.

However, if the five-factor model is accepted, then we can be sure that some researchers will add momentum, and we will have a six-factor model to explain stock price movements. It probably won't be very useful for obtaining market-beating returns.

The format most often used now in academic research has the simulated portfolio long the best 20% of the strategy being evaluated and short the worst 20%. This approach is effective for comparisons, but doesn't help predict real-world outcomes for the strategy.

Academic research also typically sets weights for the various factors based on regression analysis. Linear regression analysis is itself suspect in real-world distributions based on the concepts discussed in Chapter 1.

O'Shaughnessy Research

Fortunately, "What Works on Wall Street" (2012) by James O'Shaughnessy has taken these various factors that promise market-beating returns and simulated long-term portfolio returns. He tests the individual factors, as well as many combinations of them. This book is an essential source for any investor wishing to develop actively managed portfolios.

The only problem with the book is that it eliminates, with a few exceptions, the use of smaller-capitalization stocks because O'Shaughnessy feels that only institutions will be doing this type of active investing. His cutoff of $200 million in market capitalization would be appropriate for institutions, but most individual investors can effectively include stocks with market caps of $50 million, and in many cases even lower. The Model Shadow Stock Portfolio goes down to $30 million if there is reasonably active trading and acceptable bid/ask spreads.

I think any of the approaches O'Shaughnessy is testing would perform even better with a lower market-cap limit. As it turns out, the few tests he did with micro-cap stocks turned out to be the most effective approaches. When O'Shaughnessy does use micro caps, he goes down to $50 million with restrictions that eliminate stocks individual investors wouldn't be able to buy.

"What Works on Wall Street" isolates some additional decision factors but really expands past research by looking at multiple combinations of factors used in portfolio decision-making.

A word of caution: When putting together this type of simulation, it is difficult to include the cost of investing in the real world. Researchers sometimes add estimates of the impact of bid/ask spreads and commissions, but they generally are too low, particularly for small- and micro-cap stocks.

Most simulations use "last" price in calculations, which distorts reality for less-active stocks. The price that determines your return is the price you would get if you sold and the price you would pay when you buy; this is the "ask" price when you buy and the "bid" price when you sell. For example, if a stock is trading with an inside spread of $8.44 bid and $8.66 ask, a purchase of 100 shares would cost $866 ignoring the commission cost. If you were to turn around and sell the stock, you would only get $844 for your 100 shares (again ignoring commission costs and now SEC transaction fees). This quick change from a "buy" or ask price to a "sell" or bid price represents a 2.5% reduction in the reported price of last two transactions, even though the price of the bid/ask spread did not change.

The market can move dramatically since a last price occurred. Simulations should use the bid price, the ask price, or an average of the two rather than last price. Many rules require frequent turnover and adjustments, which multiply the cost impact of the bid/ask spread.

Based on my own portfolio experience, I would estimate that an approach that indicates a return of 20% in O'Shaughnessy's research might be closer to 16% when actually implemented, but there is no way to verify this.

Accordingly, I would suggest focusing on O'Shaughnessy's approaches that indicate returns of over 15% in order to exceed both the market return and the return possible from a passive approach. There are over 60 approaches that provide that return or better in his book, although many of them are very similar. His book covers most of the combinations of strategies that have been discussed in research.

The bottom line is that O'Shaughnessy's research shows that stocks with small and micro capitalizations, value factors and momentum are the winners. However, the devil is in the details and the specific combinations of value factors is important to get the results he shows.

O'Shaughnessy's research shows that stocks with small and micro capitalizations, value factors, and momentum are the winners.

In addition, there are value components that, when combined with larger-cap stocks, can also provide significantly above-market returns and useful diversification at the same time.

I believe studying "What Works on Wall Street" is a first step to any active portfolio management.

The most recent edition (fourth) of the book is 2012 and the data is through December 31, 2009. That includes the Great

Recession and the successful strategies have been consistent over the years.

Some of O'Shaughnessy's simulations are based on data back to 1927 and some only to 1965. Some of this is due to the databases with CRSP (Center for Research in Security Prices, Booth School of Business, University of Chicago) going all the way back to 1926 and Compustat, which has additional details only going back to 1965 for quarterly data. Wilshire data goes back to 1971 for both cap-weighted and equal-weighted portfolios.

As I have discussed previously, I do not believe the circumstances that brought about the Great Depression could occur again, and I feel that data that goes back far enough to include the bear market of the 1970s is a better predictor of the future than data based on the markets more than 50 years ago.

AAII Stock Screens

The American Association of Individual Investors (AAII) also evaluates multiple strategies through its stock screening series available to members. AAII stock screens include the most researched of the anomalies in academic literature and simulations of the approaches of numerous gurus such as Warren Buffett, Benjamin Graham, Joseph Piotroski, Josef Lakonishok, William O'Neil, Peter Lynch, John Neff and many more.

Evaluation of the more than 60 AAII stock screens in January 2016 showed more than half besting the S&P 500 over the past 10 years.

Wayne Thorp's evaluation of the more than 60 strategies in the January 2016 *AAII Journal*, showed more than half besting the S&P 500 over the past 10 years. Even after adding the 4% transaction cost estimate I mentioned above, 17 strategies beat the S&P 500. However, when dealing with micro-cap stocks or strategies that require very short-term adjustment periods (monthly or quarterly), the transaction costs may be higher than 4% a year.

The AAII stock screens research is available to AAII members on-line and is updated regularly. There is certainly overlap between the AAII stock screens and the simulations in O'Shaughnessy's book, and factors that have shown to be successful in both should be strong contenders for any active approach.

INTERMEDIATE APPROACHES

Intermediate approaches would be a combination of the passive and active approaches described. For the individual investor who has the time and temperament to do some active management, the ideal combination would be to use passive approaches for large-cap stocks and actively manage a micro-cap portfolio.

This would be optimal because the best-performing stock portfolios are in various forms of micro-cap value stocks, but there is no truly effective passive way to invest in them.

For the individual investor who has the time and temperament to do some active management, the ideal combination would be to use passive approaches for large-cap stocks and actively manage a micro-cap portfolio.

While there are a few micro-cap value mutual funds, most are closed to new investors. There is also a significant problem with micro-cap funds. In severe down markets, investors tend to panic and sell. While the long-term individual investor can hold on or even buy on downdrafts, many individuals panic. If they sell their shares of a micro-cap fund, the fund must liquidate in a narrow market, which drives prices even lower than they would normally go; the fund must then sell at that price. So even if you as a fund investor have a long-term discipline, the other fund holders' behavior hurts you.

If you choose to run your own micro-cap value portfolio, there are multiple approaches for determining value. Research indicates that it is better to use several determinants of value rather than a single one such as the price-to-book ratio.

The rules demonstrated in O'Shaughnessy's "What Works on Wall Street" can provide a starting point, as can the rules of AAII's Model Shadow Stock Portfolio (provided in the Appendix). Any combination of the factors discussed previously may provide market-beating portfolios. The website that accompanies this book, **Level3investing.com**, lists the O'Shaughnessy approaches that appear to offer the best chance of exceeding the passive approach returns.

THE USE OF LEVERAGE

All the market returns and potential returns discussed up to this point have assumed there has been no leverage that could come from using borrowed funds to augment returns.

The basic approach to using leverage is to borrow funds at a rate of return that is less than the anticipated return on the portfolio. Generally this would be accomplished by the process of investing on margin through a broker (only allowed in regular accounts, not IRAs).

The basic approach to using leverage is to borrow funds at a rate of return that is less than the anticipated return on the portfolio.

I have already gone way out on a limb by suggesting that long-term investors should be 100% in equities during the accumulation, wealth-building stage. To suggest the use of margin for individual investors would make me a heretic. But I think it is something that should be discussed, even if I wouldn't advocate it for most investors.

Let's look at the math. Assume a long-term return on our strategy of 12%, a margin loan of 25% of our equity, and a margin loan rate of 4% (estimate based on net cost of loan after tax deduction).

Return on the leveraged portion of the portfolio would equal

25% of the portfolio rate of return minus net cost of the margin loan:

$$= (12\% - 4\%) \times 0.25$$
$$= 8\% \times 0.25$$
$$= 2\%$$

The total portfolio return is then the sum of the return on portfolio plus the return on the leveraged portion:

$$= 12\% + 2\%$$
$$= 14\%$$

The return calculation assumes 25% margin is maintained. If 25% margin was solely taken initially, the margin percentage would decrease over time in relation to the overall portfolio, giving extra protection.

An Example

Using the Plan Z example from the Introduction where the Smiths average holding period for pre-retirement savings of $250,000 was 18 years, at retirement they would have:

At 12%, a pretax portfolio value of $1,922,000
At 14%, a pretax portfolio value of $2,644,000

This is a significant difference and it means an approximate annual retirement income difference of $132,000 versus $96,000 at a 5% withdrawal rate.

Remember the portfolio value for the 60%/40% stock/bond portfolio of Level 2 returning 8% on average a year was only $999,000. Its 5% withdrawal rate is only $50,000.

So, if 25% margin is so great, why not leverage the full 50% that is permitted? Well, the premise of Level3 is that in the long term the market will always come back. But if you lose all your funds in the short term, the market's resurgence won't help you.

If the market goes down precipitously, you will get margin calls to replenish funds. When the market is down 50%, you are broke. And the market will drop close to 50% probably twice in your lifetime.

At 25% margin, you can stand a drop of 60+% and allow for the fact that some of your stocks may lose their marginability. But if 50% drops inspire panic without using margin, you can imagine the impact when you have lost 65%.

It is worthwhile noting that if you had invested in the stocks used by Ibbotson's SBBI 2015 Yearbook to measure the market since 1926 and used 25% margin, you could have held on straight through the Great Depression era without a margin call. Today you would have about three times as much portfolio value as if you didn't margin. This is due to the 10% maintenance requirement at that time. The maintenance requirement is 25% today. Note that brokerage firms may have higher margin maintenance requirements.

If you are able to handle such shocks, you probably should adjust your withdrawal stage strategy from four years to two years in reserve. This would be 90% equities and in 10% safe short-term investments, and would add about 1% to your annual income.

Another factor is that the cost of margin borrowing would influence any margin decision. If you estimate your long-term equity return as 12% and the margin rate as 12% or higher (as it sometimes has been), then margin makes no sense.

Once again, I hesitate to suggest most investors use margin in this way because only a few investors would be able to stay focused and adhere to a strategy in worst-case bear markets.

Chapter 7 covers the various psychological forces that impact our ability to follow an optimal investing approach, but right here we have an example of how we develop concepts based on our surroundings.

Margin as Emergency Fund

We have been taught that margin is bad, but actually even if we choose not to use margin regularly it can still fill a role in our financial plans.

It is often suggested that we maintain a safe reserve in a bank account or other safe place where over the long run we earn 2% to 3% at best. The most common suggestion is a reserve of six months' income. This is to provide for emergencies such as losing a job or medical expenses.

Suppose we have 10 such emergencies in our investing lifetime (which should be on the high side) and each one takes us a year to fully recover from financially. Because we recover gradually, we have need for funds only for six months on average. Say six months' income is $50,000 currently and has averaged $20,000 (going back in time) over the years. Putting that away at 3% instead of having it invested at 12%, we have paid $1,800 a year for a lifetime (9% of $20,000) to avoid the interest on 10 loans of $20,000 with an average duration of six months. At an interest rate of 4%, that's a total cost of about $8,000:

$$= (0.04 \times \$20,000) \times 10$$
$$= \$800 \times 10$$
$$= \$8,000$$

The above assumes using margin loans, which are generally tax deductible and charge much lower interest than consumer or credit card loans. The psychological puzzle here is that margin at a net 4% has a negative connotation while credit card installment loans at 16% seem to be acceptable as a normal way to even out high expenses.

There is no better place to get short-term loans than from your broker: No application, likely tax deductibility, and low interest rates. Plus, if you have dividends or take some capital gains, there is automatic repayment.

Even if you don't use margin to leverage, it can be the best source of funds to meet emergencies and further justifies 100% in equities.

> *Even if you don't use margin to leverage, it can be the best source of funds to meet emergencies and further justifies 100% in equities.*

While on the topic of leverage, it is worthwhile to look at how leverage might impact professional investors. The reason high margin would be deadly for individuals in severe down markets is that there is a Federal Reserve requirement that the amount of a new margin loan is limited to an amount where initially the loan is no more than 50% of the portfolio value. If the market goes down, it is only necessary to maintain 25% to 30% of the portfolio value. But you can't maintain 30% if the market goes down 50% or more, and you will be wiped out.

However, if the market always comes back and you had a loan that did not require maintaining a certain equity amount, then you could use extreme leverage and get market-beating results from average investments. It has been suggested that that is, at least partially, how Warren Buffett gets his returns.

MARKET TIMING

In addition to the selection process, many advisers suggest going in and out of your stock investments over time. Some market timing is long term, with the objective of avoiding major downturns, and some is very short term, involving day trading.

Timing decisions are sometimes based on macroeconomic events related to the business cycle or the economic strength of the U.S. It can be based on particular measures such as money supply or Federal Reserve activity. While this approach makes sense and there are a number of models based on economic events, I find little convincing evidence that long-term results can be meaningfully improved with timing models, particularly when factoring in transaction costs and tax consequences.

They all seem to work some of the time and then taper off. On balance, it seems that the risk of missing a dramatic up move in the market is just as big as the risk of being stuck in a down move.

I find little convincing evidence that long-term results can be meaningfully improved with timing models, particularly when factoring in transaction costs and tax consequences.

However, it would be worthwhile to have an approach that would predict only major collapses such as 1929, 1974 and 2008 but ignore the others. Unfortunately, I am not aware of any such indicator.

Another timing approach is based on technical analysis, which predicts up and down moves for individual stocks and stock indexes based on various configurations of price and volume. The most popular indicators for stock indexes would be various forms and lengths of moving averages, by themselves and in relationship to each other.

As discussed in Chapter 2, in my view, the various technical approaches do not work out in the long run, and those that are most touted were discovered after the fact.

Individual investors, I believe, can do so much better than their advisers and so much better than they have been doing without attempting market timing.

Remember that "buy and hold" refers to the overall portfolio. Buying and selling of the securities within the portfolio always takes place based on the strategy being followed.

POSSIBLE SCENARIOS

So what does it all mean? What are the choices? What are the possibilities? I want to make one thing very clear: The suggested approaches are just that, suggestions or starting points. As an investor, you must find an approach that is reasonably comfortable for you regarding the exposure to volatility and risk. I say "reasonably" because no sane person can watch their life savings bounce around in value without some anxiety.

The approach you choose must also be within your level of ability—not intelligence or even education as much as discipline. Investing, particularly the active approaches, requires effort applied diligently. If you commit to a diet and exercise program and then slough off, you will get fat. If you slough off on adhering to your chosen investment strategy, you will go broke.

Choosing a valid strategy and following it faithfully can lead to a retirement nest egg two or four times as great as what you might have if you let an adviser manage your money who is stuck at Level 2 or has other loyalties.

Choosing a valid strategy and following it faithfully can lead to a retirement nest egg two or four times as great as what you might have if you let an adviser manage your money who is stuck at Level 2 or has other loyalties.

I meet a lot of people who are certainly capable of managing their own money but don't. They mostly fall into three groups.

- The first group is the one that makes the most sense. They are younger professionals making good money and directing all of their efforts into their careers. It is likely that the financial return from concentrating on their career is higher than the increased return would be from managing their portfolios while the portfolios are still relatively small.

  Even if you are in this group, I would suggest considering Level3 Plan Z or the Level3 Passive Portfolio, which probably involves less effort than interacting with an adviser and will provide much higher returns.

- The second group consists of individuals who have been convinced that it is better to let experts manage their money. It seems sensible. After all, you wouldn't perform surgery on yourself or represent yourself in court. I hope that this book points out the fallacy in that thinking. Only a limited number of this group is likely to read this book, but I firmly believe they are the ones who could be most helped.

- The third group is the most puzzling to me. Many of my friends and acquaintances are members of this group. These are successful individuals, active or retired, who believe that successful people farm out whatever work they can. They are entitled to have other people serve them; it is a status symbol to have an adviser.

  Just as they might comment that the doctor who replaced their hip is the best in the field, they feel that their adviser is tops. They enjoy saying, "Well so-and-so runs my money and he has done really well for me." Unfortunately, they mostly don't know what "doing well" is.

Let's review some alternative paths. I won't bother with Level 1 investing, which is inconsistent investing largely dependent on casual conversations and quick advice online, in print or on TV and is devoid of any underlying consistent strategy.

But let's look at three possible scenarios. We use some of the same assumptions we used for the Smiths in the Introduction to this book. You are 70 years old and are about to retire. You have been saving for 48 years, but more was saved later so that the average dollar has been invested for 18 years. For the sake of modeling the assumptions, I assume that $250,000 was invested for 18 years and any income was reinvested.

Remember, all the results discussed here are expected results—the annualized average return expected. Real returns will vary around this expected return, but this will only be important if you need to withdraw funds during periods of significant downward divergence.

Scenario 1

This is a version of what would be considered best practice by the typical adviser. The adviser has kept your portfolio allocation 60% in stocks at a 10% (S&P 500) return and 40% in bonds of various maturities that provide a 6% compound average return. The blended return is 8.4% [(0.60 × 10%) + (0.40 × 6%)], and annual commissions and fees of 0.4% provide an 8.0% net return.

That historical return on the $250,000 initial investment gives you a portfolio of $999,000 at retirement. Let's assume that any return earned on the portfolio is subject to an average annual tax rate of 20%.

Suppose your adviser is slightly more aggressive than average when you retire and switches you to 40% stocks and 60% varied duration long-term bonds, for a combined return of 7.6% less 0.4% commissions and fees, or 7.2% [(0.40 × 10%) + (0.60 × 6%) − 0.4%] Assuming that the portfolio's return is subject to 20% tax will reduce the aftertax rate of return to 5.8% [7.2% × (1 − 0.20)]. But 3% must be put away for next year's inflation, which means if you only withdraw your average return, you can spend 2.8% a year, or $27,900, if you don't want to use up capital. (Note that we are simplifying the inflation adjustment by subtracting the annual inflation rate from the aftertax return.)

If you are willing to reduce your long-term capital to supplement your income and assume a 30-year life, the $27,900 becomes approximately $49,700. (You can obtain this from a loan amortization table or financial calculator.) Another way of stating this is that if you are consuming your capital as well as your return at a rate of $49,700 per year, your $999,000 portfolio will have run dry after 30 years if you earn a long-term aftertax return of 2.8% on your portfolio.

Scenario 2

This is a midrange of Level3 Investing, using mostly passive strategies with a 12% average return. With the same background assumptions of $250,000 put aside, you have invested

100% in equities earning 12% until four years before retirement and then have taken out 5% a year for four years and put it in very safe short-term investments earning 4%. At retirement and after, there will be 80% in the 12% stock strategy and 20% in safe investments (short-term bonds) that earn 4% on average over the long term for a blended return of 10.4% [(0.80 × 12%) + (0.20 × 4%)]. Advisory fees are not a factor for the Level3 investor.

A $250,000 all-equities portfolio would have grown to $1,922,000 invested at 12% over 18 years. Moving a portion of the portfolio to safe investments over the last four years reduces the ending value to $1,855,000. The difference is the lower return generated by the safe investment over the last four years. (This figure will vary depending on when the money was shifted.)

Following the suggested withdrawal strategy of Chapter 5 (moving 5% into safe investments for four years before retirement) with the blended return of 10.4%, if you want to withdraw only anticipated average earnings, you would have 10.4% less 20% in taxes, or 8.3% [10.4% × (1 – 0.20)]. Reducing the aftertax return by 3% for next year's inflation, a 5.3% would provide an income of $98,300 per year without using capital and $124,800 per year if you consume capital and return over the next 30 years.

Scenario 3

This represents the potential results if you are willing to accept more volatility and use 25% margin until you reach retirement. Also, during retirement, it assumes you only use a two-year safe reserve rather than the four years suggested in Chapter 5 and utilized in Scenario 2 (margin will be maintained until two years before retirement, when you start to build the safe reserve). Such an aggressive investor would reach retirement with $2,525,000. Annual income would be $151,500 without using capital and $183,400 using up capital. This is based on a blended rate of 11.2% (90% of portfolio at 12% and 10% of portfolio at 4%). The return would be reduced by 20% for taxes to 9.0%. Putting away 3% for next year's inflation, brings the potential withdrawal to 6.0%. Again, advisory fees are not a factor.

So the three scenarios result in annual retirement incomes of:

	Income Only	**Income & Capital**
Scenario 1	$27,900	$49,700
Scenario 2	$98,300	$124,800
Scenario 3	$151,500	$183,400

These will be very different retirement experiences.

Annual retirement income figures can be calculated using Microsoft Excel functions or a loan amortization schedule calculator (readily available online). The "income and capital" figures in the examples here are calculated using the "payment" function in Excel; it represents the sum of interest and principal in a loan. The "income only" figure is the beginning balance of the loan (in these examples, the beginning balance in the retirement account) multiplied by the per period interest rate.

I certainly don't want to suggest that most investors should pursue Scenario 3, but I do want to point out and emphasize the high cost of reducing volatility.

And what is the worst that could happen to you as a Scenario 3 investor, based on what has happened in the past 50 years, assuming you follow the rules? Expected returns are based on long-term results, so they allow for the two 40+% portfolio drops for all scenarios that are likely to occur.

However, at what point in time the bear growls makes a difference. If the downturn comes when you are withdrawing, that portion never recovers.

Suppose that starting on retirement day your portfolio faced one of those 30-year horrible markets and in each of the following four years the portfolio was below the retirement-day level by an average of:

- 25% the first year,
- 40% the second year,
- 20% the third year, and
- 10% the fourth year.

You had budgeted to withdraw the $151,500 indicated above each year. That means that you took a loss of 25% on the $151,500 withdrawn the first year, or $37,875. The loss was $60,600 the second year (on the planned $151,500 withdrawal), $30,300 the third year and $15,150 the fourth year, for a total of $143,925.

Now, this is money that is gone. When the market goes way up the following year, these funds will not recover like the rest of the portfolio. This means your basic expected portfolio level is now $2,381,075 instead of $2,525,000 and your expected withdrawal will have to be adjusted to:

	Income Only	Income & Capital
Scenario 3A	$142,900	$173,000

That's still a significantly better retirement than the other scenarios, and once again emphasizes that what we usually pay to avoid volatility is far greater than any loss the volatility can generate.

ADDRESSING THE RARE RISKS

For many years, there has been an ongoing conflict, sometimes bitter, over what matters the most when managing investments. On one side are those who believe that the criteria for choosing investment strategies should be the mean return and variance (or standard deviation) model—the best return at a given level of risk, the lowest risk for a given return, or some combination, such as the Sharpe ratio.

Opposing this is the view that what really counts is the terminal wealth—what you have when you sell your investments for consumption. It should be obvious by now that this is my view.

Paul Samuelson (now deceased), a Nobel laureate and renowned economist, was a vociferous supporter of the mean/standard deviation model. An interesting history of the struggle between the mean/standard deviation group and the terminal wealth group that is ongoing can be found in the book "Fortune's Formula" (2005), by William Poundstone.

While I am in the terminal-wealth camp, there is one argument used by Samuelson and others that must be considered. I have continually used the assumption that the market will always come back for the investor. Those in the other camp would say I use the word "always" when I mean "almost always." They are right and even though the "almost" is to me a very rare probability, it is there and should be considered.

What could happen that would prevent the market and our portfolios from coming back? There are two general possibilities. First, something could happen to the market itself or the world it operates in. Any of the things we see in science-fiction movies leading to a dystopia would close the market, but in most of those scenarios nothing would be a safe investment.

Second, and of more concern, is that some unusual event would force us out of the market at the wrong time. Death would be one example: If our heirs had to sell for taxes or other compelling reasons at the market bottom, the market would not come back for the part withdrawn.

Another possibility would be an extended period of unemployment that requires us to sell our equities at a market low. Though rare, this is a real risk and deserves attention. The problem is to assess such a risk and see if changing to a more conservative strategy is justified.

Going to a more conservative strategy has significant cost, and that cost must be compared with the likely loss from such a scenario.

As the analysis we have just gone through shows, going to a more conservative strategy has significant cost, and that cost must be compared with the likely loss from such a scenario. Remember that the loss we are concerned with is only the difference between what we would lose in the safer 60%/40% (Level 2) strategy versus the Level3 approaches.

A SUMMARY OF THE APPROACHES

Figure 6.3 provides a graphical presentation of different strategies and possibilities. It visually summarizes the approaches we have been discussing. More importantly, reflecting on it occasionally can provide reinforcement when we are tempted, usually in bear markets, to depart from the planned strategy.

The risk of the rare but possible drop in the market at the exact time when some circumstance requires us to withdraw funds even with our intended long-term strategy needs to be considered.

As discussed earlier, the worst time for a severe market downturn (50%) and a need to withdraw funds would be right before retirement. We can examine the impact. Assume that Year 24 in Figure 6.3 is just before we start to put some funds in safe investments preparing for retirement: The market drops 50%, and we have the unemployment situation mentioned above.

Say we had to withdraw $200,000 to cover two years of unemployment or had to sell everything for taxes. We would still be better off with a 12% return, even if our portfolio lost 50%, than having been in safe longer-term investments (5% line). And even though the traditional Level 2 investing approach of 60%/40% allocation would only drop 30% when the market dropped 50%, we'd be better off with the 12% return.

With historical returns, this would be true after only 10 years of investing. Once again, the cost of giving up higher return is too high for the value of the risk reduction. Remember, we are looking at an extreme case in this example. With the Level3 strategies discussed earlier in the chapter, there is little chance of a 50% drop in portfolio value and, it is hoped, little chance you would be laid off for an extended period just before retirement. But it could happen.

The short-cut way of calculating how much you can withdraw from your portfolio follows these steps:

1. Select your expected return: 11.2% if 90% in Level3 equities and 10% in the two-year protection plan, 10.4% if following the Level3 four-year protection approach, and 7.2%

FIGURE 6.3

A Comparison of the Approaches

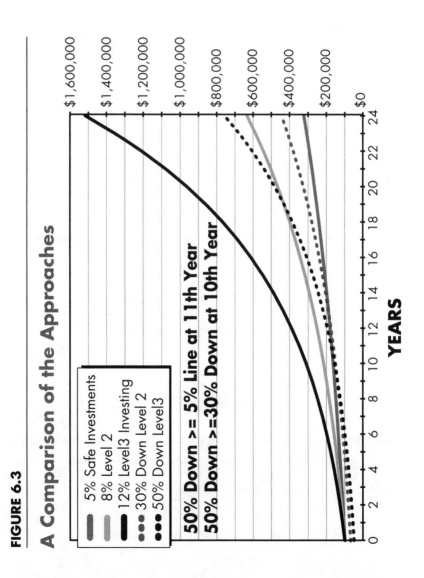

with a traditional (aggressive traditional) retirement portfolio of 40% equities/60% bonds and fees of 0.4%.

2. Reduce by 20% for taxes. This is our estimated blend of
    capital gains, qualified dividends, required or necessary
    distributions from tax-deferred retirement funds across the
    income typical of an AAII member. You can substitute your
    own tax demands for the 20%. In tax-deferred accounts,
    you should keep track of what portion will be yours and
    what portion must go for taxes when you withdraw.

3. Inflation averages 3% a year. You must put aside 3% of
    each year's return to pay for next year's inflation. (We are
    simplifying by subtracting the inflation rate from the ex-
    pected return.)

4. You are left with the return that you can spend without di-
    minishing your portfolio value. In our three examples:

Scenario 3: $11.2\% \times (1 - 0.2) - 3\% = 6.0\%$
Scenario 2: $10.4\% \times (1 - 0.2) - 3\% = 5.3\%$
Scenario 1: $7.2\% \times (1 - 0.2) - 3\% = 2.8\%$

This keeps the basic portfolio value for emergencies, for an unusual market drop, or for passing on to heirs.

If you choose to or need to withdraw as much as you can by
utilizing capital and figure you might live 30 more years, you
can withdraw in our three examples approximately:

Scenario 3:   7.3%   instead of   6.0%
Scenario 2:   6.7%   instead of   5.3%
Scenario 1:   5.0%   instead of   2.8%.

These withdrawal rates are calculated by dividing the Income
& Capital figures on page 217 by the portfolio value at retirement for each scenario.

Remember that the return on equities is way above what it
should be, based on the moderate risk I have shown equities to

have in this and preceding chapters. It is like the economics professor saying the $10 bill on the ground can't be real or someone would have picked it up. You hope that everyone else ignores the free profit that equities offer, but don't pass up that gift yourself.

All of the possibilities for the increased success of the long-term investor are meaningless unless the long-term view is maintained and the strategy discipline is followed. The strategies can be effective, but only if we follow them. And that is not always easy.

In Chapter 7, I look at the barriers challenging our efforts and give some suggestions on how to avoid the multitude of pitfalls.

All of the possibilities for the increased success of the long-term investor are meaningless unless the long-term view is maintained and the strategy discipline is followed.

IMPLEMENTING AND CONTROLLING LONG-TERM INVESTMENT STRATEGIES

"Everyone has a plan until they get punched in the mouth."

—Mike Tyson

The success of the strategies of Level3 Investing discussed in the previous chapters depends on the assumption that you will obey two rules.

- **Rule 1.** You, the investor, must choose a well-defined strategy or strategies that you have the skill and time to implement.

  Certainly as time passes you will become more skillful and time availability may change. So you may adjust the allocation between active and passive approaches based on your current situation.

- **Rule 2.** You stick to the strategy or strategies chosen even through extremely volatile markets. In this rule, you must focus on the overall strategy, which determines the allocation of assets.

RULE 1: CHOOSE A WELL-DEFINED STRATEGY

Following Rule 1 will be less of a problem than following Rule 2, although it is very important. Only you can determine how much time you have available. The only problem should be estimating how much time different active approaches might take.

The Level3 passive approach described in Chapter 6 should

take virtually no time. At the other extreme, a complex screening approach with frequent rebalancing might require a full day every month and a quick review of positions once every week to be sure there is no news requiring action on your part, and you must check brokerage statements for errors.

Some approaches will require action only at fixed time periods such as annually, quarterly or monthly; others can require action at any time when a specific event occurs, such as a stock holding no longer meeting the necessary criteria. To a certain extent, you may be able to adapt your strategy to the time you have available. For example, in the Model Shadow Stock Portfolio, holdings are only adjusted once a quarter. There is no reason an investor couldn't update this portfolio monthly or weekly, but I felt that quarterly was enough and I wanted to make the portfolio easy to maintain (less rebalancing also lowers transaction fees).

You may be able to adapt your strategy to the time you have available.

Deciding whether you have the skill to implement one or more approaches to stock selection—such as the ones in O'Shaughnessy's "What Works on Wall Street" or those in AAII's stock screens—should almost be apparent when you read the description of the approach. If you understand what the terms mean and how the various measures are combined into a screen, you probably have the necessary intellectual skill. In fact, I think anyone who has gotten this far in the book has the basic intellectual skill to implement most of the approaches I have discussed.

However, studies in behavioral economics indicate there may be personality and special conceptual abilities necessary to succeed in implementing and sticking with some of the strategies. (More on this later.)

Having access to the data necessary for a particular approach may also limit the choice of rules to be used. Some databases such as CRSP (Center for Research in Security Prices, Booth

School of Business, University of Chicago) or the Standard & Poor's database are extremely expensive (thousands of dollars per month depending on selections). AAII's *Stock Investor Pro* fundamental stock screening and research database program has over 2,000 data points on around 7,000 stocks (see the Appendix for a complete description). Daily updates are available. There are a number of online databases with less extensive coverage, but one of them may cover all the data you need for some portfolio management rules. [See *Computerized Investing's* "Best of the Web" at www.computerizedinvesting.com for the top stock screening websites.]

While behavioral concerns are likely to be more important when it comes to following Rule 2, they also can have an impact on the implementation of Rule 1. Some of the same behavioral phenomena that appear when implementing strategies could also cause problems when choosing suitable strategies. I point out such possibilities when discussing the behavioral impacts on our investing actions later in the chapter.

RULE 2: STICK TO THE STRATEGY

Once you have decided on an approach, or combination of approaches, as your strategy for managing your portfolio, you must implement it. It is essential that you strictly follow your established decision rules and that you keep records of what you are doing and when. Note that this rule doesn't say that you can't change strategies, but you should know the difference between a complete change of strategy and making exceptions to the rules. There are two areas of action where you will face the greatest temptation to deviate from the straight and narrow:

> *It is essential that you strictly follow your established decision rules and that you keep records of what you are doing and when.*

1. Special situations in the short term that make you think you can add value by tweaking your strategy.

2.   A significant down market that makes you nervous.

You will be tempted on a regular basis to deviate from the approach you have adopted because you see a special situation or have "feelings" about short-term market behavior. A typical situation is one where, according to your rules, you should sell Stock A and buy Stock B. Instead of carrying this out simultaneously, you decide the market looks weak and so you sell Stock A today and wait until the market pulls back to buy Stock B. Alternatively, you think the market looks strong and decide to buy today and wait to sell.

Another version of this mistake can occur when you make an execution error (as everyone does occasionally). Instead of correcting it instantly and taking a small loss, you are tempted to offset the small loss by waiting for the market to go up or down so you can correct the error at a profit or at worst break even.

You would think that even if your insight was wrong, you would have a 50% chance of it working out well. But the stock market gods are mean, and you will lose more often than you gain. Even more likely, you will lose larger amounts than you gain.

What will happen is that 50% of the time you will be right and you will save a quarter of a point. But 50% of the time you will be wrong. And some of the time one of the stocks will run away, you will resist giving in and you will wind up with either a significant loss on the transaction compared to the earlier price, or in some cases the transaction may not fit your rules anymore and you will have to abandon the part of the trade you have already completed—likely at a loss.

The greatest stress will come with significant down markets. The more the market declines and the longer it stays down, the greater the stress. As I explained in earlier chapters, there have only been three collapses that would approach 50% using the portfolio selection rules of Chapter 6 in the last 100 years (1929, 1974, and 2008). This means most investors will be caught in one or two of them during their investing lifetime. You have probably already experienced one, maybe two.

There have been other bear markets, generally defined as down 20% or more. Most of these have been of short (one to two years) duration and were easier to cope with.

The greatest stress will come with significant down markets.

Chapter 4 described how to use the following rules to mitigate severe pullbacks:

- Strategic but limited diversification across individual equity holdings and sectors,

- Time diversification (limited) and

- Equal weighting rather than capitalization weighting of holdings.

These rules will reduce the drop in portfolio value, but the psychological impact will still make it difficult to adhere to the long-term strategy.

The rest of this chapter addresses two topics: the psychological processes that push us to investing behavior that is suboptimal and in many cases disastrous (behavioral economics), and practical ways to help combat the psychological impulses that endanger our investment success.

BEHAVIORAL CHALLENGES TO LEVEL3 INVESTING

A basic assumption of traditional economical models is that human beings are rational. That is, that they will make decisions based on what is best for them. In finance or investing, the assumption underlying decision processes is that the investor wants to maximize returns at a given level of risk or minimize risk at a given level of return.

Behavioral economics/finance is the study of how individuals really make decisions in their economic life or, in our case, their investing life. Research over the past 40 years has brought into question the validity of rationality in economic decision-making.

> *Research over the past 40 years has brought into question the validity of rationality in economic decision-making.*

Psychologists are interested in the entire span of human behavior and economists are interested in economic decision-making. We then have a subset of academics who might come from economics or finance or psychology disciplines who are examining how individuals really make economic/investing decisions and what the factors are that influence them.

While this has only been an organized area of research for less than 40 years, some of the concepts probably go back into prehistory when some wise tribal leader discovered he could change people's food preferences by managing scarcity or suddenly realized that pupil dilation indicated preferences.

While "post-purchase dissonance" is a 20th century term, "buyer's remorse" has likely been understood almost as long as the selling process has existed. The significance of psychological factors on the rational man model started to be noted by John Maynard Keynes and others back in the 1940s, but there was a strong move back to the rational man model in the 1950s. Not until "Judgment Under Uncertainty: Heuristics and Biases" (Daniel Kahneman and Amos Tversky) was published in Science in 1974 did economists begin to accept psychological factors in economic decision-making.

It is important to note that this overlooking of behavioral influences did not exist in all business areas. The field of marketing, even at the academic level, has continually accepted that psychological processes impact economic decisions. That is what advertising and other forms of promotion are all about. In one study, economists were amazed to find that adding the picture of an attractive woman to an ad had more impact that lowering the price of the product for sale. Anyone involved in advertising could have told them that it was extremely likely. Have you noticed how many TV ads now have dogs? It's the latest thing.

Kahneman and Tversky followed up with "Prospect Theory: An Analysis of Decision Under Risk" in Econometrica (1979). This engendered much support in the economic community because of the intensive underlying research. Nevertheless, to this day, many adherents to the rational man model do not accept behavioral factors except as a kind of deviation that should average out.

The purview of behavioral economics is very broad and I am only interested in a limited part of it. However, it is a fascinating area and I would recommend reading "Thinking, Fast and Slow" by Daniel Kahneman (2013). While the book is principally about conscious and unconscious thinking, it reviews much of the work of behavioral economics—particularly the groundbreaking work that Kahneman did with the late Tversky. The examples are entertaining as well as informative, and he has a uniquely pleasant writing style.

The following are a number of behavioral observations based on research that show why effective investing behavior faces some tough hurdles.

Heuristics

All through life we use rules of thumb or past experiences to get estimates of various data. These approaches can be used as first estimates, though in many cases they are used instead of complete analyses. In many cases, particularly under time pressure, we depend completely on our heuristic approach, which gives us flawed estimates.

In many cases, particularly under time pressure, we depend completely on our heuristic approach, which gives us flawed estimates.

In their earlier work, Kahneman and Tversky (1974) concentrated on three heuristic approaches that caused judgment errors in economic decisions: representativeness, availability and anchoring.

Representativeness is an approach where we jump to judgment about something because it resembles something else. For example, our past experience with a certain class of stock such as convertible preferreds might lead us to assume a similar experience with a new stock of that class.

Availability indicates that we estimate the probability of an event based on the ease with which similar events can be brought to mind. An example would be an upcoming stock split where we recall numerous cases of splits that caused the stock price to rise and we assume that that would be the case again.

Anchoring, the third of the prominent heuristics, is based on the observation that when making a numerical judgment people usually start their analysis with a rough estimate and that estimate biases their final decision. The initial estimate might come quickly from their own experience, or it could be induced by outside factors. For example, if I ask you how well your portfolio performed last year, I will get one answer. But if I first say, "compared to the market's x% return," I will get a different answer, and that answer will vary with the value of x%.

Prospect Theory

In their subsequent work (1979), Kahneman and Tversky expanded their research into how probabilities affect decisions. In examining how individuals choose from alternative combinations of probabilities, it was discovered that severe deviations from classical utility theory occurred. Choices could be significantly altered by the way the choices were framed.

> The most important aspect of framing in investing is that losses are more important to the risk-taker than gains.

Probably the most important aspect of

framing in investing is that losses are more important to the risk-taker than gains. Losses hurt us more emotionally than gains make us feel good. Prospect theory shows that investors will accept lower returns to avoid a small probability of a loss than they will to get an equal or even a larger gain that has as great or greater probability of occurring. The most significant outcome of this theory in portfolio management is the behavioral propensity to sell winners and keep losers. And this is not the optimal strategy from an investment or taxation strategy.

Prospect theory explains the observations that:

- Individual mutual fund holders have lower returns than the funds themselves,

- In the trading records of online brokerage accounts of individual investors, stocks sold do better than the new stocks purchased, and

- When mutual funds change positions, the stocks sold do better than those purchased.

Losing on a purchase/sale transaction causes psychological regret, which is more powerful than the positive impact of a gain of equivalent size, and this reinforces the negative feelings when the market and our holdings go down in value.

Other Behavioral Influences

There are numerous other behavioral factors that impede our efforts to effectively follow a strategy, including the herd effect, personality and cognitive characteristics, and physical characteristics.

Herd Effect

While it has been shown that individuals collectively can be very accurate in estimating a wide range of values, this ability disappears if they are in contact with each other. The leaders tend to dominate decisions, and others simply follow. We have all seen examples of experiments where individuals seek to be in compliance even when it requires sensory distortion.

Individuals seek to be in compliance even when it requires sensual distortion.

The most common example is when members of a selected group one after another say that the shorter of two lines is longer, the propensity of the next group member, who is not in on the experiment, is to go along. In many cases of this type of experiment, the actual senses become distorted.

Personality and Cognitive Characteristics

There is evidence that the individual personality traits and cognitive characteristics of investors significantly influence investment behavior. Certain aspects of intelligence influence investment success, and there are personality characteristics, such as compulsive gambling or other addictions, that can lead to disaster.

Kahneman's book "Thinking, Fast and Slow" shows ways that cognitive ability can influence decision-making ability, but it is a certain kind of intelligence that turns out to be important, and the ability is partly related to personality characteristics.

Intelligence or cognition can influence our ability to make effective judgments in the face of behavioral pressures. The Cognitive

Intelligence or cognition can influence our ability to make effective judgments in the face of behavioral pressures.

Reflection Test developed by Shane Frederick (2005), and now discussed in most expositions of behavioral economics, measures a certain kind of cognitive ability that is significantly different from other measures of intelligence. Consider the three problems from the Cognitive Reflection Test box.

COGNITIVE REFLECTION TEST SAMPLE

A bat and a ball cost $1.10 in total. The bat costs $1.00 more than the ball. How much does the ball cost? _____cents.

If it takes 5 machines 5 minutes to make 5 widgets, how long would it take 100 machines to make 100 widgets? _____minutes.

In a lake, there is a patch of lily pads. Every day the patch doubles in size. If it takes 48 days for the patch to cover the entire lake, how long would it take for the patch to cover half the lake? _____days.

I will let you figure out the correct answers, but they are not: $0.10, 100 minutes, or 24 days, respectively. (If you can't figure out the answers, see the footnotes at the end of this chapter.) The important aspect of these problems is that they offer a quick obvious answer that is wrong. In the study, even those answering correctly thought of the wrong answer first.

Answering these problems incorrectly is an indication, not a certainty, that you are overconfident and impatient, neither of which is a desirable trait for implementing investment strategies. If you didn't answer two or three of the problems correctly, you might consider a passive Level3 strategy. However, of those who took the test in the original research, only 17% got them all correct. Even at MIT, less than half had all three correct.

Individuals with significant self-control problems or addictions should choose a passive strategy where the only major decision area will be dealing with market downturns.

Individuals with significant self-control problems or addictions should choose a passive strategy where the only major decision area will be dealing with market downturns.

Overconfidence will lead to bad judgments both in the stock se-lection process and in sticking with the selected strategy rather than believing you can wisely deviate based on your unique ca-pabilities. Impatience will lead you to avoid necessary research and make it easy to accept the unexamined opinions of others.

There is another test by Tim Richardson that has been used to uncover overconfidence and look for practical judgment. I am not including the entire test here since it is available online at **tim-richardson.net/misc/estimation_quiz.html**, but I am includ-ing a sample question to show the intent of the test.

> Give a high and a low estimate so you feel you have a 90% chance of the correct answer being within your estimates.
>
> What is deepest known point in the oceans?
>
> Low: _____ feet
>
> High: _____ feet
>
> Please commit to estimates before checking on your smartphone or the answer in the footnotes at the end of this chapter.

This sample question and answer should give you some idea of what the test measures, but please take the full test and if your score is below the levels described in the end of test comments, consider using a passive strategy—at least to start.

Physical Characteristics

There is some evidence that variations in our DNA can impact our investing ability. Dopamine levels and changes in levels when making decisions may influence the effectiveness of those decisions. The highs reached when compulsive gamblers win are so positive that it makes the risk and losses bearable. Any signs of addictive behavior should be a warning that passive approaches are best. Slot machines are cleverly designed to give reinforcement. The participation, the noises, the whirling wheels with "almost" wins and the occasional wins all make it hard to stop. I thought one of the strongest reinforcements was the noisy falling of the coins, but the machine makers had to find a substitute reinforcement for efficiency now that the machines are all electronic.

Many of the trappings of investing provide similar reinforcement. The ticker, the shouting gurus on TV and the frequency of profits (just not as high as they could be) all reinforce active participation. Perhaps the strongest motivational aspect is that losers (relative to chance) can win.

Distortions

There are all kinds of individual characteristics, personality and cognitive abilities that influence our ability to invest successfully. While the entire area of behavioral economics/finance is interesting and worth examining, the real task in Level3 Investing is making sure that the behavioral impacts do not reduce the effectiveness of our strategies.

> *The real task in Level3 Investing is making sure that the behavioral impacts do not reduce the effectiveness of our strategies.*

An enjoyable way to observe many of the behavioral phenomenon we have discussed, and many others that relate to other aspects of your life, is to watch "Brain Games" on the National Geographic channel (available from Amazon.com). In most cases, they also explain how the behavioral activity is related to the functions of the different parts of the brain. While the content is educational, the presentations are both interesting and fun. Because this is late-night TV with late-night TV ads, I usually record episodes so I can zip through the long commercials.

Now let us think back to technical analysis, particularly chart-ing—what a perfect Rorschach test. There is nothing there except what you imagine there. It's just a bunch of points and figures and bars and candlesticks with no real meaning. It's a great opportunity for your behavioral impulses to see what-ever they want to see and justify whatever course they wish to pursue.

Another behavioral distortion that I find myself guilty of is con-centrating on the big winner. Somehow a $10,000 or $100,000 gain from a position seems much more important than six $2,000 or $20,000 gains. Small gains and moves seem trivial if you have a large portfolio, but they add up if you stop to reflect that all you need to do to be an exceptional investor is to earn 2% more than the market.

Many small gains make that objective a lot easier. It is hard to keep that focus. At social gatherings, I have heard much brag-ging about the 100% racked up from Apple (AAPL) or Google (GOOG) trades. I have never heard anyone brag about the 15% a year they made investing in Ennis Inc. (EBF) or other little-known stocks.

Gaining From Behavioral Missteps

Before discussing ways to overcome behavioral impulses that will divert you from the desired behavior, let's look at the posi-tive side of all the inferior investing behavior.

The poor investing decisions made by individuals and institu-tions alike that lead to the wild fluctuations in equity prices are what provide the opportunity for some of us to obtain substan-tially above-average returns. There is even more opportunity when this is combined with the aversion to loss that leads peo-ple to sacrifice high returns and invest in inferior instruments.

You must avoid the pitfalls discussed in this book and look at the crazy market and the underlying crazy behavior of most in-vestors and think to yourself, "They are trying to contribute to my ultimate wealth, let me be wise enough to accept their contributions." In the next section, I look at ways to stay at Level3 in order to be a receiver of excess returns and avoid becoming part of the Level 1 and 2 contributors.

Tom Howard of AthenaInvest (2014) takes this a step further by developing strategies based on the behavioral mistakes of other investors. His approaches provide another source for active portfolio strategies.

OVERCOMING PSYCHOLOGICAL PRESSURES

The first decision is whether to pursue a passive or active portfolio, or a combination of the two. This is probably the easiest decision, but it is not unimportant. The major problem that might be encountered is that overconfidence might push you to take on a more demanding approach than is suitable. That will lead to taking shortcuts and the breakdown of the strategy.

Overconfidence might push you to take on a more demanding approach than is suitable.

One approach would be to start out with a passive strategy consisting of mutual funds and ETFs. Once that is comfortable, begin with some active strategy if you feel you have the time and interest. I think that for many investors, particularly those who are still working full time, a passive strategy will be the most practical. Mutual funds are even using ETFs for part of their portfolio in the belief that it is harder and harder to select winning individual stocks.

In a passive strategy, choosing which ETFs to use will be the main initial problem. Any decisions about leverage can wait until you are comfortable with your portfolio. The suggestions in Chapter 6 can serve as a beginning.

Whether your strategy is passive or active, you will be faced with the need to overcome behavioral pressures. These pressures become strongest in significantly down markets. When your portfolio value is down, there is increasing pressure to do something. This can lead to either selling out to reduce the negativity or taking a different investing direction in the hope it will do better. Either of these responses can lead to disaster.

We all know from personal experience or from observation that the "waiting to get even" syndrome is also a disaster. Losses are unlimited and gains are limited to zero. However, the aversion to loss is such that even the thought of getting back to even is a positive reinforcement and we forget that we could have gotten back to even by not investing in the first place. We also forget that, if the stock comes roaring back to get us even, it probably continues up after we sell it.

Behavioral pressures become strongest in significantly down markets.

There are a number of practical things we can do to overcome the dangers that our emotions bring to our investment strategy. They must be done before the problems occur, which in itself is also a problem because when everything is going well there is little motivation to take protective action. It is very similar to various problems of health. Why worry about weight, exercise and nutrition if you aren't sick?

The actions I suggest to offset the psychological barriers to success need to be planned before our portfolios start to drop in value. The major barriers to success will arise when we encounter those drops. The deeper the loss of value, the more difficult it will be to avoid tampering.

Most of us still remember 2008 and what we went through in our portfolio management at the time.

Willpower, or Stick-to-It-iveness

Focusing on the proper strategy and sticking to your rules will help at some level. But as any student of human behavior will tell you, when it's your emotional self against your rational self the rational self will only win if the emotional drive is a lot weaker than the rational propensity.

Willpower, steadfastly following the rules, can be effective for overcoming slight impulses but will not be effective against the strong impulses coming from a fear of loss. Emotional drives can distort our view of reality and even our senses. In criminal investigations, it is known that eyewitnesses are unreliable not only for identifying suspects but also for descriptions of what happened.

For an example of how even our senses can be distorted, search online for a video showing the McGurk Effect. I still find this audio/visual misperception mind-boggling. The previously mentioned TV program "Brain Games" also shows examples of how emotions can dominate our behavior.

> *When it's your emotional self against your rational self the rational self will only win if the emotional drive is a lot weaker than the rational propensity.*

Reinforcing Intended Investing Behavior

There are a number of ways you can reinforce the behavior you intend in your selected strategy. Through these techniques, you can either strengthen the appropriate behavior or weaken the impact of psychological forces pushing you to ineffective investment behavior.

My Level3 Worksheet

Your first level of reinforcement should be the spreadsheet with chart available for download at **Level3investing.com**. Figure 7.1 shows a sample chart from the My Level3 Worksheet.

The chart shows the cumulative value of average expected growth of a Level3 portfolio at an annualized return of 11% over 24 years, called the Level3 LRE line (remember that LRE stands for line of reasonable expectations). It also shows where that value could be if the market fell 40% at any point (Worst-Case Level3 LRE Drop line).

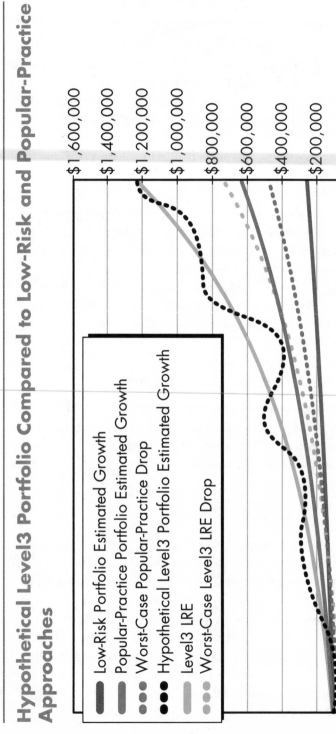

FIGURE 7.1

Hypothetical Level3 Portfolio Compared to Low-Risk and Popular-Practice Approaches

Our estimate of current popular practice, or Level 2 (60% stocks, 40% bonds), at a return of 8% is shown along with the estimated maximum loss envisioned (25%) with this approach (Popular-Practice Portfolio Estimated Growth and Worst-Case Popular- Practice Drop lines).

We also show where a very safe short-term U.S. Treasury portfolio would be (Low-Risk Portfolio Estimated Growth line). All of these are long-term estimates.

The dotted line is just an illustration of how an actual portfolio value might progress. When you download the spreadsheet and enter your portfolio figures, that line will be replaced by the actual progress of your portfolio over the years.

I strongly suggest that you download the spreadsheet at Level3investing.com. It allows you to set up your own estimates and equivalent future plan on a quarterly or yearly basis. The inputs that are needed are shown on the spreadsheet.

From the beginning and through the years, you will be able to view your average expectation, look at what the worst-case scenario might be, and record your actual performance.

The spreadsheet at Level3investing.com allows you to set up your own estimates and equivalent future plan on a quarterly or yearly basis.

This becomes your first level of reinforcement. You should look at the chart in your My Level3 Worksheet regularly and visualize the possibility that no matter where you are you could—and, at least once in your investing experience, probably will—be down to the worst-case LRE drop line.

You should also remind yourself that after eight years, even if you see a 50% overall market drop, you will be ahead of a very safe portfolio as well as a portfolio based on current popular practice.

This regular review of what you are doing and what you want to do will help guide you in bad markets.

Avoid Noise

All around us—and particularly in the financial publications, TV (notably CNBC) and radio programs—there is noise. It is of no particular value when it is opinions because in a few minutes there will be someone appearing with an opposite opinion. Many of these "talking heads" run various funds that are underperforming the market. Watch news items and data, but try to avoid listening to opinions.

> **Watch news items and data, but try to avoid listening to opinions.**

The hidden danger in listening to opinions is that in tough times your emotional inclination will find support in an opinion, even if it is the minority opinion, somewhere on the news.

The financial news is full of buzzwords and ideas that sound good but don't make any sense. The problem is that when you are being tempted to deviate from your long-run strategy, those buzzwords support the wrong action.

One of the key mistakes investors make is to sell winners and keep losers. Why in the world then would anyone want to promote the idea that it is smart to take some winnings off the table? In extreme cases, your strategy might call for some rebalancing, but in general momentum is one of the strongest anomalies.

Think about it: If you sell some shares of your best holding because it went up, what do you do with the money? Maybe you find another stock on your list but, gosh, that went up also. The only difference between the new stock and the one you sold is that you didn't own the new one when it went up. So you look for a stock that went down? That's crazy.

As the saying goes, "bulls make money, bears make money, but pigs get slaughtered." It's another way to get you to sell winners. Originally this expression referred to commodity traders who would get on a trend and keep increasing their position via leverage as it continued going up. That behavior is the same as doubling up continuously until you lose, and it does lead to your slaughter.

That is not the same as staying with winners. We are constantly reminded of how well some investors have done by sticking with a stock for the long term—Berkshire Hathaway (BRK.A), Amazon (AMZN), Google (GOOG), etc. Warren Buffett has not taken anything off the table, and he has not been slaughtered. While there are a few exceptions, the basic rule is: The only reason to sell a stock (unless you are consuming wealth) is if there is something better to buy.

> *The only reason to sell a stock (unless you are consuming wealth) is if there is something better to buy.*

In fact, what you paid for a stock should not be a factor in deciding when to sell. I know that in rare cases your capital gain situation may make you want to modify your decisions, but it should not make you depart from your strategy significantly. A stock does not know what you paid for it and what you paid does not influence the future price.

"You never go broke taking a profit." No. But you don't get rich, either. Imagine Procter & Gamble Co. (PG) with a policy of selling off products as soon as they become popular. They would have some large one-time profits, but over the long term they would shrink and shrink.

Another common phrase is "this time is different." Sure, every move in the stock market is a bit different, but the major trends keep recurring. Past performance may not be an indication of future results for money managers, but I believe it is a good guide for evaluating the market.

"Don't fight the tape." What does that even mean? Should you go along with every short-term trend in the market? It's more gobbledygook.

Keep a Portfolio Focus

Try to avoid contemplating price drops in individual stocks. Always review whether a stock is due to be sold based on your strategy, but avoid second-guessing yourself. It will be hard enough to stay on the straight and narrow when you have port- folio problems, but worrying about individual stocks will really distract you from your strategy.

Avoid contemplating price drops in individual stocks.

Remember that if you have a diversified portfolio, it may be that certain condi- tions that make some stocks go up may make others go down. The loss in one stock may have helped the overall portfolio. Sure, the drop in oil prices hurt one of your stocks, but it helped most of the others.

Keep a Long-Term Perspective

While there are factors that require you to check your portfolio regularly (e.g., splits, dividends, spin-offs), you will find that life is easier if you don't follow the value of your portfolio on a daily or weekly basis. Many pullbacks recover in a few days and you don't need extra strain. It would probably be wise if you only checked your portfolio annually, but I know that is too much to ask. I am not able to do it myself.

Compared to What?

In every area of life, we hear experts tell us some action is good or bad. In investing, we hear that approaches are good or bad, but anything we do is done instead of something else. Look at your results and any criticisms in terms of what the alternatives were.

I call the Low-Risk Portfolio line in Figure 7.1 (safe investment) the "Is this what I should have done, dear?" alternative. When the hypothetical Level3 portfolio hits that bottom shown in the illustration in year 16 you may hear "Dear, why are we in the stock market? I happened to look at our monthly statement and we have lost half our savings!" That is when you take out the chart from your My Level3 Worksheet and point out that you still have considerably more than you would have had if you weren't in stocks.

That may not end the discussion, but it should temper it. Historically, that would probably be a wife nudging and a husband defending, but in contemporary life it could be either way. It may be a good idea if both are involved in investment decisions.

Another way of reducing the emotional impact of portfolio collapses is to think in terms of "how many years of profit did I just give back?" At any low point of your portfolio value, you can look at when you were at that level the last time and see how long ago it was. Giving back

Look at your results and any criticisms in terms of what the alternatives were.

five years of profit is a different animal psychologically than a 50% loss. I discussed "framing" before and here we are doing our own framing to mitigate the aversion to loss.

Oversight & Record-Keeping

The most effective way to ensure we follow our planned strategy is to permit some level of oversight—even the minimal oversight that might occur if in an investing group such as those at AAII Local Chapters (see Appendix). While you can limit the specifics you discuss when talking about your approach, there will be some pressure to adhere to the approach you have espoused, which will help maintain discipline.

The most effective way to ensure we follow our planned strategy is to permit some level of oversight.

We can share what we do with another person, either partly or completely. There will always be a resistance to do this because oversight of our decisions opens the possibility of criticism, which everyone wants to avoid. The most logical person to share with is our mate. There are various levels of joint involvement.

- You can jointly decide on the strategy and share implementation duties. This will almost guarantee the strategy will be followed. Not only will this avoid deviations, unless you conspire to deviate together, but in bad times you can reinforce each other. This is ideal when possible.

- Because of time or interest constraints, such a partnership may not be possible. But some level of involvement by both should be attempted. If the primary investor takes time to explain the approach and the justification for the approach including exposure to risk that, in itself, will create pressure to follow the rules.

Older investors might want to include children in the discussion of strategy for a variety of reasons:

- teaching good investment habits,

- preparing heirs to take over in the case of death or incapacity, and

- providing some oversight, which leads to following the rules.

One final way of overcoming the pressures to deviate or panic is to keep a record of your investing decisions. Of course, there will be the chart in your My Level3 Worksheet that you should maintain and there will be brokerage records. But recording your reasons for actions when it is not obvious will help you maintain discipline. It may also help you improve your strategy. It is important, however, not to nitpick individual stock picks within your strategy. Everything is a probability and some positions will turn out badly by chance alone.

Recording your reasons for actions when it is not obvious will help you maintain discipline.

Because the horse you bet on got boxed in and didn't win as you expected doesn't mean it was a bad bet. Good bets don't always win individually, but cumulatively they do.

As a final consideration, realize that human mental processes, even when specified by brain activity, are not simple. As I have pointed out, it is not really possible to model the price movements of stocks successfully. We are much less likely to ever model the processes of the human mind. While I feel that the breakthroughs of behavioral economics in the last decade are useful and represent progress in understanding investor behavior, they are likely to be dismissed as simplistic down the road, just as was most of modern portfolio theory.

Let me pose a question that I don't know the answer to. Look at Figure 7.2. It represents the portfolio of two investors A and B. They reach retirement day at age 70. Which investor is happiest with his or her investing?

FIGURE 7.2

Two Paths to Retirement

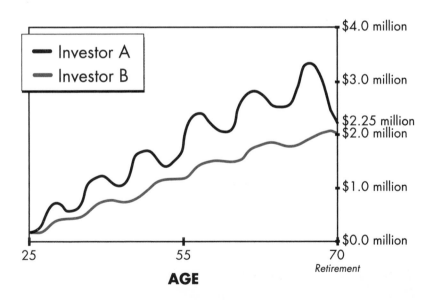

SUMMARY

All of the efforts we put into discovering strategies that will exceed market returns and provide a satisfactory level of risk are wasted if we let psychological pressures deflect us from our intended course. Throughout this book, I have suggested approaches that would have unjustifiable risk if implemented by a short-term investor. You must be committed to the long view, or else you must look to a less-aggressive approach. To be able to stay the course, you must be aware of the psychological pressures you will face and be ready for them.

> *The failure of others to take and be faithful to a long view toward investing is what provides the opportunity for you.*

On the bright side, the failure of others to take and be faithful to a long view toward investing is what provides the opportunity for you. Don't let it slip by.

Footnotes:

Cognitive Reflection Test answers: The ball costs five cents, and the bat costs $1.05. It would take 100 machines five minutes to make 100 widgets. It would take 47 days for the patch to cover half the lake.

Tim Richardson Overconfidence Test answer: Deepest point in oceans is 36,198 feet.

POSTSCRIPT

Thank you for buying and reading this book! I know that many of the ideas I have presented are challenging and contradict much of what you have heard in the past. I want to emphasize once again that these are my own thoughts put together as I contemplate retirement and reflect all that I have been exposed to over the years.

I respect the many views of investing that AAII has covered in the *AAII Journal* and seminars for the past 38 years, and believe that AAII has helped the two million investors who have been members during that time become more organized and analytic investors.

I am not sure exactly how much above the 10% market return you can realize—it's an area that is difficult to measure. But I believe strongly that modern portfolio theory and its many off-shoots have taken risk avoidance to ridiculous levels. And that has more impact on the real risk of not having enough to retire comfortably than all the market volatility. I believe we as long-term investors are being led to pay ridiculously more for risk reduction through lower returns compared to the actual risk we face.

If you take only one thing away from this book, let it be the resolve to examine the worst that could happen over the long term based on market history and use that to help you decide whether investing in lower-return vehicles makes any sense. My belief that many of you will do that has been my motivation for writing this book.

—*James B. Cloonan*

APPENDIX: AAII RESOURCES

AAII Model Shadow Stock Portfolio   253

AAII Stock Screens   261

Stock Investor Pro   263

AAII Local Chapters   265

Related Articles   267

AAII MODEL SHADOW STOCK PORTFOLIO

The Model Shadow Stock Portfolio provides guidance for investing in the micro-cap value sector of the market. The portfolio was initially conceived to show the membership of AAII how to capitalize on the most promising academic research to manage a stock portfolio without having to commit a great deal of time and effort to day-to-day monitoring. In fact, AAII manages this real-money stock portfolio (it is not a hypothetical portfolio) by simply reviewing holdings on a quarterly basis. Figure A.1 shows the actual return of the Model Shadow Stock Portfolio over various time periods.

The Model Shadow Stock Portfolio reflects the following beliefs:

- The best stocks for individual investors are not the same stocks that are best for institutions.

- Over the long run, research indicates that value stocks outpace the market, as do small (and micro-cap) stocks.

- Excessive trading of small-cap stocks hurts your bottom line; you can achieve solid returns by simply adjusting your portfolio quarterly.

- Success comes more from concern for the overall portfolio

than for individual stocks.

Model Shadow Stock Portfolio Performance

	Annual Return (%)				Annual
Portfolio	1-Year	3-Year	10-Year	Since Incep	Std Dev (%)
Model Shadow Stock Portfolio	(15.2)	8.8	11.1	15.4	18.9
Vanguard 500 Index (VFINX)	1.3	15.0	7.2	8.9	10.5
Vanguard Small Cap Index (NAESX)	(3.8)	12.4	7.8	9.7	12.5

Data as of 12/31/2015. Inception date 1/1/1993.
Source: AAII

A Do-It-Yourself Model

To pick the right stocks for AAII's Model Shadow Stock Portfolio, we focus primarily on portfolio formation and risk reduction. The stocks in the AAII Model Shadow Stock Portfolio may look volatile when evaluated separately. But when taken together as a portfolio, most of that individual stock volatility has been diversified away. The central point of the Model Shadow Stock Portfolio is that the risk of any individual stock is not important if your portfolio is well diversified. What is important is how the addition of that stock affects the risk of your overall portfolio. If you are not following the full portfolio but instead use the list of stocks as a tool to generate investment ideas, it is suggested that you adhere to the overall strategy by selecting and monitoring a portfolio that consists of at least 10 stocks. Choosing stocks in different sectors will provide added diversification and protect your portfolio from some sector volatility. Furthermore, be sure to consider fees when making your investments. While there is no recommended minimum, investments should be large enough so that fees are insignificant.

While the Model Shadow Stock Portfolio reduces long-term risk, it is still prudent to take into account your personal risk tolerance. Investors are rightly worried about the amount they invest in a micro-cap strategy. The worst time to sell a stock is at the bottom, so be sure not to put so much weight into your micro-cap portfolio that you cannot stomach the losses. Keep in mind that due to the nature of the Model Shadow Stock Portfolio, it will offer very little income in the form of dividends. As in all Level3 Investing approaches, higher returns are the most effective defense against real risk.

Two Ways to Build Your Own Shadow Stock Portfolio

Follow the guidance provided here and issued in the AAII Model Portfolios columns in the January, April, July and October *AAII Journals*—remember, this portfolio was designed to require only simple modifications on a quarterly basis when company fundamentals change.

~ OR ~

Utilize the resources offered at **www.aaii.com/stockportfolio** where monthly updates are provided on the "Passing Companies." The Passing Companies list shows the companies that meet the criteria for the Shadow Stock screen on the "data as of" date. This list is not to be confused with the Actual Portfolio list, which shows the companies that AAII currently holds in the Model Shadow Stock Portfolio. This screen is run monthly, so please check the website for the most current list of stocks.

Ongoing Management of Your Stock Portfolio

AAII's Model Shadow Stock Portfolio is not intended to be an advisory service in the usual sense of that term—it is not intended to be a list of individual stock recommendations. Instead, the model portfolio serves to show you how to use a value-oriented approach to select micro-cap stocks in an effort to build your own Shadow Stock Portfolio. Profitable micro-cap investing requires extra care. The portfolio construction and monitoring rules were developed over the years to minimize real-world costs and maximize profits.

The *AAII Journal* provides quarterly commentary on the Model Shadow Stock Portfolio (it has been running for 23 years) and suggestions on how you can vary the approach to build a portfolio suitable for your own specific needs. The detailed rules for building and managing a Shadow Stock Portfolio, as well as a monthly list of stocks that meet the criteria for inclusion, can be found at **www.aaii.com/stockportfolio**.

Ongoing performance of AAII's Model Shadow Stock Portfolio is tracked online, but keep in mind that a portfolio can be built by simply following the investment moves outlined in the AAII Model Shadow Stock Portfolio columns found quarterly in the *AAII Journal*.

Stock Portfolio Management Criteria

A quarterly review of the following purchase, sale and management criteria is all that is needed to build your own Shadow Stock Portfolio. Simply review your holdings on a quarterly basis to see if any fundamental changes make them candidates for sale (see sell rules below). If you have new investment funds available or cash from sales, you can look at the list of Passing Companies (**www.aaii.com/stockportfolio**) to see if any companies meet your needs for inclusion in your Shadow Stock Portfolio.

Stock purchases must meet these criteria:

- Price-to-book-value ratio must be less than or equal to 1.00. If the price-to-book-value ratio moved up a bit since the stock was included in the portfolio, it is OK to purchase the stock unless this ratio goes above 1.00.*

- Market capitalization must be between $30 million and $300 million.*

- Price-to-sales ratio must be less than 1.2.*

- The firm's last quarter and last 12 months' earnings from continuing operations must be positive.

- The share price must be greater than $4.

- No bulletin board or pink sheet stocks will be purchased.

- No financial stocks or limited partnerships will be purchased.

- No foreign stocks will be purchased because of different accounting and/or withholding tax on dividends. Foreign stocks traded primarily on U.S. exchanges are OK with one exception: The stock of any company whose primary business is in China will not be purchased.

- Any stock that was sold within two years will not be rebought.

- Note second item under stock order guidance (below) concerning spreads when buying shares.

- Eliminate any company that failed to file a 10-Q (quarterly) report in the last six months.

These figures will change gradually as market values change. Any changes will be noted in the AAII Journal and online.

Stocks are sold if any of the following occur:

- The stock reports a string of negative earnings: If last 12 months' earnings from continuing operations are negative, the stock is put on probation; if a subsequent quarter has negative earnings prior to 12-month earnings from continuing operations becoming positive, the stock is sold.

- The stock's price increases so that it is no longer

considered a small/micro-cap value stock:

- The stock's price-to-book-value ratio goes above three times the initial criterion.

- Market capitalization goes above three times the initial maximum criterion.

In summary, stocks are sold when the market recognizes the value of one of our holdings, thus driving up the price so that it no longer remains in the "shadows" of Wall Street.

Stock order guidance

- These rules are for general guidance. Your own experience, market conditions and size of position will impact decisions.

- Market orders are not used. Instead, if the quoted bid/ask spread is less than 2% (ask price minus bid price, divided by ask price), place a limit order at the ask price for a buy and at the bid price for a sell. If the bid/ask spread is more than 2%, try to place a limit order between the bid and ask prices to keep transaction costs low. If necessary, build a position gradually. With low commissions, it is often better to place partial orders than to try to establish a large position all at once. Be patient.

- The average daily dollar volume should be at least 10 times the amount needed for your position. This will ensure liquidity to get in and out of the position, even if you need to grow the position gradually and sell gradually. This will result in a varying number of qualifying stocks for each investor.

- If price changes cause a stock to become ineligible (due to changes in the price-to-book-value ratio or market capitalization) when only part of the order has been filled, shares already purchased are kept but the balance of the order is canceled.

Management rules

- Equal dollar amounts are invested in each stock initially.

- Decisions are made only at the end of each quarter. In order to react to the majority of earnings reports as soon as possible, quarterly reviews are made in February, May, August and November.

- Best judgment is used for tenders or mergers, but all criteria must be obeyed.

- At the end of a quarter, if receipts from stocks sold exceed requirements for new purchases, the excess receipts—up to 5% of the portfolio's value—are kept in cash until the next quarter. If the excess receipts are greater than 5% of the total portfolio value, the amount above 5% is distributed to smaller holdings that still qualify as buys. Efficient quantities are purchased: If over 10% of the portfolio is in cash, the price-to-book-value ratio can be moved up, but never over 0.90.

- At the end of a quarter, if receipts from stock sales are insufficient to buy all newly qualifying stocks, purchases are made in order of lowest bid/ask spreads.

- Note that if you are managing your own portfolio, it should consist of at least 10 stocks. If you are developing the portfolio gradually you can do it stock by stock, but don't put more than 10% of your funds in each additional stock. More than 20 stocks are not needed until the portfolio exceeds $1 million.

Getting Started: AAII Model Shadow Stock Portfolio

AAII communicates information about the Shadow Stock Portfolio to membership via both print and online methods. Ongoing print coverage is provided through James Cloonan's AAII Model Portfolios column in the *AAII Journal*. Performance information and commentary are always posted and kept up-to-date at www.aaii.com/stockportfolio.

AAII STOCK SCREENS

AAII has been developing, testing and refining a wide range of screening strategies over the years. Many of the screens follow the approaches of popular investment professionals, while others are tied to basic principles of investing. These approaches run the full spectrum, from those that are value-based to those that focus primarily on growth, while most fall somewhere in the middle.

Screens following the approach of an investment professional do not represent their actual stock picks. The rules of each screen are defined by our interpretations of their respective investment approaches. The results of the screening strategies, as well as the criteria for each screen, are programmed into the *Stock Investor Pro* program and are also posted in the Stock Screens area of AAII.com (free access for AAII members).

Each month over 60 separate screens are performed using AAII's *Stock Investor Pro* and the current companies passing each individual screen are reported. *Stock Investor Pro* subscribers can run the screens themselves on a daily basis, while AAII members can access the screening results by going to the Stock Screens area of AAII.com (**www.aaii.com/stock-screens**). The results are posted to AAII.com on the 15th of each month (excluding holidays and weekends) using data from the previous month's end. The AAII Stock Screens Update email will notify you when the strategies have been updated on AAII.com and provide a more in-depth look at a featured screen each month. AAII members can sign up for this complimentary newsletter at **www.aaii.com/email/signup**.

The performance of the stocks passing each screen is tracked on a monthly basis. The month-to-month closing price is used to calculate the return, with equal investments in each stock at the beginning of each month assumed. The impact of factors such as commissions, bid/ask spreads, cash dividends, time slippage (the time between the initial decision to buy a stock and the actual purchase) and taxes is not considered. This overstates the reported performance, but all approaches are subject to the same conditions and procedures. Higher turnover portfolios typically benefit more from these simplified rules.

Sell rules are the same as the buy rules: The hypothetical portfolios are completely reallocated using each subsequent month's data. Thus, a stock is sold (no longer included in the portfolio) if it ceases to meet the initial criteria, and new stocks are added if they qualify.

Stocks that no longer qualify are dropped even if the strategist behind a particular approach suggests different sell rules versus buy rules. This may shorten the holding period and increase the turnover relative to what the strategist would suggest for an actual portfolio.

See the January *AAII Journal* each year for a review of the AAII Stock Screens performance, including best and worst screens of the past year and best and worst screens over the long term.

AAII Stock Screens: **www.aaii.com/stock-screens**

STOCK INVESTOR PRO

Stock Investor Pro is a Windows-based fundamental stock screening a research database that is offered by AAII as a subscription product. Timely data is combined with in-depth data (over 2,000 data fields per company) to help you keep abreast of the market.

Stock Investor Pro allows you to easily conduct company-specific research, build customized stock filters or quickly tap into the program's more than 60 powerful stock screens. The program contains how-to articles, online tutorials and valuable data from Thomson Reuters. You can learn successful stock-picking methodologies and also see the winning companies that pass each screen.

Screening

More than 60 screens are preprogrammed into *Stock Investor Pro* that cover most of the approaches tracked as AAII Stock Screens. Many of the preprogrammed screens follow the approaches of popular investment professionals, while others are tied to basic principles of investing. These approaches run the full spectrum, from those that are value-based to those that focus primarily on growth, while most fall somewhere in the middle.

Preprogrammed screens can be run and the results saved as a portfolio for further review. Screen criteria can also be modified to your specifications and saved.

The program allows you to create and save your own screens, run crosstab reports, and combine screens. Several statistical summaries and reports can be generated.

Database

Data with *Stock Investor Pro* includes:

- Database of around 7,000 NYSE, Amex, NASDAQ, and

OTC stocks

- Consensus earnings estimates

- Eight quarters and seven years of cash flow statements, income statements and balance sheets

- Relative price strength for 4, 13, 26 and 52 weeks

- Percentile rankings, ratios, multiples and growth rates

- Ten full years of monthly price data

- Over 2,000 data fields per company

New information is continuously updated, such as recent insider buy and sell decisions and operating & investing cash flows, plus research & development expenses and discontinued operations and extraordinary items from the income statement.

How to Subscribe

To order, go to www.aaii.com/store/sipro or call AAII Member Services at 1-800-428-2244.

AAII LOCAL CHAPTERS

AAII local chapters are grassroots organizations led by volunteer AAII members. They allow AAII to extend its mission "person to person" to individual investors in their own communities by programming meetings that provide unbiased investment education in a social context. In over 40 locations around the country, AAII members gather to hear from some of the most renowned experts in the field of investing. Local chapter meetings also give AAII members the chance to interact with other members to discuss investment trends and share opinions.

For a list of chapters, go to **www.aaii.com/chapters**.

AAII members can sign up to receive meeting announcements from a nearby local chapter at **www.aaii.com/chapter/signup**.

RELATED ARTICLES

Go to Level3investing.com for links to these articles from the AAII archives.

AAII Model Shadow Stock Portfolio:

AAII Model Portfolios Commentary, by James B Cloonan, *AAII Journal.*

AAII Sentiment Survey as Indicator:

"Analyzing the AAII Sentiment Survey Without Hindsight," by Charles Rotblut, CFA, *AAII Journal*, June 2014.

Advisory Services:

Investment Newsletters columns, by Mark Hulbert, *AAII Journal.*

Robo-Advisers section, *Computerized Investing*, www.computerizedinvesting.com.

"What Exactly Do Online Investment Advisory Services Offer?" by Jaclyn McClellan, *AAII Journal*, January 2015.

Asset Pricing Models:

"Is Outperforming the Market Alpha or Beta?" by Larry E. Swedroe and Andrew L. Berkin, *AAII Journal*, July 2015.

Anomalies:

"Momentum's Role as a Driver of Stock Prices," by Charles Rotblut, CFA, *AAII Journal*, May 2016.

Behavioral Finance:

"Driving Emotions From Your Investment Process: A 12-Step Program," by C. Thomas Howard, *AAII Journal*, September 2014.

Higher-Return Strategies:

"Finding Value and Financial Strength Based on 'What Works

on Wall Street,'" by John Bajkowski, *AAII Journal*, March 2014.

"Investment Wisdom From Wall Street's Legends," by Frederik Vanhaverbeke, *AAII Journal*, November 2014.

"The Magic Formula Approach to Stockpicking," by John Bajkowski, *Computerized Investing*, January 2006.

"Why a New Allocation Approach Is Needed," an interview with James B. Cloonan, *AAII Journal,* June 2016.

Index Investing:

"Achieving Greater Long-Term Wealth Through Index Funds," and interview with John C. Bogle by Charles Rotblut. *AAII Journal*, June 2014.

Options Strategy:

"Assembling a Covered Call Portfolio on Dividend-Paying Stocks," by Ben Branch, *AAII Journal*, June 2014.

Retirement Strategies:

"A Pseudo-Life Annuity: Guaranteed Annual Income for 35 Years," by Robert Muksian, *AAII Journal,* June 2012.

"The Sequence in Which Returns Occur Affects Your Wealth," by Charles Rotblut, CFA, *AAII Journal,* May 2015.

Stock Screening

"AAII Stock Screens 2015 Review: Small-Cap Wins During a Large-Cap Year," by Wayne A. Thorp, CFA *AAII Journal*, January 2016.

"Best of the Web: Stock Screening." *Computerized Investing*, December 2015.

"Constructing Winning Stock Screens, by John Bajkowski, *AAII Journal*, December 2012.

LEVEL3 INVESTING WEBSITE

Go to Level3investing.com for more information, links and tools related to this book.

More on the Level3 Approaches

- The Hulbert Financial Digest's list of stock advisory letters that outperformed the S&P 500 by 3% or more for at least 15 years
- Best approaches from "What Works on Wall Street" by James O'Shaughnessy
- Details on the Model Shadow Stock Portfolio

My Level3 Worksheet

- A downloadable spreadsheet with a chart that readers can use to follow their own Level3 portfolio
- Full explanation on how to use the spreadsheet

Links to Sources

- Research papers and articles
- Websites
- AAII resources

Enhancements and Updates to Book Content

- Downloadable full-size versions of Figures and Tables
- New ETFs recommended by James Cloonan
- New research
- Errata to book

GLOSSARY

401(k) plan

A defined-contribution retirement plan that allows an employee to contribute pretax dollars to a company pool that is invested in stocks, bonds or money market instruments. Named after the section of the Internal Revenue Code that created it.

529 educational savings plan

A tuition program that allows you to build up savings to pay for qualified higher education at eligible institutions using tax-free dollars. Named after a section of the tax code and offered through states.

alpha

A coefficient measuring risk-adjusted performance, considering the risk due to the specific security rather than the overall market. A large alpha indicates that the stock or mutual fund has performed better than would be predicted given its beta (market volatility).

annuity

A series of fixed-amount payments paid at regular intervals over the contract period of the annuity.

anomaly

Returns higher than explainable by the efficient market hypothesis.

arbitrage

A type of trading that tries to capitalize on market inefficiencies and helps keep prices close to their fair value. In general, involves buying and selling a security simultaneously, or taking long and short positions in similar securities, to try to profit from price differences. Risk arbitrage involves potential mergers and acquisitions and is a strategy often used by hedge funds.

arithmetic mean

The sum of a series of numbers divided by their number.

artificial neural networks (ANN)

Computer models made up of groups of interconnected nodes used to estimate functions involving a large number of inputs. ANN systems solve problems through simulation based on the structure of the brain.

ArXiv

A clearinghouse for research papers in physics.

ask price

The price a seller is willing to accept for the security; also called the offer price.

asset

A resource that has economic value to its owner. Examples of assets are cash, accounts receivable, inventory, real estate and securities.

asset allocation

Dividing your investment portfolio among the major asset categories such as stocks, bonds and cash.

bear market

Market decline of 20% or more.

beta

A measure of a stock's risk relative to the market, usually the

S&P 500 index. The market's beta is always 1.0; a beta higher than 1.0 indicates that, on average, when the market rises the stock will rise to a greater extent, and when the market falls the stock will fall to a greater extent. A beta lower than 1.0 indicates that, on average, the stock will move to a lesser extent than the market. The higher the beta, the greater the risk (volatility).

bid/ask spread

See spread.

bid price

The price a buyer is willing to pay for a security.

Black Scholes (B/S) model

A financial model for calculating the fair price of a stock option.

bond

A security that obligates the issuer to repay the principal amount upon maturity and to make specified interest payments over specified time intervals to the bond holder. The issuer can be a corporation or a governmental entity. A bond is a debt obligation; the bondholder is a lender to the issuer and there is no ownership position.

bond call

Early redemption of a bond by the issuer. A callable bond is a bond with an embedded call option. If a bond is called, the issuer has exercised its option to redeem a bond prior to maturity.

book value

Total stockholder's equity minus preferred stock and redeemable preferred stock. Also known as common stock equity. Tangible book value subtracts goodwill and intangible assets from book value.

book value per share

The accounting value of a share of common stock. It is determined by dividing the net worth of the company (common stock plus retained earnings) by the number of shares outstanding.

broker-dealer

A firm that places trades of securities between parties and makes markets in securities. Commonly called stockbrokers, brokers or registered representatives. Must be registered with the Securities and Exchange Commission (SEC) and pass various exams that relate primarily to state and federal law and regulations.

bull market

Market rise of 20% or more.

buy-and-hold approach

A strategy in which the stock portion of your portfolio is fully invested in the market at all times.

call option

The right to purchase stock at a specified (exercise) price within a specified time period.

CalPERS

California Public Employees Retirement System. Agency that manages the pension and health benefits of California public employees. Manages the largest public pension fund in the U.S.

capital asset pricing model (CAPM)

A model for defining risk and how it drives expected returns used in the pricing of securities. The CAPM equation estimates a required return on equity for a particular company based on its systematic risk (beta), the risk-free rate and an equity risk premium (the premium that investors require for investing in equities).

capital gain

An increase in the value of a capital asset such as common stock. If the asset is sold, the gain is a "realized" capital gain. A capital gain may be short term (one year or less) or long term (more than one year.)

capitalization

See market capitalization.

capitalization-weighted

Weighting the holdings of a fund or index based on market capitalizations (larger companies take a larger position in the portfolio). Also called market-cap weighted.

cash flow per share

Earnings after taxes plus depreciation and amortization, on a per share basis. A measure of a firm's financial strength.

cash and equivalents

The most liquid of a firm's assets and carefully watched by equity and credit analysts. A company's cash component includes marketable securities and other cash-equivalent interest-bearing accounts.

CBOE Volatility Index (VIX)

A market index that gives an indication of the market's expectation of volatility over the next 30 days. Based on prices of short-term puts and calls on the S&P 500 index (approximately the one-year standard deviation). Called the "fear index" since it gauges perceived market risk going forward.

certificate of deposit (CD)

Savings certificate that entitles the holder to the receipt of interest. CDs are issued by commercial banks and savings and loans (or other thrift institutions).

chartered financial analyst (CFA)

A professional designation conferred by the CFA Institute on investment professionals who demonstrate professional, educational and ethical excellence by passing three levels of exams covering accounting, economics, ethics, money management and security analysis.

chartered market technician (CMT)

Professional designation given to individuals who demonstrate proficiency in technical analysis by passing a series of tests administered by the Market Technicians Association (MTA).

churning

Excessive trading in a customer account by a broker, usually in order to generate commissions. Churning violates SEC rules and securities laws.

closed-end fund

A pooled investment fund that has a fixed capitalization after the initial issue. Fund shares are traded on an exchange. As the stock price fluctuates with the market, the fund can trade at a discount or premium to its net asset value. (See mutual fund for definition of open-end fund.)

commission

Broker's fee for buying or selling securities.

common stock

A security issued by a corporation that represents ownership.

compounding

The ability of an asset to generate earnings that are then reinvested and generate their own earnings (earnings on earnings).

conversion

A hedge fund strategy that attempts to profit from pricing errors between a firm's convertible bonds and its stock by purchasing the convertible security and taking a short position in the same company's common stock.

correlation

The relationship between two assets. Correlation coefficients are used to measure how closely a pair of asset classes tends to move in relation to each other. A perfect positive correlation of 1.0 indicates identical fluctuations: both classes tend to move up and down at the same time by similar amounts. The lower the correlation, the better the diversification; –1.0 means perfect negative correlation.

cost basis

Purchase price of a security adjusted for stock splits, dividend and return of capital distributionsused to calculate capital gain for tax purposes.

covered call

Selling the right to buy a stock (call option) that you own at a predetermined price within a specified period of time. With a covered call strategy, the investor holds a long position in (buys) an asset and writes (sells) call options on that same asset to try to increase their income from the asset.

credit rating

Evaluation of credit risk issued to debt obligations to indicate probability that debt will not be repaid on time in full. Best-known agencies that specialize in evaluating credit quality are Moody's, Standard & Poor's (S&P) and Fitch.

debt-to-equity ratio

Long-term debt divided by stockholder's equity. The ratio identifies the relationship of debt to ownership interest in the firm's financial structure. A measure of financial risk.

defined-benefit plan (DB plan)

Pension plan that pays a specified amount to employees who retire after a set number of years of service. Plans do not pay taxes on investments; usually all contributions are made by the employer.

defined-contribution plan (DC plan)

A type of retirement plan where the ultimate benefits that are paid out depend on the level of contributions made to the plan and the investment performance of those contributions.

discount broker

A stockbroker who charges a reduced commission and provides no investment advice.

diversification

The process of accumulating securities in different investments, types of industries, risk categories and companies in order to reduce the potential harm of loss from any one investment.

dividend discount model

A method of stock valuation that discounts projected dividends back to their present value. The model generates an estimated value of a stock, assuming that dividends are paid into infinity and are not cut. The basic formula is stock price = $D_1 \div (k - g)$, where: D_1 is the dividend for the coming year, k is the required rate of return; g is the long term growth rate of dividends.

dividend payout ratio

Annual indicated dividend per share (most recent quarterly dividend multiplied by four) divided by annual earnings per share. A ratio of 100% means that the company is paying all of its earnings out to shareholders via dividends.

dividend yield

Annual indicated dividend per share (most recent quarterly

dividend multiplied by four) divided by price per share. An indication of the income generated by a share of stock. Dividend yield plus capital gains percentage equals total return.

Dodd-Frank Wall Street Reform and Consumer Protection Act

Law passed in 2010 that mandated rigorous standards and oversight of the financial system in order to improve accountability and transparency in the wake of the Great Recession.

dollar cost averaging

A system of putting equal amounts of money in an investment at regular time intervals to lessen the risk of investing a large amount of money at a particularly inopportune time.

Dow Jones industrial average (DJIA)

Price-weighted average of 30 actively traded blue-chip stocks, traditionally of industrial companies.

earnings surprise

The percentage by which announced earnings exceeded or fell short of the median analysts' estimate for the latest fiscal quarter. Positive earnings surprises tend to have a positive impact on stock price.

EBITDA

Earnings before interest, taxes, depreciation and amortization.

efficient market hypothesis (EMH)

An investment theory based on the belief that asset prices reflect all information about the asset, and therefore it is not possible to make an abnormal profit trading on information. The EMH asserts that stocks always trade at fair value, making it impossible for investors to either purchase undervalued stocks or sell overvalued stocks. Therefore, an investor can't outperform the overall market through fundamental or technical analysis; the only way to obtain higher returns is to purchase riskier investments. The EMH is a cornerstone of modern portfolio theory, but is heavily debated by academics and investment professionals alike.

enterprise value (EV)

A measure of a company's total value. Enterprise value is often calculated as the sum of market capitalization (historical), short-term debt, long-term debt, minority interest and preferred equity less cash. Enterprise value is sometimes referred to as a company's theoretical takeover price. In the event of a buyout, an acquirer would have to take on the company's debt, but would pocket its cash.

equal-weighted

A portfolio or index with all securities are held in the same proportion, irrespective of market capitalization. Equal-weighted indexes require rebalancing to maintain an equal-weighted position in each holding.

equity

Another word for stock, or similar securities representing an ownership interest.

equity premium puzzle

The observation of stocks realizing higher long-term returns than they should based on their riskiness compared to other investments.

excess returns

Returns in excess of the risk-free rate or in excess of a market measure such as the S&P 500 index.

exchange-traded fund (ETFs)

Open-ended funds that trade on an exchange. Unlike mutual funds, share prices of ETFs change in real time, and ETFs can be bought and sold during market hours, just like stocks. Most ETFs track indexes.

expected return

The average of a probability distribution of possible returns.

fear index

See CBOE Volatility Index (VIX).

financial planner

An investment professional generalist who helps individuals delineate financial plans with specific objectives and helps coordinate various financial concerns. A "fee-only" financial planner does not take commissions but charges a set fee, usually a percent of assets managed.

fiduciary obligation

An obligation that a financial professional must put the interests of the individual client ahead of firm or personal interests.

FINRA

Financial Industry Regulatory Authority. A self-regulatory organization (SRO) that regulates member brokerage firms and exchange markets. FINRA is a non-governmental organization; it is a not-for-profit organization authorized by Congress to protect investors by ensuring that the securities industry operates fairly and honestly.

fixed-income security

An investment vehicle that provides a return in the form of fixed periodic payments and return of principal; examples are bonds and certificates of deposit.

float

The number of freely tradable shares in the hands of the public. Computed by subtracting shares held by insiders from total shares outstanding.

framing

The tendency of individuals to respond to and interpret information depending on how it is presented.

front running

The unethical, and potentially illegal, practice of a broker buying and selling an asset ahead of clients. This includes trading based on non-public information that has yet to be released, but will likely result in client orders to trade once the information is made public.

full-service broker

A broker that provides a large variety of services to its clients, including research and advice, retirement planning, tax management and more. Full-service brokers charge more than discount brokers.

fundamental analysis

The valuation of stocks based on fundamental factors, such as company earnings, growth prospects and so forth, to determine a company's underlying worth and potential for growth.

fundamental indexing

An indexing approach that varies the weights of holdings based on fundamental measures. Commonly used factors include sales, earnings, book value, cash flow and dividends.

future value

Future value formula is present value $\times (1 + r)^n$.

GARP

A stock selection methodology that stands for growth at a reasonable price.

Gaussian distribution

See normal distribution.

geometric mean

An average based on the *n*th root of a set of numbers. An annualized return calculation that compensates for the volatility of the individual returns. The calculation is often used to determine performance results of an investment or portfolio. See example in box.

GEOMETRIC MEAN FORMULA AND EXAMPLE

Geometric mean = $[(1+r)(1+r)(1+r)(1+r)(1+r)(1+r)^{1/n}]-1$

Where,

r = return, and

n = number of compounding periods

Example:

= $[((1.12)(1.16)(1.08)(1.04)(1.11)(1.09))^{1/10}]-1$

= 10%

Alternative Formula

Geometric mean = $[(\text{Ending Value/Beginning Value})^{1/n}]-1$

Example:

= $[(\$1,766/\$1000)^{1/6}]-1$

= 10%

---

ghost risk

In this book, used as the phantom risk of short-term volatility for the long-term investor.

Great Recession

Recession that began in December 2007 in the U.S. with the bursting of the housing bubble and ended in June 2009 and became a global recession.

gross-profit-to-assets ratio

Revenue minus cost of goods sold divided by total assets.

hedge fund

A private investment limited partnership that invests a pool of money often, but not always, using alternative investments and strategies. Hedge funds are open to a limited number of accredited investors and require a large initial minimum investment and charge high fees.

herd effect

The tendency to follow the crowd. The term is often used in financial behavioral analysis and has shown that investors often follow the crowd as opposed to making sound, logical investment decisions on their own.

heuristics

Problem-solving that uses self-educating techniques to improve performance. Heuristics are often regarded as "mental shortcuts" that ease the cognitive load of decision making.

index

A statistical measure of the changes in a portfolio representing a market. The S&P's 500 is the most well-known index, which measures the overall change in the value of the 500 stocks of the largest firms in the U.S.

individual retirement account (IRA)

Personal retirement account that an employed person can set up with a deposit that is tax-deductible up to a set maximum per year. Such deposits qualify as a deduction against income earned in that year. Capital gains, dividends and interest accumulate tax-deferred until the funds are withdrawn at age 59½ or later. Early withdrawals are subject to a penalty. (See also Roth IRA.)

initial public offering (IPO)

The process of bringing private companies to the public market for the first time.

institutional advisers

Institutional advisers provide advice and guidance to institutional investors (pension funds, mutual funds, money managers, insurance companies, investment banks, commercial trusts, endowment funds, hedge funds, etc.) as opposed to individual investors.

investment adviser

A person who manages assets and makes portfolio composition and individual security selection decisions for a fee, usually a percentage of assets invested. The term "investment adviser" is often referencing advisers who assist individual investors.

Japanese candlesticks

A technical chart that plots a stock's open, high, low and closing prices as a series of candle-like figures.

kurtosis

A measure of how peaked a distribution is beyond that of a normal curve. Also called peakedness.

leptokurtic distribution

A statistical distribution where values are clustered around the mean. A distribution with high kurtosis—that is, a high peak (many observations close to the mean, more so than a normal distribution) and fat tails (more extreme values than a normal distribution).

Level 1 investing

In this book, a label for unorganized investing driven by impulse and emotion. It is influenced by random observations and advice and is in a constant state of flux.

Level 2 investing

In this book, a label for the currently accepted "best practice" investing that is a combination of modern portfolio theory and fundamental analysis. Various measures of risk and return are modeled to seek optimal outcomes. Approach used by most investment advisers.

Level3 Investing

In this book, a new approach proposed as a substitute for current investing practice. Strategies for the long-term investor based on deriving reality-based risk and return directly from actual historical data and common sense.

leverage

Leverage is the use of debt financing. Investors employ leveraged strategies in hopes of increasing returns without adding additional equity to their investment. Borrowing funds on margin is an example of using leverage.

limited partnership

A limited partnership is a type of business organization that limits the amount of liability that falls onto its partners or owners; partners are only liable to the extent of their investment. One or more general partners manage the partnership, controlling the day-to-day operations, and assume unlimited personal liability for debts. The main advantage to this business structure is that the limited partners are typically not liable for the debts of the company.

limit order

An order placed with a broker to buy or sell at a price as good or better than the specified limit price.

line of reasonable expectations (LRE)

In this book, expected long-term return plotted as a line on a portfolio chart that is based on the investing strategy chosen.

liquidity

The degree of ease and certainty of value with which a security can be converted into cash.

load

A sales commission to buyers that a mutual fund may charge.

log scale/logarithmic scale

Scaled such that equal percentage moves appear equal.

lump-sum distribution

A single payment to a beneficiary covering the entire amount of an agreement. Participants in individual retirement accounts (IRAs), pension plans, profit-sharing and executive stock option plans generally can opt for a lump-sum distribution if the taxes are not too burdensome when they become eligible.

macroeconomic analysis

A type of analysis that examines how the general economy impacts a particular company or sector. Macroeconomics is a branch of economics dealing with the performance, structure, behavior and decision-making of an economy as a whole rather than individual markets.

maintenance requirement

Equity level that must be maintained in a margin account. Currently the exchanges require a minimum of 25% of the market value of securities in the account, but individual brokers may set the minimum at a higher percentage. If the account level goes below the requirement, additional funds are requested by the broker (see margin call).

margin

The use of borrowed money to purchase securities (buying "on margin").

margin call

A broker's demand for additional money or securities to be deposited when a margin account falls below a required amount (maintenance requirement).

market capitalization

Number of common stock shares outstanding times share price. Provides a measure of firm size and value.

market risk

The volatility of a stock price relative to the overall market as indicated by beta.

market-cap weighted

See capitalization-weighted.

market maker

A broker-dealer firm that takes on the risk of holding a large number of shares of a security to ensure a liquid market for trading.

master limited partnership (MLP)

A publicly traded limited partnership. Shares are called "units" and trade on an exchange. To qualify for MLP status, a company must receive at least 90% of its income from interest, dividends, real estate rents, the sale or disposition of real property, commodities or commodity futures, and mineral or natural resources activities.

mean absolute deviation (MAD)

A measure of volatility that uses the absolute values of the dispersions in the data.

economic moat or "moat"

An element of a firm's business model that is not easily replicated by competitors.

Model Shadow Stock Portfolio

AAII's model for a portfolio of individual stocks that focuses on micro-cap value stocks.

modern portfolio theory (MPT)

Overall investment strategy that seeks to construct an optimal portfolio by considering the relationship between risk and return, especially as measured by alpha, beta and R-squared. This theory recommends that the risk of a particular stock should not be looked at on a stand-alone basis, but rather in relation to how that particular stock's price varies in relation to the variation in price of the market portfolio. The theory goes on to state that given an investor's preferred level of risk, a particular portfolio can be constructed that maximizes expected return for a level of risk.

money managers

As used in this book: mutual funds, hedge funds and investment advisers, as well as financial planner activities that involve the selection of publicly traded investment assets and the allocation of wealth among those assets.

moving average

A popular indicator used in technical analysis to determine trend direction. The moving average plots the average of a security's prices over a defined period. The time period moves forward as time passes, consequently dropping off older time periods as it moves.

momentum

Sustained stock price movement in one direction. Momentum analysis analyzes stocks based on how much their price has gone up over recent periods of time compared to the market as a whole or compared to other stocks.

mutual fund

A pool of investors' money invested and managed by an

investment adviser. Money can be invested in the fund or with-drawn at any time, with few restrictions, at end-of-day net asset value (the per share market value of all securities held) minus any loads and fees. Mutual funds are open-end funds: They continuously sell and redeem shares at current net asset value, and they have no limit to the number of shares they can issue.

mutual fund subadviser

An outside money manager hired by a mutual fund to manage part of the portfolio's assets.

NASDAQ Composite index

A market-capitalization-weighted index of the more than 3,000 companies listed on the NASDAQ stock exchange. Contains a large number of technology stocks.

no-load mutual fund

A mutual fund that does not charge an additional fee for buying (front-end) or selling (back-end) shares.

normal distribution

A distribution of probabilities where values are grouped equal-ly above and below the mean and taper off symmetrically. Also called Gaussian distribution.

odd lot

A transaction involving fewer shares than in a usual or "round" order amount, which for most stocks is 100 shares. There is no longer an additional cost for buying an odd lot of stocks.

online advisory service

See robo-adviser.

online discount broker

See discount broker.

opportunity index

In this book, redefining of CBOE Volatility Index (VIX) from "fear index" since higher volatility leads to greater long-term returns.

paretian distribution (pareto)

A distribution that implies much greater volatility than the normal distribution.

PEG ratio (P/E to EPS growth)

Stock's price-earnings ratio divided by earnings per share growth rate. Provides an indication of the price the market has put on earnings expectations relative to what the firm has actually produced. As a rule, a PEG ratio of 1.0 is considered fairly priced, while ratios below 1.0 may point to undervalued stocks and ratios above 1.0 are potentially overvalued.

pension

Fund set up by a corporation, labor union, governmental entity or other organization to pay the pension benefits of retired workers.

point & figure charting

A technical charting method that plots stock prices as a series of X's and 0's. Depicts rising and falling of price without regard to time.

portfolio manager

One responsible for managing large pools of funds. Portfolio managers may be employed by insurance companies, mutual funds, bank trust departments, pension funds and other institutional investors.

potential portfolio shortfall (PPS)

In this book, a possible drop in portfolio value below what is reasonably expected.

present value

The value today of a future payment, or stream of payments, discounted at some appropriate interest rate.

price-earnings ratio (P/E)

Market price per share divided by the firm's earnings per share. A measure of how the market currently values the firm's earnings growth and risk prospects.

price-to-book-value ratio (P/B)

Market price per share divided by book value (tangible assets less all liabilities) per share. A measure of stock valuation relative to net assets. A high ratio might imply an overvalued situation; a low ratio might indicate an overlooked stock.

price-to-cash-flow ratio (P/CF)

Price per share divided by cash flow per share. A measure of the market's expectations regarding a firm's future financial health. Provides an indication of relative value, similar to the price-earnings ratio.

price-to-sales ratio (P/S)

Current market price per share divided by the sales per share for the most recent 12 months. Used similarly to price-earnings ratios to identify "out-of-favor" stocks.

private equity fund

A fund raised and managed by investment professionals of a specific private equity firm. Private equity firms are typically structured as limited partnerships and invest in the securities of non-listed companies, or private companies.

probability density function

Density of a continuous random variable; a function that describes the relative likelihood for this random variable to take on a given value. The probability that any specific deviation from the average return will occur in a given time period as measured by the standard deviation of the portfolio.

prospect theory

The theory that gains and losses are valued differently and holds that people incur greater aggravation from losing a certain sum of money than pleasure from gaining the same amount. Also known as "loss-aversion theory." Prospect theory shows that investors will accept higher risk to avoid the probability of a loss than they will to get an equal or even a larger gain.

put/call ratio

Shows the relationship between the number of puts to calls trading on the options exchange. Buying a put gives the buyer the right (or option) to sell shares of a stock at given price. Conversely, a call gives the option buyer the right to purchase shares of stock at given price.

put option

The right to sell stock at a specified (exercise) price within a specified period of time.

quick ratio

The sum of cash, equivalents and receivables (but not inventories), divided by short-term liabilities. Tries to answer the question: If sales stopped, could this firm meet its current obligations with its most liquid assets on hand?

random walk theory

The theory that the past movement or trend of a stock price or market cannot be used to predict its future movement. Stocks take an unpredictable path and an investor cannot outperform the market without taking on extra risk.

REIT

Real estate investment trust. Invests in real estate enterprises, primarily the ownership, renting and managing of properties.

Characteristically, REITs have higher dividend yields than common stocks, although payouts are not treated as qualified dividends under U.S. tax law.

registered investment adviser (RIA)

Financial planner who gives advice to high-net worth individuals and is registered with the Securities and Exchange Commission (SEC).

regression analysis

Regression is a statistical process used to estimate the relationship between one variable and a series of other changing variables.

relative strength

Price performance of a stock divided by the price performance of an appropriate index over the same time period. A measure of price trend that indicates how a stock is performing relative to other stocks. Zero percent indicates price performance equal to that of the index.

representativeness

The behavioral tendency to believe some pattern of data is representative of a larger model.

required minimum distribution (RMD)

The minimum amount that owners of traditional IRAs (individual retirement accounts) and other qualified plans must begin distributing each year from their accounts by April 1 following the year they reach age 70½. Calculated by dividing the prior December 31 balance of an IRA or retirement plan account by a life expectancy factor.

resistance

A price level that a stock will have difficulty surpassing as identified on a technical chart.

return

Income plus capital gains earned relative to the price paid for an investment.

return on assets (ROA)

Net income divided by total assets. Provides a measure of management's efficient use of assets.

return on equity (ROE)

Net income after all expenses and taxes divided by stockholder's equity (book value). An indication of how well the firm used shareholder dolars to generate additional earnings.

risk

Traditionally, the possibility that an investment's actual return will be different than expected; includes the possibility of losing some or all of the original investment. Measured by variability of historical returns or dispersion of historical returns around their average return (standard deviation). In this book, the relevant definition of risk is the chance of financial injury, damage or loss. It is used to describe the variations in stock prices and how that impacts the availability of assets: the possibility that the assets we expected to have for consumption will not be there when we need them.

risk arbitrage

See arbitrage.

Roth IRA

A type of individual retirement plan funded by aftertax dollars, but qualified distributions are tax free. Also, no distributions are required to be taken.

R-squared

A measurement of how closely a portfolio's performance correlates with the performance of a benchmark index, such as the

S&P 500, and thus a measurement of what portion of its performance can be explained by the performance of the overall
market or index.

robo-adviser

An online financial management service that provides automat-
ed, algorithm-based portfolio management advice.

shareholder yield

Shows what percentage of total cash the company is paying out
to shareholders, either in the form of a cash dividend or through
repurchasing shares in the open market. Calculated by adding
the dividend yield and the buyback yield together. (Buyback
yield is determined by comparing the average shares outstanding for one fiscal period with the average shares outstanding for
another fiscal period.)

shares outstanding

Total number of shares held by shareholders. Provides an indication of the trading liquidity of the firm.

Sharpe ratio

A measure developed by Nobel laureate William F. Sharpe to
determine the risk-adjusted return of an investment or portfolio. The formula for the Sharpe ratio is $(R_x - R_f) \div StdDev(R_x)$,
where R_x = average rate of return from investment X,
R_f = risk-free rate, and $StdDev(R_x)$ = standard deviation of R_x.

skewness

The tendency for a distribution curve to be stretched out more
on one side (asymmetrical). The skewness can be in either direction, but in security returns the tail would be to the right.

short sale

A market transaction in which an investor sells borrowed securities in anticipation of a price decline.

spread

The difference between the bid (offer to buy) price and ask (willing to sell) price of a security.

S&P 500 index

A broad-based, market-cap-weighted index based on the average performance of approximately 500 widely held common stocks.

standard deviation

A measure of volatility that shows the degree to which returns of an asset vary around the mean.

stockbroker

An agent who handles the public's orders to buy and sell securities for a commission.

support

A price below the current price that the stock will have difficulty going below on a technical chart.

systematic risk

Risk common to almost all investments in an asset class (such as common stocks) that cannot be diversified away in a portfolio by adding additional stocks. Market risk.

survivor bias

Results that may be influenced by the dropping out of poor-performing securities and securities that have ceased trading.

target date mutual funds

A mutual fund that changes the asset mix of stocks, bonds and cash based on a time frame to reach a goal, such as retirement. Target date mutual funds invest a greater proportion of their holdings in bonds as shareholders age past their target retirement date.

technical analysis

An analysis of price and volume data as well as other related market indicators to determine past trends that are believed to be predictable into the future. Charts and graphs are often utilized.

transaction costs

Costs incurred buying or selling securities. These include brokers' commissions and dealers' spreads (the difference between the price the dealer paid for a security and the price for which he can sell it).

Treasury bill

Short-term debt security issued by the federal government for periods of one year or less.

Treasury bond

Longer-term debt security issued by the federal government for a period of seven years or longer.

Treasury STRIPS

Debt security issued by the federal government that is sold at a discount to face value and does not pay interest because it matures at par. Acronym stands for separate trading of registered interest and principal securities.

true recovery period (TRP)

In this book, a measure of how long it takes until the market and a portfolio have recovered from any collapse by returning to the line of reasonable expectations (LRE).

underwriter

Investment banker that raises capital from investors on behalf of corporations and governments that are issuing either equity or debt securities.

unsystematic risk

Risk unique to a particular company that can be diversified away by combining it with other securities in a portfolio.

utility theory

Introduced by Daniel Bernoulli in 1738, the decision-making theory that states that investors are risk-averse. Risk aversion is based on the preference of an individual to hold on to what he or she has as opposed to gaining more. The assumption of this preference is based on the concept of decreasing marginal utility of wealth. Each additional increment of wealth is worth less than the previous increment, so investors are not willing to give up a unit of wealth for the chance to gain an additional unit.

valuation

The process of determining the current worth of an asset.

value stock

Stock of companies whose price looks cheap relative to earnings, assets, dividends or cash flow.

variability

An insurance product that pays periodic payments based on the performance of various investments.

variable annuity

A life insurance company investment product that combines a savings plan with a small life insurance component to provide certain tax benefits. The savings portion can be invested in a choice of pooled vehicles, including stock funds.

volatility

Traditionally used as the measure of risk, usually calculated as the standard deviation. In this book, defined as the likelihood of returns shifting quickly and unpredictably.

Wilshire 5000 index

A broad-based, market-cap-weighted index of stocks. Includes virtually all liquid securities (about 3,800).

wrap fee

Brokerage accounts that include a range of services from research to advice to trading and charge a percent of the portfolio value each year, which includes commissions. Fees tend to run 2% or more.

working capital

Current assets minus all liabilities. A measure of a company's efficiency and its short-term financial health. A positive number signals that current assets are more than large enough to cover all short-term obligations.

BIBLIOGRAPHY

"Best of the Web: Stock Screening." *Computerized Investing,* www.aaii.com/computerized-investing/bestwebarchive?cat1 =StockScreening, December 2015.

Bachelier, Louis. "The Theory of Speculation." Annales scienti-fiques de l'École Normale Supérieure 17, no. 3 (1900): 21-86.

Bernoulli, Daniel. "Exposition of a New Theory on the Measurement of Risk." *Econometrica* 22, no. 1 (1954); 23-36. (Translation of Bernoulli, 1738.)

Bernstein, Peter L. *Against the Gods: The Remarkable Story of Risk.* New York: John Wiley & Sons, Inc., 1998.

Bogle, John C. "Achieving Greater Long-Term Wealth Through Index Funds." By Charles Rotblut. *AAII Journal* 36, no. 6 (2014): 13-17.

Bogle, John C. *Common Sense on Mutual Funds.* 10th ed. Hoboken: John Wiley & Sons, Inc., 2010.

Bogle, John C. *The Little Book of Common Sense Investing: The Only Way to Guarantee Your Fair Share of Stock Market Returns.* Hoboken: John Wiley & Sons, Inc., 2007.

Brain Games, National Geographic Channel.

CalPERS, www.calpers.ca.gov.

Cloonan, James B. AAII Model Portfolios Commentary. *AAII Journal.*

Credit Suisse Hedge Fund Index, www.hedgefundindex.com.

Edelen, Roger M., Richard B. Evans, and Gregory B. Kadlec. "Scale Effects in Mutual Fund Performance: The Role of Trading Costs." SSRN (2007).

Einstein, Albert. "Investigations on the Theory of the Brownian Movement." *Annalen der Physik* 322, no. 8 (1905): 549-560 (randomness).

Fama, Eugene F. "The Behavior of Stock-Market Prices." *The Journal of Business* 38, no. 1 (1965): 34-105.

Fama, Eugene F., and Kenneth R. French. "A Five-Factor Asset Pricing Model." *Journal of Financial Economics* 116, no. 1 (2015): 1-22.

Fama, Eugene F., and Kenneth R. French. "Common Risk Factors in the Returns on Stocks and Bonds." *Journal of Financial Economics* 33, no. 1 (1993): 3-56.

Fama, Eugene F., and Kenneth R. French. "Cross-Section of Expected Stock Returns." *The Journal of Finance* 47, no. 2 (1992): 427-465.

Fama, Eugene F., and Kenneth R. French. "Dissecting Anomalies." *Journal of Finance* 63, no. 4 (2008): 1653-1678.

Fama, Eugene F., and Kenneth R. French. "Multifactor Explanations of Asset Pricing Anomalies." *The Journal of Finance* 51, no. 1 (1996): 55-84.

Fox, Justin. *The Myth of the Rational Market: A History of Risk, Reward, and Delusion on Wall Street*. New York: HarperBusiness, 2009.

Frederick, Shane. "Cognitive Reflection and Decision Making." *Journal of Economic Perspectives* 19, no. 4 (2005): 25-42.

Graham, Benjamin, and David Le Fevre Dodd. *Security Analysis*. New York: McGraw-Hill, 1934.

Greenblatt, Joel. *The Little Book That Still Beats the Market*. Hoboken: John Wiley & Sons, Inc., 2006.

Hennessee Hedge Fund Index, Hennessee Group, **www.hennesseegroup.com**.

Howard, C. Thomas. "Driving Emotions From Your Investment Process: A 12-Step Program." *AAII Journal* 36, no. 9 (2014): 27-31.

Hulbert, Mark. "Long Term Performance Ratings." *Hulbert Financial Digest* 36, no. 5 pt. 2 (2016): 1-16.

Hulbert, Mark. *Hulbert Financial Digest* 36, no. 4 (2015): 2.

Hulbert, Mark. *Hulbert Financial Digest* 36, no. 5 pt. 1 (2016): 5-16.

Ibbotson, Roger G. and Rex A. Sinquefield. *Ibbotson SBBI 2015 Yearbook*. Stocks, Bonds, Bills and Inflation, 1982 ed. Institute of Chartered Financial Analysts, Charlottesville, Va.

Kahneman, Daniel, and Amos Tversky. "Availability: A Heuristic for Judging Frequency and Probability." *Cognitive Psychology* 5, no. 2 (1973): 207-232.

Kahneman, Daniel, and Amos Tversky. "Judgment Under Uncertainty: Heuristics and Biases." *Science* 185, no. 4157 (1974): 1124-1131.

Kahneman, Daniel, and Amos Tversky. "Prospect Theory: An Analysis of Decision Under Risk." *Econometrica* 47, no. 2 (1979): 263-292.

Kahneman, Daniel. *Thinking, Fast and Slow*. New York: Farrar, Straus and Giroux, 2013.

Keynes, John Maynard. *The General Theory of Employment, Interest, and Money*. Orlando: Harcourt, Inc., 1965.

Kurtz, Walter. "The 20-Year Performance of Hedge Funds and the S&P 500 Are Almost Identical." *Business Insider,* August 12, 2013.

Loomis, Carol J. "Warren Buffett Loses a Bit of Ground in His 'Million-Dollar Bet'." *Fortune,* February 16, 2016.

Magic Formula Investing, **magicformulainvesting.com**.

Malkiel, Burton G. *A Random Walk Down Wall Street*. 11th ed. New York: W. W. Norton & Company, Inc., 2015.

Mallaby, Sebastian. *More Money Than God: Hedge Funds and the Making of a New Elite*. New York: The Penguin Press, 2010.

Mandelbrot, Benoit, and Richard L. Hudson. *The Misbehavior of Markets: A Fractal View of Financial Turbulence*. New York: Basic Books, 2004.

Markowitz, Harry M. *Portfolio Selection: Efficient Diversification of Investments*. New York: John Wiley & Sons, Inc., 1959.

Markowitz, Harry. "Portfolio Selection." *The Journal of Finance* 7, no. 1 (1952): 77-91.

Marois, Michael B. "Calpers to Exit Hedge Funds, Divest $4 Billion Stake." Bloomberg Businessweek, September 15, 2014.

Martin, Timothy W. "Calpers' Private-Equity Fees: $3.4 Billion." *The Wall Street Journal,* November 25, 2015.

McClellan, Jaclyn. "What Exactly Do Online Investment Advisory Services Offer?" *AAII Journal* 37, no. 1 (2015): 28-32.

Model Portfolios, AAII.com, **www.aaii.com/model-portfolios**.

Morgenson, Gretchen. "Behind Private Equity's Curtain." *The New York Times*, October 19, 2014.

Muksian, Robert. "A Pseudo-Life Annuity: Guaranteed Annual Income for 35 Years." *The AAII Journal* 34, no. 6 (2012): 26-29.

O'Shaughnessy, James P. *What Works on Wall Street: A Guide to the Best-Performing Investment Strategies of All Time.* 4th ed. New York: McGraw-Hill, 2012.

Phillips, Don. "Mutual Fund Urban Myths." *MorningstarAdvisor*, June/July 2013.

Poundstone, William. *Fortune's Formula: The Untold Story of the Scientific Betting System That Beat the Casinos and Wall Street.* New York: Hill & Wang, 2005.

Richardson, Tim. "Self-Test of Overconfidence," **www.tim-richardson.net/misc/estimation_quiz.html**.

Rotblut, Charles. "Analyzing the AAII Sentiment Survey Without Hindsight." *AAII Journal* 36, no. 6 (2014): 21-25.

Rotblut, Charles. "Momentum's Role as a Driver of Stock Prices." *AAII Journal* 38, no. 5 (2016): 7-11.

Rotblut, Charles. "The Sequence in Which Returns Occur Affects Your Wealth." *AAII Journal* 37, no. 5 (2015): 6-9.

Savage, Sam L. *The Flaw of Averages: Why We Underestimate Risk in the Face of Uncertainty.* Hoboken: John Wiley & Sons, Inc., 2009.

Sharpe, William F. "Capital Asset Prices: A Theory of Market Equilibrium Under Conditions of Risk." *The Journal of Finance* 19, no. 3 (1964): 425-442.

Shiller, Robert J. "Do Stock Prices Move Too Much to Be Justified by Subsequent Changes in Dividends?" *The American Economic Review* 71, no. 3 (1981): 421-436.

Siegel, Jeremy J. *Stocks for the Long Run*. 5th ed. New York: McGraw-Hill, 2014.

Surowiecki, James. "Private Inequity." *The New Yorker*, January 30, 2012.

Swedroe, Larry E., and Andrew L. Berkin. "Is Outperforming the Market Alpha or Beta?" *AAII Journal* 37, no. 7 (2015): 11-15.

Taleb, Nassim Nicholas. *The Black Swan: The Impact of the Highly Improbable*. New York: Random House, 2007.

Vanhaverbeke, Frederik. "Investment Wisdom From Wall Street's Legends." *AAII Journal* 36, no. 11 (2014): 7-11.

Vanhaverbeke, Frederik. *Excess Returns: A Comparative Study of the Methods of the World's Greatest Investors*. Petersfield: Harriman House Publishing, 2014.

Weinberg, Neil, and Darrell Preston. "7 Ways Private Equity Is Gaming Your Pension." *Bloomberg Businessweek*, March 23, 2015.

LIST OF EXHIBITS

INTRODUCTION

HYPOTHETICAL SMITH FAMILY ASSUMPTIONS　　　　18

TABLE I.1
Potential Investment Returns for the Smiths Over the Very
Long Term　　　　19

**FUTURE VALUE FORMULA TO CALCULATE PORTFOLIO VALUE AT
RETIREMENT**　　　　20

FIGURE I.1
Equal-Weighted vs. Cap-Weighted Market ETFs　　　　28

CHAPTER 1

FIGURE 1.1
Changes in Utility as a Function of Changes in Wealth　　　40

FIGURE 1.2
Diversification and Risk　　　　42

FIGURE 1.3
Dispersion of Returns　　　　43

FIGURE 1.4
A Normal Distribution Curve　　　　45

FIGURE 1.5
Skewness and Kurtosis in a Distribution Curve　　　　46

STANDARD DEVIATION　　　　50

TERMINAL VALUE BASED ON GEOMETRIC MEAN　　　　53

TERMINAL VALUE BASED ON ARITHMETIC MEAN　　　　53

CHAPTER 2

THE MYSTERY CYCLE   78

WHAT IS SUCCESS?   84

CHAPTER 4

FIGURE 4.1
NASDAQ Composite Index After the Tech Bubble   125

FIGURE 4.2
NASDAQ Composite Index Leading Up to the
Tech Bubble   126

FIGURE 4.3
Model Shadow Stock Portfolio   129

FIGURE 4.4
Model Shadow Stock Portfolio on Log Scale   131

FIGURE 4.5
Measuring Recoveries in Model Shadow Stock Portfolio   134

FIGURE 4.6
Guggenheim S&P 500 Equal Weight ETF vs.
60% Stock/40% Bond Portfolio   141

FIGURE 4.7
Model Shadow Stock Portfolio vs. Vanguard 500
Index Fund   142

TABLE 4.1
Major Market (S&P 500) Pullbacks Since 1970   144

CHAPTER 5

FIGURE 5.1
Model Shadow Stock Portfolio
vs. Vanguard 500 Index Fund   157

TABLE 5.1
Accumulated Wealth at Retirement for Level 2 Versus
Level3   158

TABLE 5.2
Annual Cost of Risk Reduction During Retirement   160

TABLE 5.3
Establishing a Defensive Strategy   165

TABLE 5.4
Application of Defensive Strategy During Great Recession 166

TABLE 5.5
100% Equity Strategy During Great Recession   170

CHAPTER 6

FIGURE 6.1
Comparing Domestic and Foreign Stock Performance   183

FIGURE 6.2
Equal-Weighted vs. Cap-Weighted Market ETFs   189

FIGURE 6.3
A Comparison of the Approaches   221

CHAPTER 7

COGNITIVE REFLECTION TEST SAMPLE   235

FIGURE 7.1
Hypothetical Level3 Portfolio Compared to Low-Risk
and Popular-Practice Approaches   242

FIGURE 7.2
Two Paths to Retirement   249

APPENDIX

FIGURE A.1
Model Shadow Stock Portfolio Performance   254

GEOMETRIC MEAN FORMULA AND EXAMPLE   283

INDEX

401(k), 98

AAII, 1, 4–5, 9, 23, 81, 86, 128, 140, 172, 195, 205, 207, 222, 251, 253–254, 261, 263

AAII.com, 261

AAII Journal, 1, 26, 98, 172, 174, 187, 193, 205, 251, 255–256, 259, 262

AAII Local Chapters, 247, 265

AAII members, 265

AAII Member Services, 264

AAII Model Portfolios, 255, 259, 267

AAII Stock Screens, 205, 261–263, 268

abnormal returns, 1, 37, 41, 62–63

above-market returns, 66, 204

academic research, 197, 202, 253

accounting measures, 65, 198, 201

actively managed mutual funds, 185, 196

active strategy, 239

addiction, 234–235, 237

advertising, 230, 231

advisory fees, 104–106

advisory services, 97, 188, 195–197, 267

aftertax return, 215–216

allocation, 55, 156

alpha, 44, 52, 55

Amazon, 245

anchoring, 232

anomalies, 20, 37–38, 41, 48, 61–62, 64–66, 70–71, 78, 198, 202, 205, 244, 267

Apple, 238

"A Random Walk Down Wall Street", 70

arbitrage, 112

arithmetic mean, 52

artificial neural networks (ANN), 75

ArXiv, 76

ask price, 203

asset allocation, 105, 127, 152

Asset Allocation Survey, 81

asset growth, 64

AthenaInvest, 239

availability, 232

aversion to loss, 240

backtesting, 84

Bain Capital, 109

Barron's, 81

Bayesian analysis, 54

bear market, 122–123, 136, 138, 144, 146, 149–150, 152, 163, 172, 176, 229

behavioral distortion, 238

behavioral economics/finance, 15, 226, 229–231, 249, 267

behavioral factors, 67, 233

behavioral impulses/pressures, 238–239

behavioral research/science, 77, 171

Berkshire Hathaway, 245

Bernoulli, Daniel, 39, 40, 67

"Best of the Web", 227, 268

best practices, 8, 31, 33, 120, 140, 215

beta, 36, 38, 43–44, 55, 66

bid/ask spread, 84, 100, 104, 111, 115, 193, 203, 258, 261

bid price, 203

Black Scholes (B/S) model, 114

Bloomberg Businessweek, 110

Bob Brinker's Marketimer, 197

Bogle, John, 26

bond ladder, 174

bonds, 101, 105, 159–160, 180

book-to-price ratio, 48, 64

book value, 83, 199, 200

"Brain Games", 237, 241

broker-dealers, 92–93, 96, 104

brokers, 92–94

bubble, 124

Buckingham, John, 196

Buffett, Warren, 21, 82, 86, 109, 127, 205, 211, 245

business cycle, 79, 211

buy-and-hold strategy, 37

buyer's remorse, 230

buyout, 201

calendar effects, 64

California Public Employees Retirement System (CalPERS), 186

call option, 110

calls, bond, 102, 121

capital asset pricing model, 36, 38, 49, 55–56, 66, 70

capital asset pricing model (CAPM), 35, 47

capitalization size, 26, 38, 48, 64–66, 80, 201, 257–258

capitalization weighted, 25–26, 30, 145, 184, 229

cap-weighted index, 27, 145

cash and equivalents, 83

cash flow, 83, 198

CBOE Volatility Index (VIX), 121

CDs, 133, 174, 180

certified financial planner (CFP), 97

CFP Board, 97

chaos theory, 54

Chartered Financial Analyst (CFA), 96

chartered market technician (CMT), 74

charting, 13, 74, 80, 87, 238

Chicago Board of Options Exchange (CBOE), 54

churning, 92–93

closed-end funds, 102

CNBC, 13, 80, 112, 244

cognitive characteristics, 234

Cognitive Reflection Test, 234

commission-free, 102

commissions, 84, 93, 95, 100–102, 104, 111, 203, 261

commodities markets, 79

commodity traders, 245

company risk, 41

competitive strengths, 83

composition, 184

compound return, 122

compulsive gambling, 234

Compustat, 205

Computerized Investing, 227

computerized trading platforms, 74

conditional value at risk (CVaR), 54

conservative investors, 150

Consumer Protection Act, 92

contrarian indicator, 81

conversion, 112

convertible preferreds, 232

correlation, 44, 59, 121

covered call writing, 113–114, 268

credit ratings, 83

Credit Suisse Hedge Fund Index, 186

CRSP (Center for Research in Security Prices), 205, 226

day trading, 211

debt-to-equity ratio, 83

defensive portfolio, 173

defined-contribution plan, 98

density function, 156

directors of a mutual fund, 105

discount broker, 93, 101

distortions, 237

distressed bonds, 180

distribution, 11, 35, 61

diversification, 41, 55, 59, 76, 121, 123–124, 127, 138, 156, 190, 229

dividend discount model, 62

dividend ratio, 83

dividends, 63, 83, 199, 246, 261

dividend yield, 199

Dodd-Frank Wall Street Reform, 92

dollar cost averaging, 125

Dow Jones Credit Suisse Hedge Fund Index, 108

down market, 228, 240

downturn, 138, 149–150, 153, 193, 211, 217, 236

earnings, 198, 201

earnings estimates, 264

earnings growth, 200

earnings surprises, 63, 200

earnings-to-assets ratio, 201

EBITDA, 201

effective strategies, 66

efficient market hypothesis, 11, 20, 36–37, 47, 61–62, 64–66, 70, 73, 75, 185, 202

election cycle, 78

endowments, 106

Ennis Inc., 238

enterprise value, 201

equal-weighted, 140, 145–146

equal-weighted index, 27, 30

equal weighting, 133, 138, 229

equities, 180

equity premium puzzle, 133

E*Trade, 21

excessive trading, 253

excess returns, 41, 61, 66

exchange-traded funds (ETFs), 101–103, 105–106, 111–112, 114, 140, 180, 188, 239

execution error, 228

exercise price, 111, 113

expansion/contraction, 83

expected return, 221

expense ratio, 104, 107

expiration date, 111, 115

Fama, Eugene, 37–38, 52, 71

Fama/French models, 48, 66

Fama/French studies, 24, 66, 133, 202

fear index, 25, 121–122

Federal Reserve, 211

fee-only financial planners, 90

Fibonacci, 79

Fidelity Investor, 197

fiduciary obligation, 91–93

financial adviser, 105

financial engineering, 75

financial planners, 14, 16, 90, 95–96, 98

financials, 191

FINRA, 92

five-factor model, 202

Fortune magazine, 109

Fox, Justin, 53

framing, 68, 233, 247

Frederick, Shane, 234

French, Kenneth, 38, 71

Friedman, Milton, 1

front running, 92

full-service broker, 93–94, 101

fundamental analysis, 3, 12, 37, 81–87, 88

fundamental indexing, 30

fund expenses, 105, 114

future values, 59

fuzzy logic models, 54

GARCH, 54

GARP, 86

geometric mean, 52, 122

geometric returns, 58

ghost risk, 7, 25, 84, 120, 147

Google, 238, 245

government bonds, 102

Graham, Benjamin, 12, 82, 86, 205

Great Depression, 69, 143, 163, 186, 205, 209

Great Recession, 1, 142–143, 146–147, 167, 171–172, 204

Greenblatt, Joel, 196

gross profit, 65, 83

gross profit-to-assets ratio, 201

growth, 263

Guggenheim S&P 500 Equal Weight ETF, 22, 25, 27, 140, 143, 145, 164, 188, 190–193, 197

Guggenheim S&P 500 Equal Weight Real Estate ETF, 193

Hansen, Lars, 37

health care, 125, 191

health care mutual funds, 103

hedge funds, 16, 21–22, 75–76, 107–109, 186

hedging, 113

Hennessee Hedge Fund Index, 108

herd effect, 68, 233

heuristic approaches, 232

heuristics, 231

higher-return strategies, 267

Horizons S&P 500 Covered Call ETF, 114

Howard, Tom, 239

Hulbert Financial Digest, 23, 97, 196–197

Hulbert, Mark, 97, 267

Ibbotson's SBBI, 133, 191, 209

indexes, 111

index funds, 102, 105, 185, 187–188

indexing, 26, 30, 268

indicators, 74

individual investor, 9–10, 15, 29–30, 57, 80

inflation, 215–216, 222

inside information, 62

insiders, 37

insider trading, 37

inside spread, 203

institutional advisers, 94–95

institutional investors, 9, 31

institutions, 9, 13, 25, 29, 81, 88, 132

insured assets, 174

interest rates, 102

intermediate approaches, 206

Internal Revenue Service (IRS), 99

international stocks, 182

investment advisers, 14, 16, 96, 108

investment horizon, 58

Investment Quality Trends, 197

investment services industry, 9, 14–15, 33

Investor Advisory Serivce, 197

iPath CBOE S&P 500 BuyWrite ETN, 114

irrational behavior, 67, 69

iShares 1-3 Year Treasury Bond ETF, 192

Japanese candlesticks, 13, 74

Jensen's alpha, 55

judgment errors, 232

Kahneman, Daniel, 67, 230–232, 234

Keynes, John Maynard, 230

Kondratieff cycle, 79

kurtosis, 47, 52, 54–55

Lakonishok, Josef, 205

large-cap stocks, 26, 104, 142, 187

last price, 203

leptokurtic, 54

Level 1 investing, 7–8, 19, 31, 214, 239

Level 2, 7–8, 19, 29, 31, 120, 123, 127, 137, 158, 220, 239, 243

Level3, 99, 128, 138, 146, 149, 151, 160, 239

Level3 approaches, 129, 135–136, 143, 158–159, 181, 220

Level3 defensive strategy, 169–170, 176

Level3 Investing, 7–8, 19, 23, 29, 31, 99, 119, 130, 132, 137–138, 146, 149, 151–152, 156, 160, 175, 179, 215, 225, 239

Level3investing.com, 22, 193, 197, 207, 241, 267

Level3 passive approach, 188, 225, 235, 237, 239

Level3 Passive Portfolio, 193–194, 213

Level3 withdrawals, 22, 161

leverage, 112, 123, 185–187, 207, 211, 239, 245

leveraged ETFs, 123

Levy distribution/function, 52, 55

limited partnerships, 91, 107

line of reasonable expectations, 133, 135–137, 139–141, 149, 241

liquidity effect, 63

loads, 104

lognormal distribution, 47, 114

log normality, 54

log scale, 128

long term, 84, 128, 138, 149, 150

long-term investor, 21, 31, 33, 51, 106, 119, 121, 124, 130, 132, 134, 136–137, 149–150, 156, 179–180, 185, 223, 251

long-term return, 151, 185

low-priced stocks, 63

Lynch, Peter, 86, 205

macroeconomic analysis, 81

Madison Covered Call & Equity Income A, 114

Madoff, Bernard, 14

Magic Formula, 196, 268

maintenance requirement (margin), 209

Malkiel, Burton G., 70

Mallaby, Sebastian, 109

management fees, 102

Mandelbrot, Benoit, 53–54, 61

margin, 207, 209

margin calls, 123, 209

margin loans, 210

marketing, 230

market makers, 94, 100

market risk, 41

market timing, 211

Markowitz, Harry, 2, 35, 49, 82

master limited partnerships (MLPs), 180

mathematical distribution model, 59

McClellan, Jaclyn, 98

mean, 131–132

mean absolute deviation, 51

mean return and variance, 218

Medicare, 125, 155

mergers, 259

micro-cap stocks, 85, 105, 193, 203, 205

micro-cap strategy, 255

micro-cap value stock, 258

micro-cap value stocks, 128, 133, 140, 206, 253

mid-cap stocks, 191, 192

MIT, 235

model portfolios, 195, 196

Model Shadow Stock Portfolio, 23, 38, 128–129, 131, 133–134, 140, 142–143, 145, 157, 195–196, 203, 207, 226, 253–257

modern portfolio theory, 2, 10–11, 33, 35–71, 73, 75, 82, 84, 148, 156, 249, 251

momentum, 48, 61–62, 64–66, 80, 85, 87, 106, 132, 200, 202, 244

momentum analysis, 13

money managers, 15–16

Monte Carlo simulation, 54, 172

Morgenson, Gretchen, 110

Morningstar, 104

Morningstar StockInvestor, 197

moving average, 79

moving averages, 74, 87, 212

Muksian, Robert, 174, 268

Munger, Charles, 7

mutual funds, 14, 16, 22, 86–87, 94–95, 101, 103, 105, 107–108, 114, 180, 233, 239

My Level3 Worksheet, 241, 243, 248

Mystery Cycle, 77–78

naked put, 112

NASDAQ Composite, 103, 124, 126, 144, 190

National Geographic channel, 237

Neff, John, 86, 205

New York Stock Exchange (NYSE), 101

New York Times, 110

Nikkei index, 147

noise, 244

normal curve, 45, 52, 114, 120, 156

normal distribution, 11, 48, 56

O'Neil, William, 86, 205

online advisory services, 98

online brokerage accounts, 102, 233

opportunity index, 25, 121, 122

options, 85, 101, 110

order backlogs, 83

O'Shaughnessy, James, 24, 86, 202–204, 206–207, 226

Outstanding Investments, 197

outstanding shares, 199

overconfidence, 68, 235–236

oversight, 247

owner/manager effect, 63

Paretian distribution, 38, 55–56

Pareto function, 52

PEG ratio, 86

pension funds, 79

pensions, 93, 155

personality traits, 234

Piotroski, Joseph, 86, 205

Plan Z, 19, 25, 140, 188, 208, 213

point & figure charting, 13, 74

portfolio diversification, 181

portfolio managers, 94–95, 98

portfolio optimization, 56

portfolio volatility, 58

potential portfolio shortfall, 134

Poundstone, William, 219

PowerShares Russell 1000 Equal Weight Portfolio, 191–192

PowerShares S&P 500 BuyWrite ETF, 114

presidential election, 77–78

Preston, Darrell, 110

price, 83

price-earnings ratio, 63, 83, 200

price-to-book-value ratio, 38, 64–66, 80, 146, 200, 207, 256, 258

price-to-cash-flow ratio, 63, 198

price-to-sales ratio, 63, 133, 199
primary adviser, 95
primary advisory firm, 105
private equity, 21, 109–110, 180, 186
probability, 137, 232
probability density function, 45, 52
Procter & Gamble Co. (PG), 245
profit margins, 199
prospect theory, 232–233
protection period, 153
Protégé Partners, 109
pseudo-life annuity, 268
psychological impulses/processes, 15, 229
pullbacks, 126, 133, 135, 139, 143, 171, 229
put/call ratio, 80
puts, 121
qualitative measures, 82
quantitative measures, 82
Quantopian, 76
quick ratio, 83
random walk, 39, 60, 62, 70
rational man model, 230–231
real risk, 7, 11, 33, 58, 119–120, 128, 148, 156–158, 171, 175, 179, 190, 219, 251
rebalancing, 27, 244
record-keeping, 247
recovery period, 135, 139, 143
registered investment advisers (RIAs), 93, 96
registered representatives, 92
regression analysis, 202
REITs, 180, 191
relative price strength ranks, 200
relative strength, 64, 200
representativeness, 67, 232
research, 188, 195
resistance levels, 74, 79

retirement accounts, 93
return on assets, 64, 201
risk, 11, 50–51, 57–58, 123
risk aversion, 39, 48, 58, 67
risk/reward trade-off, 127
RIZM, 76
robo-advisers, 98
Romney, Mitt, 109
Rotblut, Charles, 172
rule, 225
Russell, 190
Russell 1000, 193
Russell 2000 index, 193
Russell 3000, 182
Russell Strategic Call Overwriting S, 114
safe investments, 161, 168, 171, 176, 180
safe period, 154
safe portfolio, 243
safe portion, 174, 192
safe reserve, 210
sales, 199
Samuelson, Paul, 219
Savage, Sam L., 131
savings accounts, 180
scenario analysis, 54
Schwab, 21, 98
Scottrade, 21
screening, 226
SDPR S&P 500 ETF, 26
Securities and Exchange Commission, 92–96
Seides, Ted, 109
self-control problems, 235
sensory distortion, 234
Sentiment Survey, 81, 267
shareholder yield, 199
Sharpe ratio, 10, 55–56, 218
Sharpe, William, 35

Shiller, Robert J., 37, 62

short term, 30, 151

short-term investments, 152, 216

short-term investor, 121, 132, 137, 148, 184, 250

short-term market behavior, 228

short-term risk, 31, 151, 156

short-term strategy, 156

short-term volatility, 158, 162

Siegel, Jeremy, 148, 181

skew index, 54

skewness, 47, 54

small cap, 63, 106

small-cap effect, 37

small-cap stocks, 26–27, 64, 66, 104, 138, 142, 147, 193

small-cap value investing, 26

small-cap value stocks, 23

small-stock effect, 146

Social Security, 155

Sortino ratio, 55

Sound Advice, 197

S&P 500, 23, 25, 27, 78, 103, 114, 121, 138, 140, 143–144, 146, 148, 153, 155, 162–164, 167, 172–173, 177, 180, 182, 184, 186–189, 191–192, 215

S&P 500 Equal Weight Index, 22

special situation, 228

spin-offs, 246

splits, 246

standard deviation, 40, 44–45, 48, 50–52, 55–56, 114, 120–121, 131–132, 137, 218

Standard & Poor's database, 227

stock buyback yield, 199

Stock Investor Pro, 86, 227, 261, 263

stocks, 101, 105, 111–112, 124, 180

"Stocks for the Long Run", 148, 181

stock split, 232

Student's t-distribution, 54

subadvisers, 95, 104

suitability standard, 92

support, 74, 79

Surowiecki, James, 110

survivor bias, 84

swaps, 54

systematic risk, 41, 59, 82

Taleb, Nassim Nicholas, 53–54

target date mutual funds, 182

tax consequences, 211

taxes, 201, 222, 262

tax-free municipal bonds, 102

tax strategies, 99

T-bills, 133

TD Ameritrade, 21

tech, 124, 145

tech bubble, 190

tech collapse, 139, 144–145

technical analysis, 2, 13, 37, 73–81, 87, 212, 238

technology, 103

Templeton, John, 86

tenders, 259

terminal wealth, 52, 57, 122, 218

The Big Short, 54

The Buyback Letter, 197

The Oxford Club, 197

The Prudent Speculator, 23, 196

"The Wolf of Wall Street", 14, 91

"Thinking, Fast and Slow", 231, 234

Thomson Reuters, 263

Thorp, Wayne, 205

time diversification, 125, 127, 229

time slippage, 261

TradeStation, 74

transaction costs, 84, 100–101, 105, 114–115, 187, 205, 211

Treasuries, 174

Treasury STRIPS, 174

Treynor ratio, 55

true recovery period, 135, 141, 149

Tukey, John, 35, 49, 121

Tversky, Amos, 67, 230, 231

underwriters, 94

unsystematic risk, 41, 48, 59, 123

U.S. Congress, 125

U.S. government, 180

U.S. Labor Department, 93

utility theory, 39, 232

valuations, 200

value, 26, 48, 106, 192, 200–201, 263

value at risk (VaR), 54

value factors, 201

value stocks, 26, 253

Vanguard, 26, 98

Vanguard 500 Index fund, 109, 141–142, 157, 182

Vanguard Mid-Cap Value, 192

Vanguard REIT ETF, 191, 193

Vanguard Total International Stock Index fund, 182

Vanhaverbeke, Frederik, 24, 187, 268

volatility, 11, 33, 35–36, 44–45, 48, 50–52, 54, 56–57, 59, 66, 114, 119–120, 130, 137, 148, 156, 175, 251

volatility, fear of, 25

Weinberg, Neil, 110

"What Works on Wall Street", 24, 202–204, 207, 226

willpower, 241

Wilshire, 205

Wilshire 5000, 23, 27, 138, 145–146, 148, 154, 164, 182, 186–187, 190

withdrawal stage, 190, 194, 209

withdrawal strategy, 216

working capital, 83

wrap fees, 93–94

Zacks Premium, 197

ABOUT THE AUTHOR

James B. Cloonan is the founder and chairman of AAII. He earned his MBA from the University of Chicago and his B.A. and Ph.D. from Northwestern University. After teaching for several years, in 1974 Cloonan helped found and served as CEO of Heinold Securities, a brokerage firm specializing in options. After selling his interest in that firm, he returned to teaching and began the preliminary work leading to the founding of the American Association of Individual Investors in 1978.

Cloonan is the author of books and articles on investing and writes the Model Portfolios column for the *AAII Journal*. He created and manages the Model Shadow Stock Portfolio, which has realized an annualized return of over 15% for the past 23 years.

Cloonan has served on several industry and regulatory panels, including the Consumer Advisory Council of the National Futures Association, the Advisory Panel on Securities Markets and Information Technology of the Congressional Office of Technology Assessment, the NASD Special Committee on the Quality of Markets, the New York Stock Exchange Panel on Market Volatility and Investor Confidence, the Chicago Mercantile Exchange Financial Instruments Advisors Committee, the New York Stock Exchange Individual Investors Advisory Committee, and The Consumer Affairs Advisory Committee of the Securities and Exchange Commission.

He lives with his wife Edie in Chicago.

ABOUT AAII

The American Association of Individual Investors (AAII) is a nonprofit educational organization that provides the tools, resources and know-how investors need to successfully build and manage investment wealth. AAII members receive the monthly *AAII Journal*, model portfolios, access to over 40 local chapters and the comprehensive investment education available on our website at www.aaii.com.

James Cloonan founded AAII in 1978 because he firmly believed that individual investors armed with effective investment education materials and a bit of dedication could outperform most professional managers. Over 30 years later, the 170,000 members of AAII report equity returns that are higher than those of the stock market as a whole.

For information on AAII membership, please visit www.aaii.com/join.